# PRENTICE HALL
# *LITERATURE*

# Common Core Companion

## *Grade Ten*

Pearson
Upper Saddle River, New Jersey
Boston, Massachusetts
Chandler, Arizona
Glenview, Illinois

**Copyright © Pearson Education, Inc., or its affiliates.** All Rights Reserved. Printed in the United States of America. This publication is protected by copyright, and permission should be obtained from the publisher prior to any prohibited reproduction, storage in a retrieval system, or transmission in any form or by any means, electronic, mechanical, photocopying, recording, or likewise. For information regarding permissions, write to Pearson Curriculum Group Rights & Permissions, One Lake Street, Upper Saddle River, New Jersey 07458.

Pearson, Prentice Hall, and Pearson Prentice Hall are trademarks, in the U.S. and/or other countries, of Pearson Education, Inc., or its affiliates.

ISBN-13: 978-0-133-19067-0

ISBN-10:     0-133-19067-6

6 7 8 9 10 V016 15 14 13

# Table of Contents

The instruction and activities in this book are organized around the Common Core State Standards for English and Language Arts.

## Reading Standards for Literature      1

# Reading Standards for Informational Text    83

# Writing Standards                                           178

**Writing 1:** Write arguments to support claims in an analysis of substantive topics or texts, using valid reasoning and relevant and sufficient evidence.

  a. Introduce precise claim(s), distinguish the claim(s) from alternate or opposing claims, and create an organization that establishes clear relationships among claim(s), counterclaims, reasons, and evidence.

  b. Develop claim(s) and counterclaims fairly, supplying evidence for each while pointing out the strengths and limitations of both in a manner that anticipates the audience's knowledge level and concerns.

  c. Use words, phrases, and clauses to link the major sections of the text, create cohesion, and clarify the relationships between claim(s) and reasons, between reasons and evidence, and between claim(s) and counterclaims.

  d. Establish and maintain a formal style and objective tone while attending to the norms and conventions of the discipline in which they are writing.

  e. Provide a concluding statement or section that follows from and supports the argument presented.

**Writing 2:** Write informative/explanatory texts to examine and convey complex ideas, concepts, and information clearly and accurately through the effective selection, organization, and analysis of content.

  a. Introduce a topic; organize complex ideas, concepts, and information to make important connections and distinctions; include formatting (e.g., headings), graphics (e.g., figures, tables), and multimedia when useful to aiding comprehension.

  b. Develop the topic with well-chosen, relevant, and sufficient facts, extended definitions, concrete details, quotations, or other information and examples appropriate to the audience's knowledge of the topic.

  c. Use appropriate and varied transitions to link the major sections of the text, create cohesion, and clarify the relationships among complex ideas and concepts.

  d. Use precise language and domain-specific vocabulary to manage the complexity of the topic.

  e. Establish and maintain a formal style and objective tone while attending to the norms and conventions of the discipline in which they are writing.

  f. Provide a concluding statement or section that follows from and supports the information or explanation presented (e.g., articulating implications or the significance of the topic).

**Writing 3:** Write narratives to develop real or imagined experiences or events using effective technique, well-chosen details, and well-structured event sequences.

a. Engage and orient the reader by setting out a problem, situation, or observation, establishing one or multiple point(s) of view, and introducing a narrator and/or characters; create a smooth progression of experiences or events.

b. Use narrative techniques, such as dialogue, pacing, description, reflection, and multiple plot lines, to develop experiences, events, and/or characters.

c. Use a variety of techniques to sequence events so that they build on one another to create a coherent whole.

d. Use precise words and phrases, telling details, and sensory language to convey a vivid picture of the experiences, events, setting, and/or characters.

e. Provide a conclusion that follows from and reflects on what is experienced, observed, or resolved over the course of the narrative.

**Writing 4:** Produce clear and coherent writing in which the development, organization, and style are appropriate to task, purpose, and audience. (Grade-specific expectations for writing types are defined in standards 1–3 above.)

**Writing 5:** Develop and strengthen writing as needed by planning, revising, editing, rewriting, or trying a new approach, focusing on addressing what is most significant for a specific purpose and audience. (Editing for conventions should demonstrate command of Language standards 1–3 up to and including grades 9–10.)

**Writing 6:** Use technology, including the Internet, to produce, publish, and update individual or shared writing products, taking advantage of technology's capacity to link to other information and to display information flexibly and dynamically.

**Writing 7:** Conduct short as well as more sustained research projects to answer a question (including a self-generated question) or solve a problem; narrow or broaden the inquiry when appropriate; synthesize multiple sources on the subject, demonstrating understanding of the subject under investigation.

**Writing 8:** Gather relevant information from multiple authoritative print and digital sources, using advanced searches effectively; assess the usefulness of each source in answering the research question; integrate information into the text selectively to maintain the flow of ideas, avoiding plagiarism and following a standard format for citation.

**Writing 9:** Draw evidence from literary or informational texts to support analysis, reflection, and research.

a. Apply grades 9–10 Reading standards to literature (e.g., "Analyze how an author draws on and transforms source material in a specific work [e.g., how Shakespeare treats a theme or topic from Ovid or the Bible or how a later author draws on a play by Shakespeare]").

b. Apply grades 9–10 Reading standards to literary nonfiction (e.g., "Delineate and evaluate the argument and specific claims in a text, assessing whether the reasoning is valid and the evidence is relevant and sufficient; identify false statements and fallacious reasoning").

**Writing 10:** Write routinely over extended time frames (time for research, reflection, and revision) and shorter time frames (a single sitting or a day or two) for a range of tasks, purposes, and audiences.

# Speaking and Listening Standards    273

**Speaking and Listening 1:** Initiate and participate effectively in a range of collaborative discussions (one-on-one, in groups, and teacher-led) with diverse partners on grades 9–10 topics, texts, and issues, building on others' ideas and expressing their own clearly and persuasively.

a. Come to discussions prepared, having read and researched material under study; explicitly draw on that preparation by referring to evidence from texts and other research on the topic or issue to stimulate a thoughtful, well-reasoned exchange of ideas.

b. Work with peers to set rules for collegial discussions and decision-making (e.g., informal consensus, taking votes on key issues, presentation of alternate views), clear goals and deadlines, and individual roles as needed.

c. Propel conversations by posing and responding to questions that relate the current discussion to broader themes or larger ideas; actively incorporate others into the discussion; and clarify, verify, or challenge ideas and conclusions.

d. Respond thoughtfully to diverse perspectives, summarize points of agreement and disagreement, and, when warranted, qualify or justify their own views and understanding and make new connections in light of the evidence and reasoning presented.

**Speaking and Listening 2:** Integrate multiple sources of information presented in diverse media or formats (e.g., visually, quantitatively, orally) evaluating the credibility and accuracy of each source.

**Speaking and Listening 3:** Evaluate a speaker's point of view, reasoning, and use of evidence and rhetoric, identifying any fallacious reasoning or exaggerated or distorted evidence.

**Speaking and Listening 4:** Present information, findings, and supporting evidence clearly, concisely, and logically such that listeners can follow the line of reasoning and the organization, development, substance, and style are appropriate to purpose, audience, and task.

**Speaking and Listening 5:** Make strategic use of digital media (e.g., textual, graphical, audio, visual, and interactive elements) in presentations to enhance understanding of findings, reasoning, and evidence and to add interest.

**Speaking and Listening 6:** Adapt speech to a variety of contexts and tasks, demonstrating command of formal English when indicated or appropriate. (See grades 9–10 Language standards 1 and 3 for specific expectations.)

# Language Standards                                     309

**Language 1:** Demonstrate command of the conventions of standard English grammar and usage when writing or speaking.

a. Use parallel structure.*

b. Use various types of phrases (noun, verb, adjectival, adverbial, participial, prepositional, absolute) and clauses (independent, dependent; noun, relative, adverbial) to convey specific meanings and add variety and interest to writing or presentations.

**Language 2:** Demonstrate command of the conventions of standard English capitalization, punctuation, and spelling when writing.

a. Use a semicolon (and perhaps a conjunctive adverb) to link two or more closely related independent clauses.

b. Use a colon to introduce a list or quotation.

c. Spell correctly.

**Language 3:** Apply knowledge of language to understand how language functions in different contexts, to make effective choices for meaning or style, and to comprehend more fully when reading or listening.

a. Write and edit work so that it conforms to the guidelines in a style manual (e.g., *MLA Handbook*, Turabian's *Manual for Writers*) appropriate for the discipline and writing type.

**Language 4:** Determine or clarify the meaning of unknown and multiple-meaning words and phrases based on grades 9–10 reading and content, choosing flexibly from a range of strategies.

a. Use context (e.g., the overall meaning of a sentence, paragraph, or text; a word's position or function in a sentence) as a clue to the meaning of a word or phrase.

b. Identify and correctly use patterns of word changes that indicate different meanings or parts of speech (e.g., analyze, analysis, analytical; advocate, advocacy).

c. Consult general and specialized reference materials (e.g., dictionaries, glossaries, thesauruses), both print and digital, to find the pronunciation of a word or determine or clarify its precise meaning, its part of speech, or its etymology.

d. Verify the preliminary determination of the meaning of a word or phrase (e.g., by checking the inferred meaning in context or in a dictionary).

**Language 5:** Demonstrate understanding of figurative language, word relationships, and nuances in word meanings.

• Interpret figures of speech (e.g., euphemism, oxymoron) in context and analyze their role in the text.

• Analyze nuances in the meaning of words with similar denotations.

**Language 6:** Acquire and use accurately general academic and domain-specific words and phrases, sufficient for reading, writing, speaking, and listening at the college and career readiness level; demonstrate independence in gathering vocabulary knowledge when considering a word or phrase important to comprehension or expression.

# Performance Tasks                                                      336

## About the *Common Core Companion*

The Common Core Companion student workbook provides instruction and practice in the Common Core State Standards. The standards are designed to help all students become college and career ready by the end of grade 12. Here is a closer look at this workbook:

### Reading Standards

Reading Standards for Literature and Informational Texts are supported with instruction, examples, and multiple copies of worksheets that you can use over the course of the year. These key standards are revisited in the Performance Tasks section of your workbook.

### Writing Standards

Full writing workshops are provided for Writing standards 1, 2, 3, and 8. Writing standards 4, 5, 6, 8, 9, and 10 are supported with direct instruction and worksheets that provide targeted practice. In addition, writing standards are revisited in Speaking and Listening activities and in Performance Tasks.

### Speaking and Listening Standards

Detailed instruction and practice are provided for each Speaking and Listening standard. Additional opportunities to master these standards are provided in the Performance Tasks.

### Language Standards

Explicit instruction and detailed examples support each Language standard. In addition, practice worksheets and graphic organizers provide additional opportunities for students to master these standards.

### Performance Tasks

Using the examples in the Common Core framework as a guide, we provide opportunities for you to test your ability to master each reading standard, along with tips for success and rubrics to help you evaluate your work.

# Reading Standards for Literature

# Literature 1

> 1. **Cite strong and thorough textual evidence to support analysis of what the text says explicitly as well as inferences drawn from the text.**

## Explanation

When you read a work of literature, you should take note of and analyze **explicit** details (those that are directly stated and provide basic information) to determine which are significant (such as those that advance the plot or describe a conflict, setting, or characters). By summarizing important explicit details, you can get an overall sense of what the text says.

Other story details are not stated directly and are only understood through making **inferences,** or drawing conclusions. To get an overall sense of what a text says, you must combine the significant explicit details you noted and the inferences you made. These details and inferences help you form your overall understanding and serve as support for the conclusion you have drawn.

In your analysis of a text, you should cite the most important details, or **textual evidence,** to support your conclusion. Think of the process as describing to your reader how the important explicit details and inferences you made support your overall understanding of what the text says.

## Examples

- **Explicit details** are directly stated and provide basic information. "The wind howled through the trees," "The cabin door slammed," and "Jesse shrieked in fear" are explicit details.
- When you make an **inference,** you draw a conclusion based on what the author tells you and what you already know about life. For example, suppose you read a story in which a girl receives a phone call and then starts grinning and shouting, "Yes! I did it!" You can infer that the girl has received good news about an important achievement.
- You use **strong textual evidence,** the most important details in the story, to support the conclusions you draw about a text. For example, think of describing a favorite movie to friend who has not seen it. You would relate the major events (the explicit details) and then explain why these are significant (how they add to the plot, affect the main characters, and so on). You would then relate the inferences you made, explaining how some details were not given directly, but were understood by drawing conclusions (such as how you think a character must feel after certain events).

## Academic Vocabulary

**inference** conclusion reached from evidence and reasoning

**textual evidence** details in the text that support a conclusion

## Apply the Standard

Use the worksheets that follow to help you apply the standard as you read. Several copies of each worksheet have been provided for you to use with a number of different selections.

- Identifying Strong Textual Evidence
- Making Inferences

Name _____ Date _____ Selection _____

# Identifying Strong Textual Evidence

Use this organizer to identify the most important details the author provides in a story or passage.

| Detail About Character, Setting, Conflict | Why It Is Important |
|---|---|
| 1. | |
| 2. | |
| 3. | |
| 4. | |
| 5. | |

A

Name _____ Date _____ Selection _____

# Identifying Strong Textual Evidence

Use this organizer to identify the most important details the author provides in a story or passage.

| Detail About Character, Setting, Conflict | Why It Is Important |
|---|---|
| 1. | |
| 2. | |
| 3. | |
| 4. | |
| 5. | |

For use with Literature 1

Name _____ Date _____ Selection _____

# Identifying Strong Textual Evidence

Use this organizer to identify the most important details the author provides in a story or passage.

| Detail About Character, Setting, Conflict | Why It Is Important |
|---|---|
| 1. | |
| 2. | |
| 3. | |
| 4. | |
| 5. | |

C

For use with Literature 1

Name _____  Date _____  Selection _____

## Identifying Strong Textual Evidence

Use this organizer to identify the most important details the author provides in a story or passage.

| Detail About Character, Setting, Conflict | Why It Is Important |
|---|---|
| 1. | |
| 2. | |
| 3. | |
| 4. | |
| 5. | |

D

Name _____ Date _____ Selection _____

# Identifying Strong Textual Evidence

Use this organizer to identify the most important details the author provides in a story or passage.

| Detail About Character, Setting, Conflict | Why It Is Important |
|---|---|
| 1. | |
| 2. | |
| 3. | |
| 4. | |
| 5. | |

For use with Literature 1

Name _____ Date _____ Selection _____

# Identifying Strong Textual Evidence

Use this organizer to identify the most important details the author provides in a story or passage.

| Detail About Character, Setting, Conflict | Why It Is Important |
|---|---|
| 1. | |
| 2. | |
| 3. | |
| 4. | |
| 5. | |

F

Name _____ Date _____ Selection _____

# Making Inferences

Use this organizer to make inferences about the characters and their conflicts. Next to each inference, write details from the text that support your inference.

| My Inferences | Textual Evidence (Supporting Details) |
|---|---|
| 1. | |
| 2. | |
| 3. | |
| 4. | |
| 5. | |

A

Name _____ Date _____ Selection _____

# Making Inferences

Use this organizer to make inferences about the characters and their conflicts. Next to each inference, write details from the text that support your inference.

| My Inferences | Textual Evidence (Supporting Details) |
|---|---|
| 1. | |
| 2. | |
| 3. | |
| 4. | |
| 5. | |

Name _____ Date _____ Selection _____

# Making Inferences

Use this organizer to make inferences about the characters and their conflicts. Next to each inference, write details from the text that support your inference.

| My Inferences | Textual Evidence (Supporting Details) |
|---|---|
| 1. | |
| 2. | |
| 3. | |
| 4. | |
| 5. | |

C

For use with Literature 1

Name _____ Date _____ Selection _____

# Making Inferences

Use this organizer to make inferences about the characters and their conflicts. Next to each inference, write details from the text that support your inference.

| My Inferences | Textual Evidence (Supporting Details) |
|---|---|
| 1. | |
| 2. | |
| 3. | |
| 4. | |
| 5. | |

D

Name _____ Date _____ Selection _____

## Making Inferences

Use this organizer to make inferences about the characters and their conflicts. Next to each inference, write details from the text that support your inference.

| My Inferences | Textual Evidence (Supporting Details) |
|---|---|
| 1. | |
| 2. | |
| 3. | |
| 4. | |
| 5. | |

E

For use with Literature 1

Name _____ Date _____ Selection _____

# Making Inferences

Use this organizer to make inferences about the characters and their conflicts. Next to each inference, write details from the text that support your inference.

| My Inferences | Textual Evidence (Supporting Details) |
|---|---|
| 1. | |
| 2. | |
| 3. | |
| 4. | |
| 5. | |

F

# Literature 2

> 2. **Determine a theme or central idea of a text and analyze in detail its development over the course of the text, including how it emerges and is shaped and refined by specific details; provide an objective summary of the text.**

## Explanation

At the end of a movie, the main character sometimes tells everyone what he or she has learned from his or her experiences. For example, the character might say, "Nothing is more important than family." This is the movie's **theme,** or central idea or message about life. In a literary work, the theme is usually not stated directly, but is implied, or hinted at. To figure out the theme, pay close attention to important details in the text and note how the author uses them to explore an overall concept or to make a comment on life. You can begin to analyze how an author develops a theme by making an objective **summary,** a brief restatement of the important details in a work.

## Examples

- To write an objective **summary**, you briefly restate the important details of a work. In "The Emperor's New Clothes," you might say, "A vain emperor seeks a unique addition to his wardrobe. Two swindlers tell him that garments they will weave will be of the most exotic kind—made of a material that will be visible only to those worthy of royal status. The swindlers pretend to weave the garments. The officers can see nothing being done, but they are afraid of appearing unworthy of their royal positions, so they say nothing. When the swindlers announce that the new garments are ready, the emperor pretends to put them on in front of the townspeople in a big public ceremony. At the ceremony, the townspeople pretend to admire the emperor's new clothes. In the crowd, however, a lone child dares to speak up and observe that the emperor is wearing nothing at all."

- To determine the **theme,** or central idea, analyze details in the text for clues about the message the writer is trying to express. These details might relate to the main characters, setting, central conflict, or even title. Pay special attention to how characters change or grow over the course of a text. Then ask yourself, "What do these details show me about life or human nature?"

## Academic Vocabulary

**theme** a story's central idea or message about life

**objective summary** a brief restatement of the important details in a work

## Apply the Standard

Use the worksheets that follow to help you apply the standard as you read. Several copies of each worksheet have been provided for you to use with a number of different selections.

- Summarizing a Text

- Analyzing a Central Idea or Theme

Name _____ Date _____ Selection _____

# Summarizing a Text

Use this organizer to identify the most important events or ideas in the text. Then, write a brief objective summary. Remember to leave your own opinions out of the summary.

| **Event or Idea** |
| --- |
|  |

↓

| **Event or Idea** |
| --- |
|  |

↓

| **Event or Idea** |
| --- |
|  |

↓

| **Final Outcome** |
| --- |
|  |

**Summary:**

.......................................................................................................................

.......................................................................................................................

.......................................................................................................................

.......................................................................................................................

.......................................................................................................................

.......................................................................................................................

.......................................................

Name _____ Date _____ Selection _____

## Summarizing a Text

Use this organizer to identify the most important events or ideas in the text. Then, write a brief objective summary. Remember to leave your own opinions out of the summary.

| **Event or Idea** |
|---|
| |

↓

| **Event or Idea** |
|---|
| |

↓

| **Event or Idea** |
|---|
| |

↓

| **Final Outcome** |
|---|
| |

**Summary:**

................................................................................................................

................................................................................................................

................................................................................................................

................................................................................................................

................................................................................................................

................................................................................................................

................................................................................................................

Name _____ Date _____ Selection _____

## Summarizing a Text

Use this organizer to identify the most important events or ideas in the text. Then, write a brief objective summary. Remember to leave your own opinions out of the summary.

| Event or Idea |
| --- |
| |

↓

| Event or Idea |
| --- |
| |

↓

| Event or Idea |
| --- |
| |

↓

| Final Outcome |
| --- |
| |

**Summary:**

........................................................................................................

........................................................................................................

........................................................................................................

........................................................................................................

........................................................................................................

........................................................................................................

........................................................................................................

C

Name _____ Date _____ Selection _____

# Summarizing a Text

Use this organizer to identify the most important events or ideas in the text. Then, write a brief objective summary. Remember to leave your own opinions out of the summary.

| **Event or Idea** |
|---|
| |

↓

| **Event or Idea** |
|---|
| |

↓

| **Event or Idea** |
|---|
| |

↓

| **Final Outcome** |
|---|
| |

**Summary:**

...........................................................................................................................

...........................................................................................................................

...........................................................................................................................

...........................................................................................................................

...........................................................................................................................

...........................................................................................................................

...........................................................................................................................

...........................................................

Name _____ Date _____ Selection _____

# Summarizing a Text

Use this organizer to identify the most important events or ideas in the text. Then, write a brief objective summary. Remember to leave your own opinions out of the summary.

**Event or Idea**

↓

**Event or Idea**

↓

**Event or Idea**

↓

**Final Outcome**

**Summary:**

................................................................................
................................................................................
................................................................................
................................................................................
................................................................................
................................................................................
................................................................................

E

Name _____ Date _____ Selection _____

## Summarizing a Text

Use this organizer to identify the most important events or ideas in the text. Then, write a brief objective summary. Remember to leave your own opinions out of the summary.

| **Event or Idea** |
| --- |
| |

↓

| **Event or Idea** |
| --- |
| |

↓

| **Event or Idea** |
| --- |
| |

↓

| **Final Outcome** |
| --- |
| |

**Summary:**

.............................................................................................................................
.............................................................................................................................
.............................................................................................................................
.............................................................................................................................
.............................................................................................................................
.............................................................................................................................
.............................................................................................................................

F

Name _____ Date _____ Selection _____

## Analyzing a Central Idea or Theme

Choose three important details from different parts of the text. Remember that these details might relate to the main characters, the setting, the central conflict, or even the title. Then use the organizer to analyze how the author uses these details to develop the text's theme, or central message.

**Analyzing Theme Development**

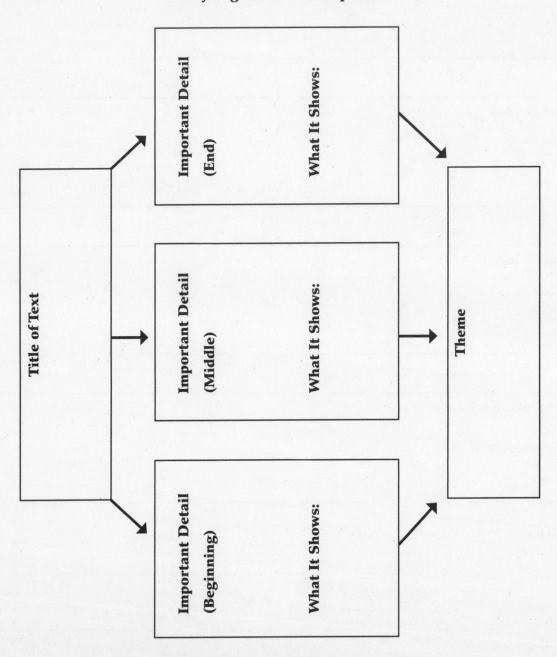

Title of Text

Important Detail (End)

What It Shows:

Important Detail (Middle)

What It Shows:

Important Detail (Beginning)

What It Shows:

Theme

Name _____  Date _____  Selection _____

## Analyzing a Central Idea or Theme

Choose three important details from different parts of the text. Remember that these details might relate to the main characters, the setting, the central conflict, or even the title. Then use the organizer to analyze how the author uses these details to develop the text's theme, or central message.

**Analyzing Theme Development**

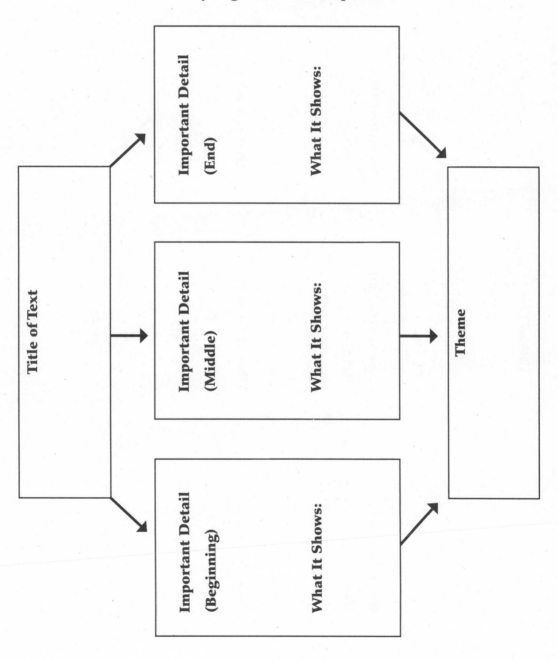

Name _____ Date _____ Selection _____

# Analyzing a Central Idea or Theme

Choose three important details from different parts of the text. Remember that these details might relate to the main characters, the setting, the central conflict, or even the title. Then use the organizer to analyze how the author uses these details to develop the text's theme, or central message.

**Analyzing Theme Development**

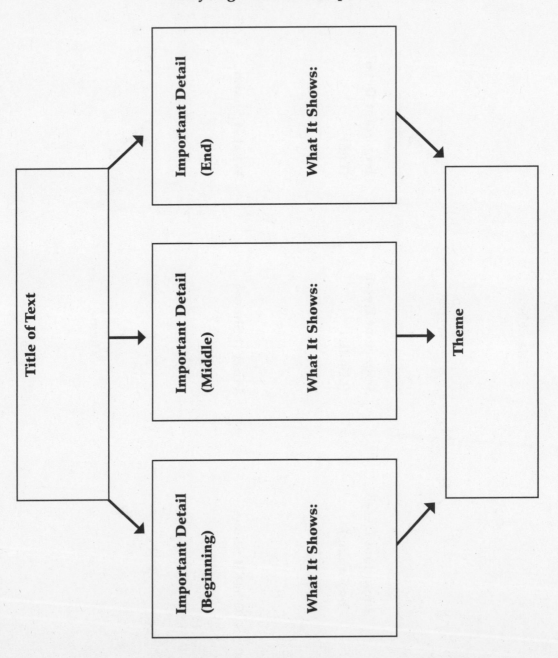

Name _____ Date _____ Selection _____

# Analyzing a Central Idea or Theme

Choose three important details from different parts of the text. Remember that these details might relate to the main characters, the setting, the central conflict, or even the title. Then use the organizer to analyze how the author uses these details to develop the text's theme, or central message.

**Analyzing Theme Development**

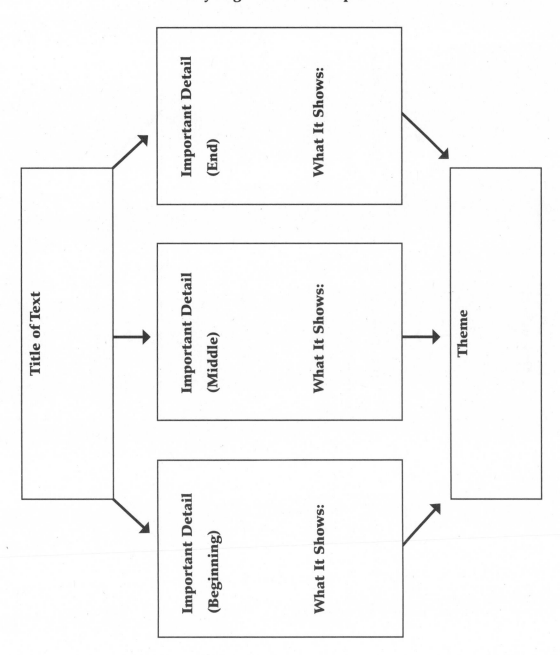

Name _____ Date _____ Selection _____

## Analyzing a Central Idea or Theme

Choose three important details from different parts of the text. Remember that these details might relate to the main characters, the setting, the central conflict, or even the title. Then use the organizer to analyze how the author uses these details to develop the text's theme, or central message.

**Analyzing Theme Development**

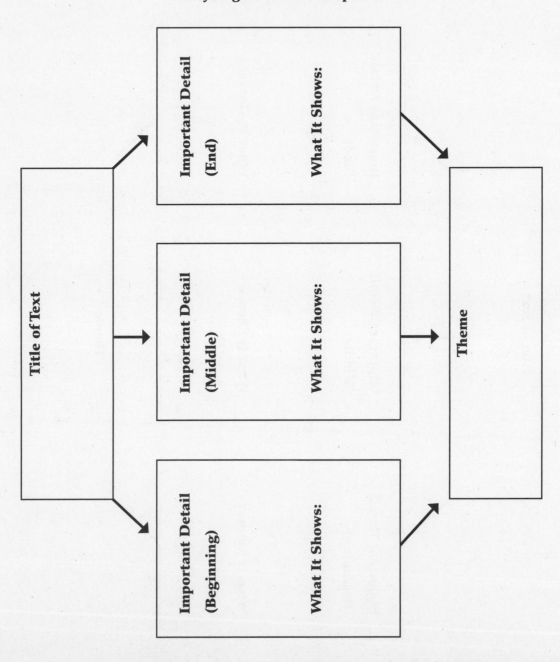

For use with Literature 2

Name _____ Date _____ Selection _____

## Analyzing a Central Idea or Theme

Choose three important details from different parts of the text. Remember that these details might relate to the main characters, the setting, the central conflict, or even the title. Then use the organizer to analyze how the author uses these details to develop the text's theme, or central message.

**Analyzing Theme Development**

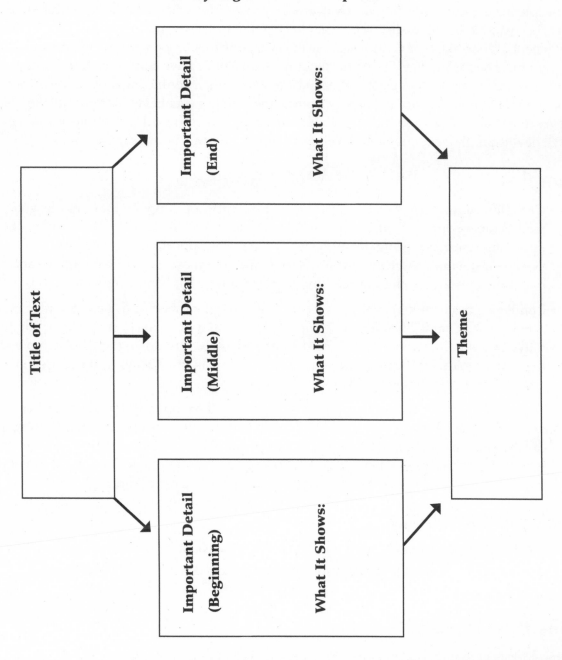

# Literature 3

3. **Analyze how complex characters (e.g., those with multiple or conflicting motivations) develop over the course of a text, interact with other characters, and advance the plot or develop the theme.**

## Explanation

Real people have many conflicting **motivations**, or reasons, for what they do. They want to be loved. They want to be successful. They want to be popular. They want to be admired for their achievements. Often, these motivations cause internal **conflicts,** as people try to figure out what they want most and what they should do about it. Good stories have **complex characters**, the type of characters who remind us of real people because of their conflicting motivations. These conflicting motivations can drive the story's **plot**—the series of events in the story. Noticing how a complex character changes and thinking about what he or she learns during the story will help you analyze how the author explores and develops the story's **theme**, or message about life.

## Examples

- **Complex characters** often have conflicting **motivations**. Suppose, for example, you read a story about a girl who wins a scholarship to study chemistry at a university where important research is being done. She really wants the opportunity to achieve her potential as a chemist. However, the university is thousands of miles away from her home, and the girl also wants to stay close to her family. This character has conflicting motivations.

- Conflicting motivations can drive the **plot** of a story by propelling a character into certain actions. For example, the girl in the story above might try to win another scholarship to a university closer to home. If she can't do that, she might turn down the scholarship but later regret her choice. Or she might accept the scholarship and find ways to stay close to friends and family, despite living far away.

- The way a character changes during a story can help develop the story's **theme**. For example, if the girl turns down the scholarship and then regrets her choice, the writer can explore the theme that denying your dreams leads to unhappiness. If she accepts the scholarship, yet stays emotionally close to friends and family, the writer can explore the theme that important relationships can survive even when people are separated.

## Academic Vocabulary

**motivation** a character's reason for doing things; what the character wants

**plot** the series of story events that establish and resolve the character's conflicts

**theme** a story's central idea or message about life

## Apply the Standard

Use the worksheet that follows to help you apply the standard as you read. Several copies of the worksheet have been provided for you to use with a number of different selections.

- Analyzing Characters

Name _____ Date _____ Selection _____

## Analyzing Characters

Use this organizer to analyze a complex character whose conflicting motivations advance a story's plot and help develop the story's theme.

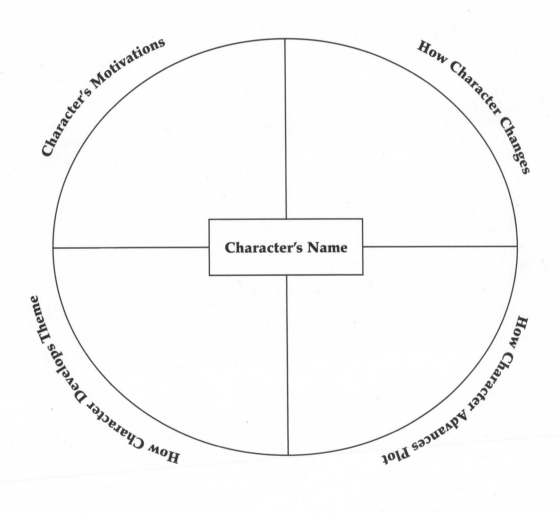

Analyzing Characters

Character's Motivations

How Character Changes

Character's Name

How Character Develops Theme

How Character Advances Plot

Name _____ Date _____ Selection _____

# Analyzing Characters

Use this organizer to analyze a complex character whose conflicting motivations advance a story's plot and help develop the story's theme.

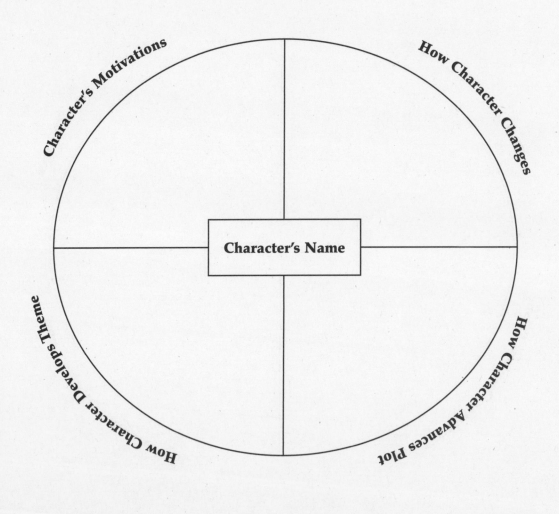

**Analyzing Characters**

Character's Motivations

How Character Changes

How Character Develops Theme

How Character Advances Plot

**Character's Name**

B

For use with Literature 3

Name _____ Date _____ Selection _____

## Analyzing Characters

Use this organizer to analyze a complex character whose conflicting motivations advance a story's plot and help develop the story's theme.

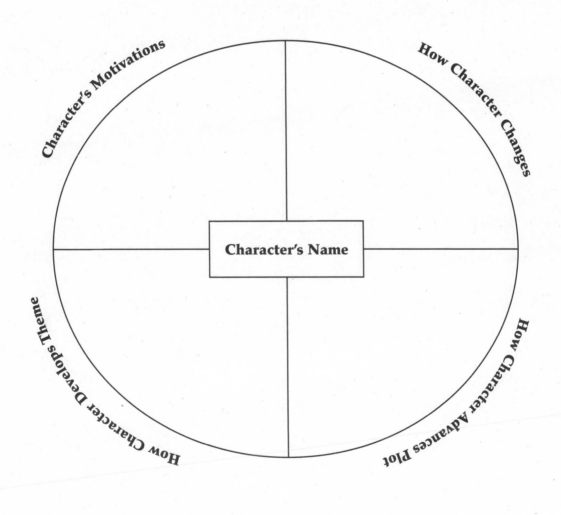

**Analyzing Characters**

Character's Motivations

How Character Changes

**Character's Name**

How Character Develops Theme

How Character Advances Plot

C

For use with Literature 3

Name _____ Date _____ Selection _____

## Analyzing Characters

Use this organizer to analyze a complex character whose conflicting motivations advance a story's plot and help develop the story's theme.

**Analyzing Characters**

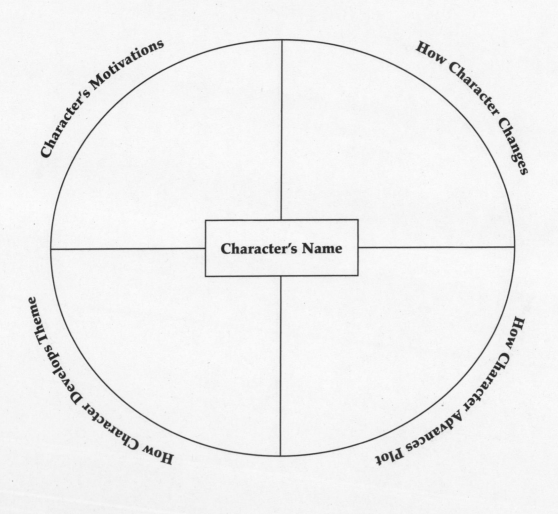

For use with Literature 3

Name _____ Date _____ Selection _____

# Analyzing Characters

Use this organizer to analyze a complex character whose conflicting motivations advance a story's plot and help develop the story's theme.

**Analyzing Characters**

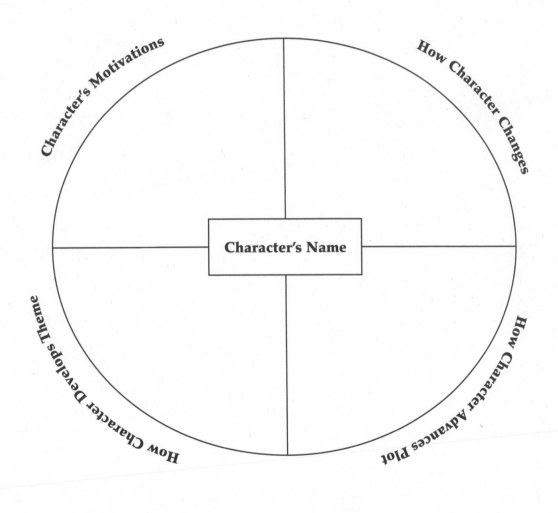

Name _____ Date _____ Selection _____

# Analyzing Characters

Use this organizer to analyze a complex character whose conflicting motivations advance a story's plot and help develop the story's theme.

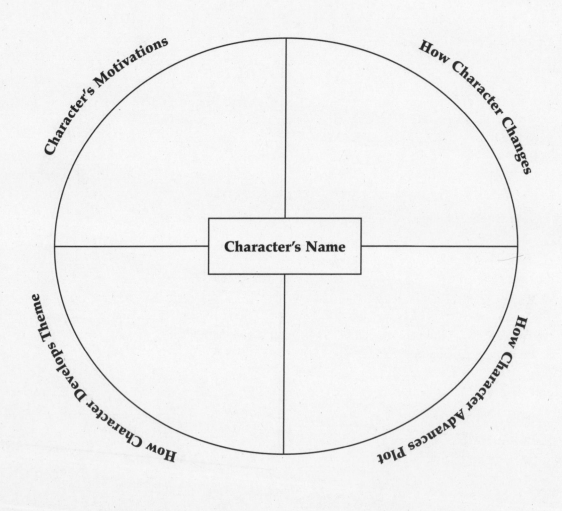

**Analyzing Characters**

For use with Literature 3

# Literature 4

> 4. **Determine the meaning of words and phrases as they are used in the text, including figurative and connotative meanings; analyze the cumulative impact of specific word choices on meaning and tone (e.g., how the language evokes a sense of time and place; how it sets a formal or informal tone).**

## Explanation

Words can express meaning and feeling. That's why writers choose their words carefully. By analyzing a writer's choice of words, you can figure out the meaning of a text and its **tone**—the attitude a writer expresses about a subject. Writers convey tone by using words with certain **connotations,** or positive or negative associations that the words suggest to the reader. Writers also convey meaning and emotion through **figurative language**—language that is used imaginatively, rather than literally. Figurative language includes such figures of speech as a simile and a metaphor.

## Examples

- Two words may have similar denotations, or dictionary meanings, but different positive or negative **connotations**. Understanding connotations in a text can help you figure out how the writer feels about a person, a place, or an idea. For example, if a writer admires someone who confidently expresses an opinion, the writer may describe that person as *bold* or *assertive*. However, if the writer wants to suggest disapproval of the person's manner or opinion, he or she might describe the person as *aggressive*, *pushy*, or *overbearing*.

- **Figurative language** expresses meaning and emotion and can also evoke a clear sense of time and place. For instance, if an author writes that a character's homework assignment "was a bear," the **metaphor** conveys the sense that the assignment was a very difficult and unwelcome task. The same author can create a very different meaning and tone by using a smile: "The homework assignment was like a game of chess."

- Once you have analyzed the most important words and phrases in a text, you are ready to figure out the cumulative effect of the author's word choices: the pattern of word choices that influences the text's overall **meaning and tone**.

## Academic Vocabulary

**connotations**  the positive or negative feelings associated with a word

**figurative language**  language that is not meant to be taken literally, including similes, metaphors, and personification

**tone**  the author's overall attitude, or feeling, toward the subject of a literary work

## Apply the Standard

Use the worksheets that follow to help you apply the standard as you read. Several copies of each worksheet have been provided for you to use with a number of different selections.

- Understanding Connotations and Figurative Language
- Analyzing Word Choices: Meaning and Tone

Name _____ Date _____ Selection _____

# Understanding Connotations and Figurative Language

Use this organizer to analyze the meaning of important words and phrases in a text, particularly the author's use of figurative language and words with positive or negative connotations.

| Word or Phrase | Connotation | Feeling It Expresses |
|---|---|---|
|  |  |  |
|  |  |  |
|  |  |  |
|  |  |  |
|  |  |  |

| Figurative Language | What It Means | Feeling It Expresses |
|---|---|---|
|  |  |  |
|  |  |  |
|  |  |  |
|  |  |  |
|  |  |  |

A

For use with Literature 4

Name _____ Date _____ Selection _____

# Understanding Connotations and Figurative Language

Use this organizer to analyze the meaning of important words and phrases in a text, particularly the author's use of figurative language and words with positive or negative connotations.

| Word or Phrase | Connotation | Feeling It Expresses |
|---|---|---|
|  |  |  |
|  |  |  |
|  |  |  |
|  |  |  |
|  |  |  |

| Figurative Language | What It Means | Feeling It Expresses |
|---|---|---|
|  |  |  |
|  |  |  |
|  |  |  |
|  |  |  |
|  |  |  |

B

For use with Literature 4

Name _____ Date _____ Selection _____

# Understanding Connotations and Figurative Language

Use this organizer to analyze the meaning of important words and phrases in a text, particularly the author's use of figurative language and words with positive or negative connotations.

| Word or Phrase | Connotation | Feeling It Expresses |
|---|---|---|
|  |  |  |
|  |  |  |
|  |  |  |
|  |  |  |
|  |  |  |

| Figurative Language | What It Means | Feeling It Expresses |
|---|---|---|
|  |  |  |
|  |  |  |
|  |  |  |
|  |  |  |
|  |  |  |

C

For use with Literature 4

Name _____ Date _____ Selection _____

# Understanding Connotations and Figurative Language

Use this organizer to analyze the meaning of important words and phrases in a text, particularly the author's use of figurative language and words with positive or negative connotations.

| Word or Phrase | Connotation | Feeling It Expresses |
|---|---|---|
|  |  |  |
|  |  |  |
|  |  |  |
|  |  |  |
|  |  |  |

| Figurative Language | What It Means | Feeling It Expresses |
|---|---|---|
|  |  |  |
|  |  |  |
|  |  |  |
|  |  |  |
|  |  |  |

D

For use with Literature 4

Name _____ Date _____ Selection _____

# Understanding Connotations and Figurative Language

Use this organizer to analyze the meaning of important words and phrases in a text, particularly the author's use of figurative language and words with positive or negative connotations.

| Word or Phrase | Connotation | Feeling It Expresses |
|---|---|---|
| | | |
| | | |
| | | |
| | | |
| | | |

| Figurative Language | What It Means | Feeling It Expresses |
|---|---|---|
| | | |
| | | |
| | | |
| | | |
| | | |

E

For use with Literature 4

Name _____ Date _____ Selection _____

## Understanding Connotations and Figurative Language

Use this organizer to analyze the meaning of important words and phrases in a text, particularly the author's use of figurative language and words with positive or negative connotations.

| Word or Phrase | Connotation | Feeling It Expresses |
|---|---|---|
|  |  |  |
|  |  |  |
|  |  |  |
|  |  |  |
|  |  |  |

**+**

| Figurative Language | What It Means | Feeling It Expresses |
|---|---|---|
|  |  |  |
|  |  |  |
|  |  |  |
|  |  |  |
|  |  |  |

F

Name _____ Date _____ Selection _____

# Analyzing Word Choices: Meaning and Tone

Use this organizer to analyze the overall impact that specific word choices have on meaning and tone in a text.

```
┌─────────────────────────────┐        ┌─────────────────────────────┐
│  ┌───────────────────────┐  │        │  ┌───────────────────────┐  │
│  │ Words and Phrases with│  │        │  │  Figurative Language  │  │
│  │     Connotations      │  │        │  └───────────────────────┘  │
│  └───────────────────────┘  │        │                             │
│                             │        │                             │
└─────────────────────────────┘        └─────────────────────────────┘
```

```
        ┌─────────────────────────────┐
        │  ┌───────────────────────┐  │
        │  │   Meaning and Tone    │  │
        │  └───────────────────────┘  │
        │                             │
        └─────────────────────────────┘
```

Name _____ Date _____ Selection _____

# Analyzing Word Choices: Meaning and Tone

Use this organizer to analyze the overall impact that specific word choices have on meaning and tone in a text.

**Words and Phrases with Connotations**

**Figurative Language**

**Meaning and Tone**

Name _____ Date _____ Selection _____

## Analyzing Word Choices: Meaning and Tone

Use this organizer to analyze the overall impact that specific word choices have on meaning and tone in a text.

> **Words and Phrases with Connotations**

> **Figurative Language**

> **Meaning and Tone**

Name _____ Date _____ Selection _____

## Analyzing Word Choices: Meaning and Tone

Use this organizer to analyze the overall impact that specific word choices have on meaning and tone in a text.

```
┌─────────────────────────────┐        ┌─────────────────────────────┐
│  ┌───────────────────────┐  │        │  ┌───────────────────────┐  │
│  │  Words and Phrases with│  │        │  │  Figurative Language   │  │
│  │      Connotations      │  │        │  └───────────────────────┘  │
│  └───────────────────────┘  │        │                             │
│                             │        │                             │
│                             │        │                             │
│                             │        │                             │
└─────────────────────────────┘        └─────────────────────────────┘
                 \                                   /
                  \                                 /
                   ↘                               ↙
              ┌─────────────────────────────┐
              │  ┌───────────────────────┐  │
              │  │   Meaning and Tone     │  │
              │  └───────────────────────┘  │
              │                             │
              │                             │
              │                             │
              └─────────────────────────────┘
```

D

For use with Literature 4

Name _____ Date _____ Selection _____

# Analyzing Word Choices: Meaning and Tone

Use this organizer to analyze the overall impact that specific word choices have on meaning and tone in a text.

**Words and Phrases with Connotations**

**Figurative Language**

**Meaning and Tone**

E

For use with Literature 4

Name _____  Date _____  Selection _____

# Analyzing Word Choices: Meaning and Tone

Use this organizer to analyze the overall impact that specific word choices have on meaning and tone in a text.

```
┌─────────────────────────────┐          ┌─────────────────────────────┐
│  ┌───────────────────────┐  │          │  ┌───────────────────────┐  │
│  │ Words and Phrases with │  │          │  │  Figurative Language  │  │
│  │     Connotations       │  │          │  └───────────────────────┘  │
│  └───────────────────────┘  │          │                             │
│                             │          │                             │
│                             │          │                             │
└─────────────────────────────┘          └─────────────────────────────┘
              │                                        │
              ↓                                        ↓
          ┌─────────────────────────────────────┐
          │  ┌───────────────────────────────┐  │
          │  │       Meaning and Tone        │  │
          │  └───────────────────────────────┘  │
          │                                     │
          │                                     │
          └─────────────────────────────────────┘
```

F

For use with Literature 4

# Literature 5

> 5. **Analyze how an author's choices concerning how to structure a text, order events within it (e.g., parallel plots), and manipulate time (e.g., pacing, flashbacks) create such effects as mystery, tension, or surprise.**

## Explanation

Authors use several techniques to create specific effects in their works, such as mystery, tension, or surprise. Typically, authors arrange the plot, or the series of events in a story, in chronological order—the order in which they take place in time—with events building to a climax, after which the conflict is resolved. However, authors sometimes choose to begin a story in the middle or to end a story with a surprise. Authors also sometimes include **parallel plots**, or two storylines. Manipulating a story's time is another technique authors use. Instead of telling events in chronological order, authors interrupt the sequence of events with **flashbacks,** scenes that occurred in the past. Authors can also vary the **pacing** of the story. By speeding up the action, an author can build excitement and tension. By slowing down the pace, the author creates room for description and character development.

## Examples

- An author chooses a **structure** and orders the events in the plot to keep readers interested in the story and wondering what will happen next. In Sir Arthur Conan Doyle's novel *The Hound of the Baskervilles*, for example, a series of mysterious events keeps readers guessing whether a vicious, gigantic dog has been killing the Baskerville family.

- An author can manipulate time in a story by including **flashbacks.** In *The Hound of the Baskervilles*, a visitor interrupts the flow of the story to tell about past events. The flashback illustrates why the Baskerville family has been cursed by the ghastly hound.

- An author can also create tension by varying the **pacing**—speeding up or slowing down the action in a story. In *The Hound of the Baskervilles*, for example, Dr. Watson gradually learns that there is a convict hiding out on the moor, and he decides to track down the criminal. When he and a friend walk across the moor at night, the pace suddenly quickens.

- A **parallel plot** is generally just as important as the main plot. Authors who use parallel plots tend to move back and forth from one to the other—often bringing both plots and sets of characters together in the end.

## Examples

**flashback** a scene that interrupts the plot to show events that happened in the past
**pacing** how quickly or slowly the action in a story unfolds
**parallel plot** a secondary storyline

## Apply the Standard

Use the worksheet that follows to help you apply the standard as you read. Several copies of the worksheet have been provided for you to use with a number of different selections.

- Analyze Author's Choices

Name _____ Date _____ Selection _____

# Analyze Author's Choices

Use this organizer to analyze the author's choices in a story. On the left, write the events that happen in each part of the story and describe any flashbacks. On the right, describe the pacing in each part of the story. At the bottom, describe how the author's choices create effects, such as mystery, tension, or surprise.

**Beginning**

Events:



Flashback?

Describe the Pacing:

**Middle**

Events:



Flashback?

Describe the Pacing:

**Ending**

Events:



Flashback?

Describe the Pacing:

Describe how the author's choices create effects such as mystery, tension, or surprise.

..............................................................................................

..............................................................................................

A

Name _____ Date _____ Selection _____

# Analyze Author's Choices

Use this organizer to analyze the author's choices in a story. On the left, write the events that happen in each part of the story and describe any flashbacks. On the right, describe the pacing in each part of the story. At the bottom, describe how the author's choices create effects, such as mystery, tension, or surprise.

**Beginning**

| Events: | Describe the Pacing: |
|---|---|
| | |
| Flashback? | |

**Middle**

| Events: | Describe the Pacing: |
|---|---|
| | |
| Flashback? | |

**Ending**

| Events: | Describe the Pacing: |
|---|---|
| | |
| Flashback? | |

Describe how the author's choices create effects such as mystery, tension, or surprise.

..........................................................................................................................

..........................................................................................................................

Name _____ Date _____ Selection _____

## Analyze Author's Choices

Use this organizer to analyze the author's choices in a story. On the left, write the events that happen in each part of the story and describe any flashbacks. On the right, describe the pacing in each part of the story. At the bottom, describe how the author's choices create effects, such as mystery, tension, or surprise.

**Beginning**

| Events: | Describe the Pacing: |
|---|---|
| | |
| **Flashback?** | |

**Middle**

| Events: | Describe the Pacing: |
|---|---|
| | |
| **Flashback?** | |

**Ending**

| Events: | Describe the Pacing: |
|---|---|
| | |
| **Flashback?** | |

Describe how the author's choices create effects such as mystery, tension, or surprise.

...................................................................................................................................

...................................................................................................................................

C

Name _____ Date _____ Selection _____

# Analyze Author's Choices

Use this organizer to analyze the author's choices in a story. On the left, write the events that happen in each part of the story and describe any flashbacks. On the right, describe the pacing in each part of the story. At the bottom, describe how the author's choices create effects, such as mystery, tension, or surprise.

**Beginning**

**Events:**

**Flashback?**

**Describe the Pacing:**

**Middle**

**Events:**

**Flashback?**

**Describe the Pacing:**

**Ending**

**Events:**

**Flashback?**

**Describe the Pacing:**

Describe how the author's choices create effects such as mystery, tension, or surprise.

................................................................................

................................................................................

D

Name _____ Date _____ Selection _____

# Analyze Author's Choices

Use this organizer to analyze the author's choices in a story. On the left, write the events that happen in each part of the story and describe any flashbacks. On the right, describe the pacing in each part of the story. At the bottom, describe how the author's choices create effects, such as mystery, tension, or surprise.

**Beginning**

| Events: | Describe the Pacing: |
|---|---|
| | |
| Flashback? | |

**Middle**

| Events: | Describe the Pacing: |
|---|---|
| | |
| Flashback? | |

**Ending**

| Events: | Describe the Pacing: |
|---|---|
| | |
| Flashback? | |

Describe how the author's choices create effects such as mystery, tension, or surprise.

.................................................................................................................................

.................................................................................................................................

E

Name _____ Date _____ Selection _____

# Analyze Author's Choices

Use this organizer to analyze the author's choices in a story. On the left, write the events that happen in each part of the story and describe any flashbacks. On the right, describe the pacing in each part of the story. At the bottom, describe how the author's choices create effects, such as mystery, tension, or surprise.

**Beginning**

Events:

Flashback?

Describe the Pacing:

**Middle**

Events:

Flashback?

Describe the Pacing:

**Ending**

Events:

Flashback?

Describe the Pacing:

Describe how the author's choices create effects such as mystery, tension, or surprise.

..................................................................................

..................................................................................

F

# Literature 6

> 6. Analyze a particular point of view or cultural experience reflected in a work of literature from outside the United States, drawing on a wide reading of world literature.

## Explanation

If you met someone from another country, you might discover that you have things in common, such as a love of video games and the Internet. You might also discover, however, that you have different beliefs, values, and customs. These differences reflect your **culture,** the way of life shared by the society in which you live. People are shaped by their **cultural experience,** the customs and expectations of their societies.

Works of literature are also shaped by culture. For example, an author's cultural experience can determine how the characters in a story act, what their motivations are, and how they respond to conflicts. Stories often reflect the **cultural point of view,** or way of seeing the world, of the society from which they arise. (This meaning of "point of view" should not be confused with the domain-specific definition of the phrase as the vantage point from which a story is told: first, second, or third person.) The more literature from around the world that you read, the better you will understand different cultural experiences and points of view.

## Examples

- Works of literature from different countries often reflect different values, beliefs, and points of view. For example, a story about a young American couple's wedding might be very different from an Indian story about the same subject. Many marriages in India are arranged by the young couple's parents. Young couples in India are expected to accept their parents' choices for the benefit of both families. The characters in the Indian story might therefore have motivations different from those of the characters in an American story.

- To analyze the point of view or cultural experience reflected in a work of world literature, ask yourself questions like these: *What does the main character do or feel? What values and beliefs motivate the character's behavior? What customs and expectations in the character's world are different from those in my world?*

## Academic Vocabulary

**culture**  way of life shared by the people living in a particular society

**cultural experience**  customs, beliefs, and expectations of a society

**cultural point of view**  way of seeing the world that is influenced by a particular culture

## Apply the Standard

Use the worksheet that follows to help you apply the standard as you read. Several copies of the worksheet have been provided for you to use with different literature selections.

- Analyzing Point of View in World Literature

Name _____ Date _____ Selection _____

# Analyzing Point of View in World Literature

Use the graphic organizer, below, to analyze the cultural point of view of a literary work from outside the United States. Identify and describe the cultural setting in the circles at the top of the organizer. Describe the characters' actions, feelings, and motivations in the circles at the bottom. In the center circle, describe the cultural point of view that the work reflects.

**Author and Title of Work:** ...............................................

**Cultural Setting**

.............................

**Customs of Culture**

.............................

**Cultural Point of View**

.............................

**Characters' Motivations**

.............................

**What Characters Do and Feel**

.............................

A

For use with Literature 6

Name _____ Date _____ Selection _____

# Analyzing Point of View in World Literature

Use the graphic organizer, below, to analyze the cultural point of view of a literary work from outside the United States. Identify and describe the cultural setting in the circles at the top of the organizer. Describe the characters' actions, feelings, and motivations in the circles at the bottom. In the center circle, describe the cultural point of view that the work reflects.

**Author and Title of Work:** ............................................

**Cultural Setting**

............................

**Customs of Culture**

............................

**Cultural Point of View**

............................

**Characters' Motivations**

............................

**What Characters Do and Feel**

............................

B

Name _____ Date _____ Selection _____

## Analyzing Point of View in World Literature

Use the graphic organizer, below, to analyze the cultural point of view of a literary work from outside the United States. Identify and describe the cultural setting in the circles at the top of the organizer. Describe the characters' actions, feelings, and motivations in the circles at the bottom. In the center circle, describe the cultural point of view that the work reflects.

**Author and Title of Work:** ...........................................

**Cultural Setting**

...........................

**Customs of Culture**

...........................

**Cultural Point of View**

...........................

**Characters' Motivations**

...........................

**What Characters Do and Feel**

...........................

C

For use with Literature 6

Name _____ Date _____ Selection _____

# Analyzing Point of View in World Literature

Use the graphic organizer, below, to analyze the cultural point of view of a literary work from outside the United States. Identify and describe the cultural setting in the circles at the top of the organizer. Describe the characters' actions, feelings, and motivations in the circles at the bottom. In the center circle, describe the cultural point of view that the work reflects.

**Author and Title of Work:** .........................................................

**Cultural Setting**
.........................

**Customs of Culture**
.........................

**Cultural Point of View**
.........................

**Characters' Motivations**
.........................

**What Characters Do and Feel**
.........................

D

Name _____ Date _____ Selection _____

# Analyzing Point of View in World Literature

Use the graphic organizer, below, to analyze the cultural point of view of a literary work from outside the United States. Identify and describe the cultural setting in the circles at the top of the organizer. Describe the characters' actions, feelings, and motivations in the circles at the bottom. In the center circle, describe the cultural point of view that the work reflects.

**Author and Title of Work:** ...............................................

**Cultural Setting**
.........................

**Customs of Culture**
.........................

**Cultural Point of View**
.........................

**Characters' Motivations**
.........................

**What Characters Do and Feel**
.........................

E

For use with Literature 6

Name _____ Date _____ Selection _____

# Analyzing Point of View in World Literature

Use the graphic organizer, below, to analyze the cultural point of view of a literary work from outside the United States. Identify and describe the cultural setting in the circles at the top of the organizer. Describe the characters' actions, feelings, and motivations in the circles at the bottom. In the center circle, describe the cultural point of view that the work reflects.

**Author and Title of Work:** ..............................................

**Cultural Setting**
.........................

**Customs of Culture**
.........................

**Cultural Point of View**
.........................

**Characters' Motivations**
.........................

**What Characters Do and Feel**
.........................

F

# Literature 7

> 7. **Analyze the representation of a subject or a key scene in two different artistic mediums, including what is emphasized or absent in each treatment (e.g., Auden's "Musée des Beaux Arts" and Brueghel's *Landscape with the Fall of Icarus*).**

## Explanation

Some subjects inspire not only authors but also painters, musicians, and other artists. For example, a character or a scene might appear in a play and also in a work in a different **medium,** or art form. Just as an author uses words to describe characters, settings, and events, other types of artists use different resources to create their own **representation,** or depiction, of a subject. By comparing an author's **treatment,** or way of presenting, a subject or key scene with that of an artist in a different medium, you can gain insights into the subject or scene itself.

## Examples

- In literary works, authors use language to describe scenes; to convey what characters say, think, and feel; and to express ideas and themes. In Act III, scene ii of Shakespeare's *Julius Caesar,* for example, the double-edged, ironic words of Marc Antony's famous funeral speech communicate a hidden message to the crowd: Caesar, accused by the conspirators of ambition, was actually a benefactor of the common people. When an actor interprets these words and accompanies them with gestures, he can give them added meaning.

- A painter depicting the same subject would of course have to do so without the use of language. The painter might choose to represent the scene just as Antony begins to turn the crowd against the conspirators. Antony could be earnestly gesturing, while members of the crowd look on, visibly interested. Some of the crowd might start to point accusingly at the conspirators, who have expressions of alarm.

- The visual depiction of the scene is therefore a kind of translation of it into a different medium. As with translations of literary works, things are both lost and gained in the process. The subtle ironies of language are replaced by one dramatic moment, portrayed with line, color, and composition.

## Academic Vocabulary

**medium**  particular form of art, such as literature, painting, sculpture, film, or music

**representation**  portrayal or depiction of a subject in a given artistic medium

**treatment**  way of presenting a given subject

## Apply the Standard

Use the worksheet that follows to help you apply the standard as you read. Several copies of the worksheet have been provided for you to use with different literature selections.

- Analyzing Representations in Different Mediums

Name _____ Date _____ Selection _____

# Analyzing Representations in Different Mediums

Use this organizer to analyze and compare the treatment of a literary character or scene in two different mediums. At the top, indicate the character or scene. Below that, enter the title and medium of both works and list the details emphasized in each work. Finally, record your comparative analysis on the lines provided.

**Literary Character or Scene:** ..................................................

```
Title:
Medium:
```

```
Title:
Medium:
```

**Emphasized Details**          **Emphasized Details**

**What key ideas, emotions, and themes are expressed or omitted in each treatment?**

....................................................................................................................

....................................................................................................................

....................................................................................................................

....................................................................................................................

....................................................................................................................

A

Name _____ Date _____ Selection _____

# Analyzing Representations in Different Mediums

Use this organizer to analyze and compare the treatment of a literary character or scene in two different mediums. At the top, indicate the character or scene. Below that, enter the title and medium of both works and list the details emphasized in each work. Finally, record your comparative analysis on the lines provided.

**Literary Character or Scene:** ................................................................

| |
|---|
| **Title:** |
| **Medium:** |

| |
|---|
| **Title:** |
| **Medium:** |

**Emphasized Details**         **Emphasized Details**

**What key ideas, emotions, and themes are expressed or omitted in each treatment?**

...................................................................................................

...................................................................................................

...................................................................................................

...................................................................................................

...................................................................................................

Name _____ Date _____ Selection _____

# Analyzing Representations in Different Mediums

Use this organizer to analyze and compare the treatment of a literary character or scene in two different mediums. At the top, indicate the character or scene. Below that, enter the title and medium of both works and list the details emphasized in each work. Finally, record your comparative analysis on the lines provided.

**Literary Character or Scene:** ...............................................

**Title:**
**Medium:**

**Title:**
**Medium:**

**Emphasized Details**

**Emphasized Details**

**What key ideas, emotions, and themes are expressed or omitted in each treatment?**

.............................................................................................................................

.............................................................................................................................

.............................................................................................................................

.............................................................................................................................

.............................................................................................................................

Name _____ Date _____ Selection _____

# Analyzing Representations in Different Mediums

Use this organizer to analyze and compare the treatment of a literary character or scene in two different mediums. At the top, indicate the character or scene. Below that, enter the title and medium of both works and list the details emphasized in each work. Finally, record your comparative analysis on the lines provided.

**Literary Character or Scene:** ............................................................

| |
|---|
| **Title:** |
| **Medium:** |

| |
|---|
| **Title:** |
| **Medium:** |

Emphasized Details          Emphasized Details

**What key ideas, emotions, and themes are expressed or omitted in each treatment?**

........................................................................................

........................................................................................

........................................................................................

........................................................................................

........................................................................................

D

Name _____ Date _____ Selection _____

# Analyzing Representations in Different Mediums

Use this organizer to analyze and compare the treatment of a literary character or scene in two different mediums. At the top, indicate the character or scene. Below that, enter the title and medium of both works and list the details emphasized in each work. Finally, record your comparative analysis on the lines provided.

**Literary Character or Scene:** ........................................................

**Title:**
**Medium:**

**Title:**
**Medium:**

**Emphasized Details**          **Emphasized Details**

**What key ideas, emotions, and themes are expressed or omitted in each treatment?**

...........................................................................................................

...........................................................................................................

...........................................................................................................

...........................................................................................................

...........................................................................................................

E

Name _____ Date _____ Selection _____

# Analyzing Representations in Different Mediums

Use this organizer to analyze and compare the treatment of a literary character or scene in two different mediums. At the top, indicate the character or scene. Below that, enter the title and medium of both works and list the details emphasized in each work. Finally, record your comparative analysis on the lines provided.

**Literary Character or Scene:** ...................................................

| |
|---|
| **Title:** |
| **Medium:** |

| |
|---|
| **Title:** |
| **Medium:** |

**Emphasized Details**          **Emphasized Details**

**What key ideas, emotions, and themes are expressed or omitted in each treatment?**

.............................................................................................

.............................................................................................

.............................................................................................

.............................................................................................

.............................................................................................

# Literature 9

> **9.** Analyze how an author draws on and transforms source material in a specific work (e.g., how Shakespeare treats a theme or topic from Ovid or the Bible or how a later author draws on a play by Shakespeare).

## Explanation

Some classic stories or literary works have a powerful hold on the human imagination and continue to inspire new authors generation after generation. Drawing on the **source material,** or original text, later writers choose which elements of the original to preserve and which elements to change or transform. By doing so, they shed new light on old characters and themes, often reinterpreting older works from the perspective of their own times.

## Examples

- Classic works of literature are often used by writers as source material for new works that are faithful to some elements of the original text but transform others. For example, the story of King Arthur first appeared in ancient British legends. In the late 1400s, these legends inspired Sir Thomas Malory to write *Le Morte d'Arthur* ("The Death of Arthur"), a series of prose tales about Arthur that reflected the values of chivalry in Malory's own medieval era. Then, in the mid-1800s, Alfred, Lord Tennyson wrote *Idylls of the King*, twelve narrative poems based largely on Malory's version of the Arthurian tales. Using characters and episodes from the ancient legends, these poems explored ideals and moral conflicts of Tennyson's own Victorian age.

- Twentieth-century authors have also been inspired by the Arthurian legends, often revising them to include contemporary perspectives. For instance, in the 1940s, T.H. White retold the Arthurian legends in a four-part novel called *The Once and Future King*. The first part focuses on the king's youth, portraying him as a mischievous, awkward boy who only reluctantly accepts his fate as a hero. More recently, the musical *Spamalot* presented a parody of the Arthurian legends, using humor to satirize the romantic, idealistic themes of the source material.

## Academic Vocabulary

**source material**  original text from which later writers draw inspiration

## Apply the Standard

Use the worksheet that follows to help you apply the standard as you read. Several copies of the worksheet have been provided for you to use with different literature selections.

- Analyzing How an Author Transforms Source Material

Name _____ Date _____ Selection _____

# Analyzing How an Author Transforms Source Material

Use the chart, below, to identify elements of a source that a later literary work drew upon. In the second column, explain how the later author transforms those elements.

**Title and author of source:** ..................................................................................................

**Title and author of later work:** .............................................................................................

| | Source Material | How Transformed in Later Work |
|---|---|---|
| **Literary Form** | | |
| **Main Characters** | | |
| **Setting** | | |
| **Conflict** | | |
| **Tone** | | |
| **Language** | | |
| **Theme** | | |

A

For use with Literature 9

Name _____ Date _____ Selection _____

# Analyzing How an Author Transforms Source Material

Use the chart, below, to identify elements of a source that a later literary work drew upon. In the second column, explain how the later author transforms those elements.

**Title and author of source:** ..................................................................................................

**Title and author of later work:** .............................................................................................

|  | Source Material | How Transformed in Later Work |
|---|---|---|
| **Literary Form** | | |
| **Main Characters** | | |
| **Setting** | | |
| **Conflict** | | |
| **Tone** | | |
| **Language** | | |
| **Theme** | | |

COMMON CORE COMPANION • COMMON CORE COMPANION • COMMON CORE COMPANION

Name _____ Date _____ Selection _____

# Analyzing How an Author Transforms Source Material

Use the chart, below, to identify elements of a source that a later literary work drew upon. In the second column, explain how the later author transforms those elements.

**Title and author of source:** .................................................................................................

**Title and author of later work:** .........................................................................................

|  | **Source Material** | **How Transformed in Later Work** |
|---|---|---|
| **Literary Form** | | |
| **Main Characters** | | |
| **Setting** | | |
| **Conflict** | | |
| **Tone** | | |
| **Language** | | |
| **Theme** | | |

C

For use with Literature 9

Name _____ Date _____ Selection _____

# Analyzing How an Author Transforms Source Material

Use the chart, below, to identify elements of a source that a later literary work drew upon. In the second column, explain how the later author transforms those elements.

**Title and author of source:** ...............................................................................................

**Title and author of later work:** ........................................................................................

|  | **Source Material** | **How Transformed in Later Work** |
|---|---|---|
| **Literary Form** |  |  |
| **Main Characters** |  |  |
| **Setting** |  |  |
| **Conflict** |  |  |
| **Tone** |  |  |
| **Language** |  |  |
| **Theme** |  |  |

D

Name _____ Date _____ Selection _____

# Analyzing How an Author Transforms Source Material

Use the chart, below, to identify elements of a source that a later literary work drew upon. In the second column, explain how the later author transforms those elements.

**Title and author of source:** ..................................................................................................

**Title and author of later work:** ............................................................................................

|  | Source Material | How Transformed in Later Work |
|---|---|---|
| **Literary Form** |  |  |
| **Main Characters** |  |  |
| **Setting** |  |  |
| **Conflict** |  |  |
| **Tone** |  |  |
| **Language** |  |  |
| **Theme** |  |  |

E

For use with Literature 9

Name _____ Date _____ Selection _____

# Analyzing How an Author Transforms Source Material

Use the chart, below, to identify elements of a source that a later literary work drew upon. In the second column, explain how the later author transforms those elements.

**Title and author of source:** ................................................................................................................

**Title and author of later work:** ..........................................................................................................

|  | **Source Material** | **How Transformed in Later Work** |
|---|---|---|
| **Literary Form** |  |  |
| **Main Characters** |  |  |
| **Setting** |  |  |
| **Conflict** |  |  |
| **Tone** |  |  |
| **Language** |  |  |
| **Theme** |  |  |

F

# Literature 10

> 10. By the end of grade 10, read and comprehend literature, including stories, dramas, and poems, at the high end of the grades 9–10 text complexity band independently and proficiently.

## Explanation

Literary works vary in their **complexity,** or the degree to which they are difficult to understand and analyze. Some works focus on familiar subjects, include explicitly stated ideas, and are written in a simple style, featuring conversational vocabulary and short sentences. However, other works introduce readers to unfamiliar concepts, have implied ideas and themes, and feature advanced vocabulary, figurative language, and long sentences.

In grade 10, you will read literary works of all genres, including stories, dramas, and poems. You will also be expected to **comprehend,** or understand the meaning and importance of, texts of increasing complexity. To comprehend complex texts, use reading strategies such as monitoring comprehension, connecting, visualizing, and paraphrasing.

## Examples

- **To monitor your comprehension** as you read, stop periodically and ask yourself questions about the text. For example, as you read Italo Calvino's story "The Garden of Stubborn Cats," you might stop to ask yourself where and when the action takes place. To find answers to your questions, reread, read ahead, or use context clues.

- **To visualize and connect** with a story, poem, or drama as you read, picture what the author describes and relate it to your own experience. For example, as you read Carl Sandburg's poem "Jazz Fantasia," picture the musicians the poet describes and relate the poem to your own feelings about music.

- **To paraphrase challenging passages** in a story, poem, or drama, restate the author's language and ideas in your own words. For example, as you read William Shakespeare's drama *The Tragedy of Julius Caesar*, check your comprehension by paraphrasing lines that are difficult to comprehend.

## Academic Vocabulary

**complexity** the degree to which a literary work is difficult to understand and analyze

**comprehend** understand the meaning and importance of something, such as a literary work

## Apply the Standard

Use the worksheet that follows to help you apply the standard as you read. Several copies have been provided for you to use with different literature selections.

- Comprehending Complex Texts

Name _____ Date _____ Assignment _____

# Comprehending Complex Texts

First, rate a story, poem, or drama you are reading in terms of its complexity and describe what makes the work complex. Then, use the table below to explain which reading strategies you used and how they helped you comprehend the work.

**Rate the Selection:** _____     1 = not complex     2 = somewhat complex     3 = very complex

**Describe the selection's complexity:** ................................................................................

| Strategy | How I Used It | How It Helped |
|---|---|---|
| monitoring comprehension | | |
| visualizing | | |
| connecting | | |
| paraphrasing | | |

For use with Literature 10

Name _____ Date _____ Assignment _____

# Comprehending Complex Texts

First, rate a story, poem, or drama you are reading in terms of its complexity and describe what makes the work complex. Then, use the table below to explain which reading strategies you used and how they helped you comprehend the work.

**Rate the Selection:** _____    1 = not complex    2 = somewhat complex    3 = very complex

**Describe the selection's complexity:** .................................................................................................

| Strategy | How I Used It | How It Helped |
|---|---|---|
| monitoring comprehension | | |
| visualizing | | |
| connecting | | |
| paraphrasing | | |

Name _____ Date _____ Assignment _____

# Comprehending Complex Texts

First, rate a story, poem, or drama you are reading in terms of its complexity and describe what makes the work complex. Then, use the table below to explain which reading strategies you used and how they helped you comprehend the work.

**Rate the Selection:** _____     1 = not complex     2 = somewhat complex     3 = very complex

**Describe the selection's complexity:** ...........................................................................................

| Strategy | How I Used It | How It Helped |
|---|---|---|
| **monitoring comprehension** | | |
| **visualizing** | | |
| **connecting** | | |
| **paraphrasing** | | |

Name _____ Date _____ Assignment _____

# Comprehending Complex Texts

First, rate a story, poem, or drama you are reading in terms of its complexity and describe what makes the work complex. Then, use the table below to explain which reading strategies you used and how they helped you comprehend the work.

**Rate the Selection:** _____    1 = not complex    2 = somewhat complex    3 = very complex

**Describe the selection's complexity:** ................................................................................

| Strategy | How I Used It | How It Helped |
|---|---|---|
| monitoring comprehension | | |
| visualizing | | |
| connecting | | |
| paraphrasing | | |

Name _____ Date _____ Assignment _____

# Comprehending Complex Texts

First, rate a story, poem, or drama you are reading in terms of its complexity and describe what makes the work complex. Then, use the table below to explain which reading strategies you used and how they helped you comprehend the work.

**Rate the Selection:** _____    1 = not complex    2 = somewhat complex    3 = very complex

**Describe the selection's complexity:** ....................................................................................

| Strategy | How I Used It | How It Helped |
|---|---|---|
| **monitoring comprehension** | | |
| **visualizing** | | |
| **connecting** | | |
| **paraphrasing** | | |

E

Name _____ Date _____ Assignment _____

# Comprehending Complex Texts

First, rate a story, poem, or drama you are reading in terms of its complexity and describe what makes the work complex. Then, use the table below to explain which reading strategies you used and how they helped you comprehend the work.

**Rate the Selection:** _____     1 = not complex     2 = somewhat complex     3 = very complex

**Describe the selection's complexity:** ...........................................................................................

| Strategy | How I Used It | How It Helped |
|---|---|---|
| **monitoring comprehension** | | |
| **visualizing** | | |
| **connecting** | | |
| **paraphrasing** | | |

F

# Reading Standards for Informational Text 1

# Informational Text 1

> 1. **Cite strong and thorough textual evidence to support analysis of what the text says explicitly as well as inferences drawn from the text.**

## Explanation

When you **analyze** an informational text, you examine it in great detail. A thorough analysis not only examines what the text says explicitly but also includes **inferences,** or conclusions you have drawn from the text. In your analysis of a text, you need to provide strong, thorough **textual evidence,** or details from the text, as support both for your analysis and inferences. Textual evidence can be quotes, facts, examples, and reasons. Be prepared to cite the textual evidence on which you base your inferences, as well as the exact words or details from the text that support your analysis.

## Examples

- Your analysis of an informational text should first examine what the text explicitly says. For example, the article "Tides" explicitly states that tides are caused by the interaction of the Earth with the moon and the sun. In your analysis, provide textual evidence that supports this point, including facts about the effect of the moon and sun's gravities on Earth's oceans. Cite also details about how the changing positions of the sun, Earth, and the moon create a monthly cycle of tides. Citing specific textual evidence such as this gives your analysis credibility.

- In your analysis, you should also make inferences and cite textual evidence that supports them. For example, after reading the article "The Spider and the Wasp," you might make the inference that the survival of the digger wasp species depends on the ability of female wasps to capture tarantulas. To support this inference, cite textual evidence stated in the article:
  - Female digger wasps hunt tarantulas to feed their larvae.
  - Digger wasp larvae eat only the captured tarantulas until they mature into adults.

These factual details provide strong, thorough support for the inference you have drawn.

## Academic Vocabulary

**analysis** a close examination of a text, including what the text states explicitly and what is implied

**inference** conclusions drawn from what is explicitly stated in a text

**textual evidence** details in the text, such as facts, examples, and reasons, on which an analysis is based

## Apply the Standard

Use the worksheets that follow to help you apply the standard as you read. Several copies of each worksheet have been provided for you to use with different informational texts.

- Identifying Strong Textual Evidence
- Making Inferences

Name _____  Date _____  Assignment _____

# Identifying Strong Textual Evidence

Use this organizer to identify textual evidence that supports what an informational text explicitly says. In the top box, write an idea that is explicitly stated in the text. Then, complete the chart by citing textual evidence to support the analysis. Finally, answer the question at the bottom of the page.

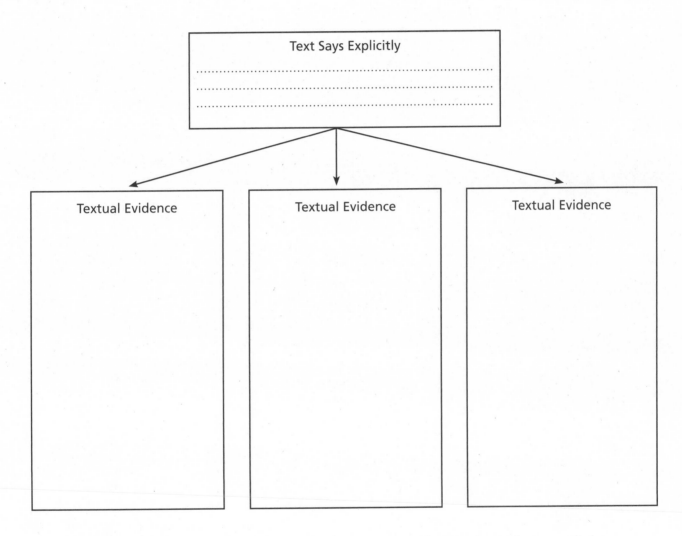

To what extent does the textual evidence cited above provide strong, thorough support?

................................................................................................................

................................................................................................................

................................................................................................................

................................................................................................................

................................................................................................................

**A**

For use with Informational Texts 1

Name _____ Date _____ Assignment _____

# Identifying Strong Textual Evidence

Use this organizer to identify textual evidence that supports what an informational text explicitly says. In the top box, write an idea that is explicitly stated in the text. Then, complete the chart by citing textual evidence to support the analysis. Finally, answer the question at the bottom of the page.

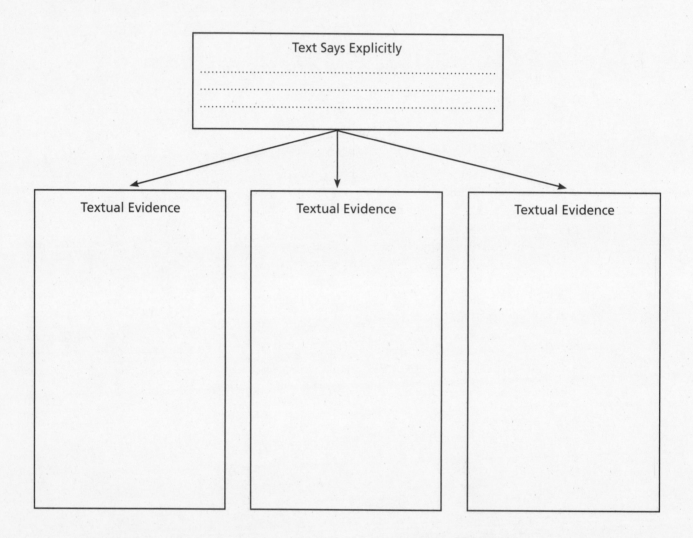

Text Says Explicitly

Textual Evidence

Textual Evidence

Textual Evidence

To what extent does the textual evidence cited above provide strong, thorough support?

........................................................................................................

........................................................................................................

........................................................................................................

........................................................................................................

Name _____  Date _____  Assignment _____

# Identifying Strong Textual Evidence

Use this organizer to identify textual evidence that supports what an informational text explicitly says. In the top box, write an idea that is explicitly stated in the text. Then, complete the chart by citing textual evidence to support the analysis. Finally, answer the question at the bottom of the page.

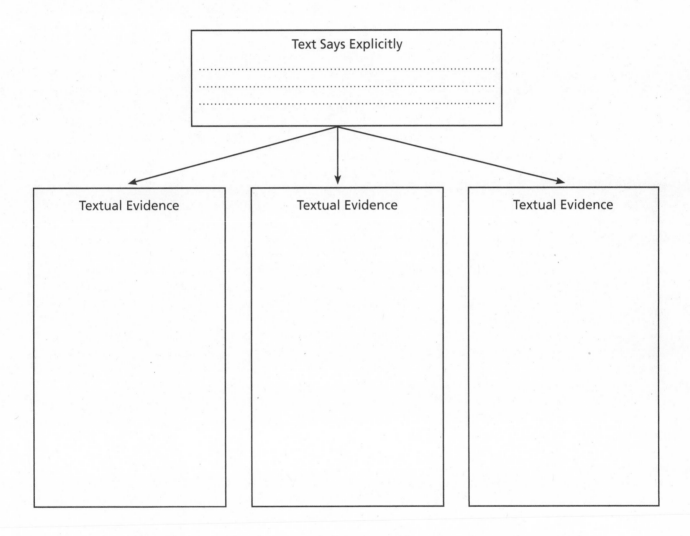

To what extent does the textual evidence cited above provide strong, thorough support?

......................................................................................................................................

......................................................................................................................................

......................................................................................................................................

......................................................................................................................................

......................................................................................................................................

For use with Informational Texts 1

Name _____   Date _____   Assignment _____

# Identifying Strong Textual Evidence

Use this organizer to identify textual evidence that supports what an informational text explicitly says. In the top box, write an idea that is explicitly stated in the text. Then, complete the chart by citing textual evidence to support the analysis. Finally, answer the question at the bottom of the page.

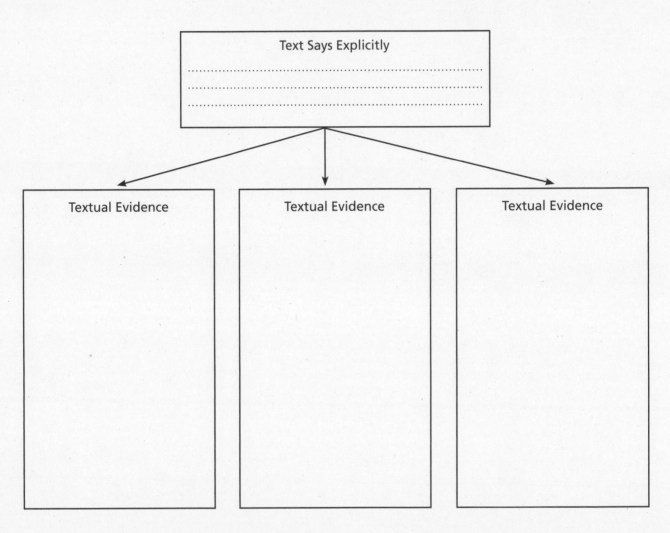

| Text Says Explicitly |
| --- |
| ...................................................... |
| ...................................................... |
| ...................................................... |

| Textual Evidence | Textual Evidence | Textual Evidence |
| --- | --- | --- |

To what extent does the textual evidence cited above provide strong, thorough support?

................................................................................................................

................................................................................................................

................................................................................................................

................................................................................................................

Name _____ Date _____ Assignment _____

# Identifying Strong Textual Evidence

Use this organizer to identify textual evidence that supports what an informational text explicitly says. In the top box, write an idea that is explicitly stated in the text. Then, complete the chart by citing textual evidence to support the analysis. Finally, answer the question at the bottom of the page.

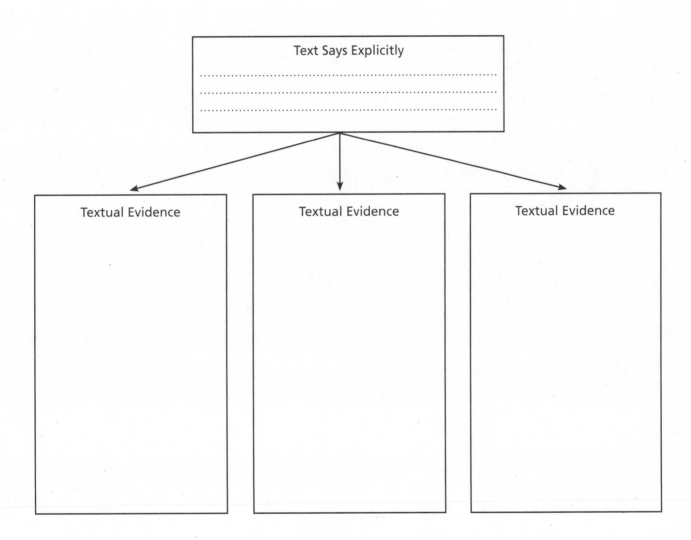

To what extent does the textual evidence cited above provide strong, thorough support?

................................................................................................................

................................................................................................................

................................................................................................................

................................................................................................................

E

Name _____ Date _____ Assignment _____

# Identifying Strong Textual Evidence

Use this organizer to identify textual evidence that supports what an informational text explicitly says. In the top box, write an idea that is explicitly stated in the text. Then, complete the chart by citing textual evidence to support the analysis. Finally, answer the question at the bottom of the page.

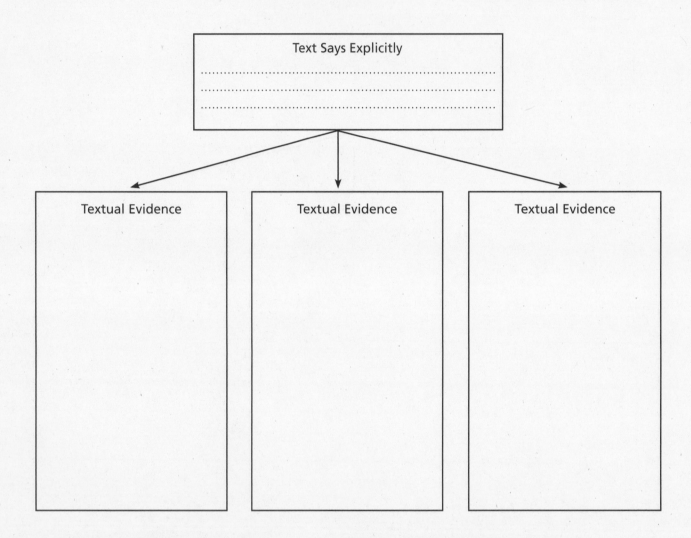

To what extent does the textual evidence cited above provide strong, thorough support?

..............................................................................................................................

..............................................................................................................................

..............................................................................................................................

..............................................................................................................................

F

Name _____ Date _____ Assignment _____

# Making Inferences

Use this organizer to make an inference and cite textual evidence to support that inference. Write your inference in the center box. Then, in the outer boxes, write textual evidence that provides strong, thorough support. Finally, answer the question at the bottom of the page.

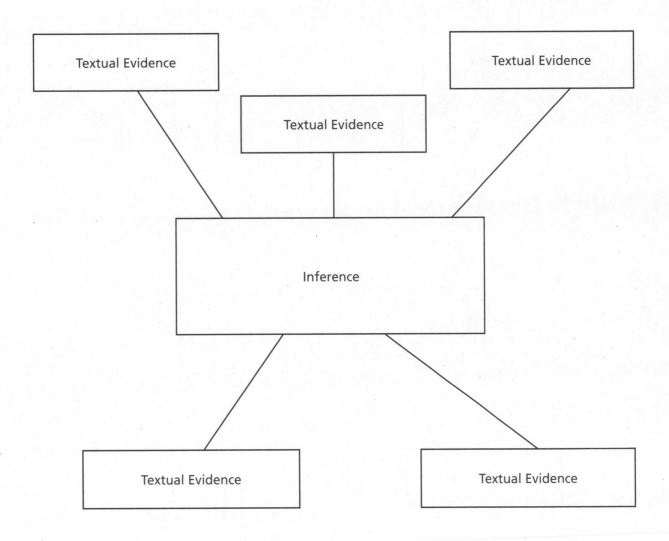

How well does the textual evidence cited provide strong, thorough support for your inference?

...............................................................................................................................

...............................................................................................................................

...............................................................................................................................

...............................................................................................................................

...............................................................................................................................

**A**

Name _____ Date _____ Assignment _____

## Making Inferences

Use this organizer to make an inference and cite textual evidence to support that inference. Write your inference in the center box. Then, in the outer boxes, write textual evidence that provides strong, thorough support. Finally, answer the question at the bottom of the page.

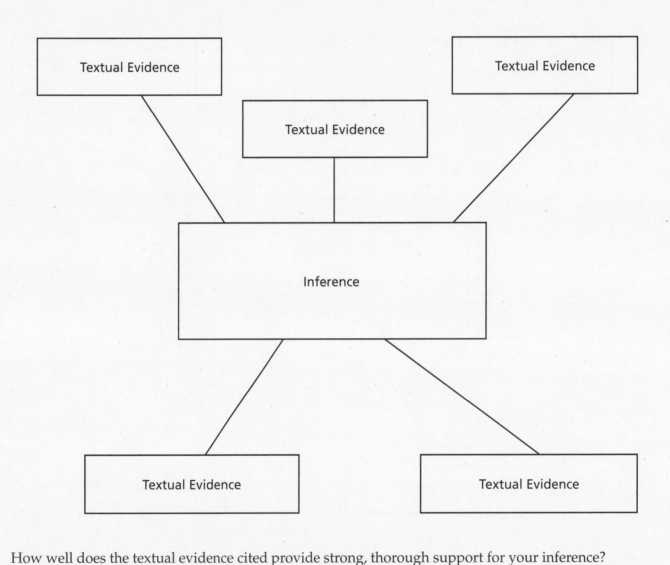

How well does the textual evidence cited provide strong, thorough support for your inference?

.................................................................................................

.................................................................................................

.................................................................................................

.................................................................................................

.................................................................................................

Name _____ Date _____ Assignment _____

# Making Inferences

Use this organizer to make an inference and cite textual evidence to support that inference. Write your inference in the center box. Then, in the outer boxes, write textual evidence that provides strong, thorough support. Finally, answer the question at the bottom of the page.

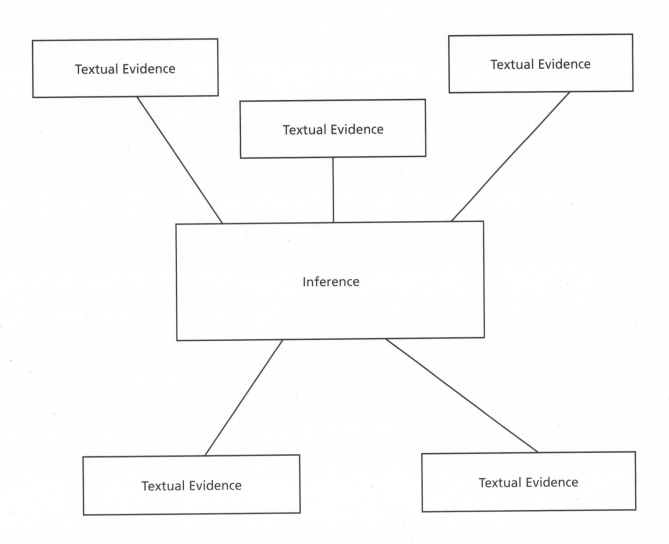

How well does the textual evidence cited provide strong, thorough support for your inference?

..........................................................................................................................

..........................................................................................................................

..........................................................................................................................

..........................................................................................................................

..........................................................................................................................

C                          For use with Informational Texts 1

Name _____ Date _____ Assignment _____

## Making Inferences

Use this organizer to make an inference and cite textual evidence to support that inference. Write your inference in the center box. Then, in the outer boxes, write textual evidence that provides strong, thorough support. Finally, answer the question at the bottom of the page.

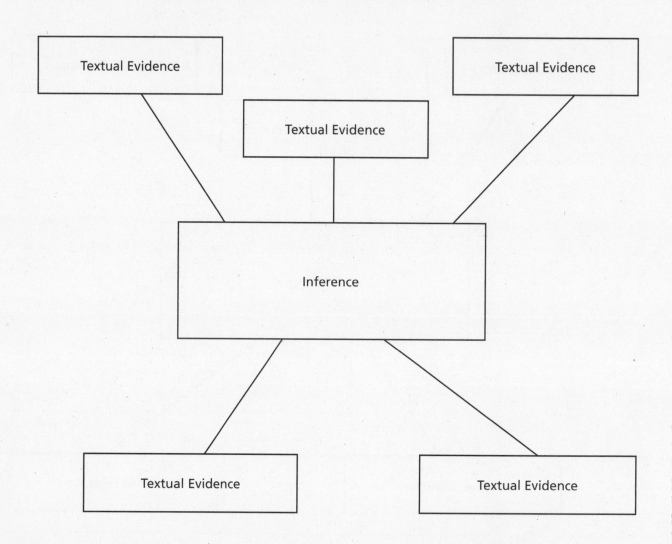

How well does the textual evidence cited provide strong, thorough support for your inference?

..........................................................................................

..........................................................................................

..........................................................................................

..........................................................................................

Name _____ Date _____ Assignment _____

# Making Inferences

Use this organizer to make an inference and cite textual evidence to support that inference. Write your inference in the center box. Then, in the outer boxes, write textual evidence that provides strong, thorough support. Finally, answer the question at the bottom of the page.

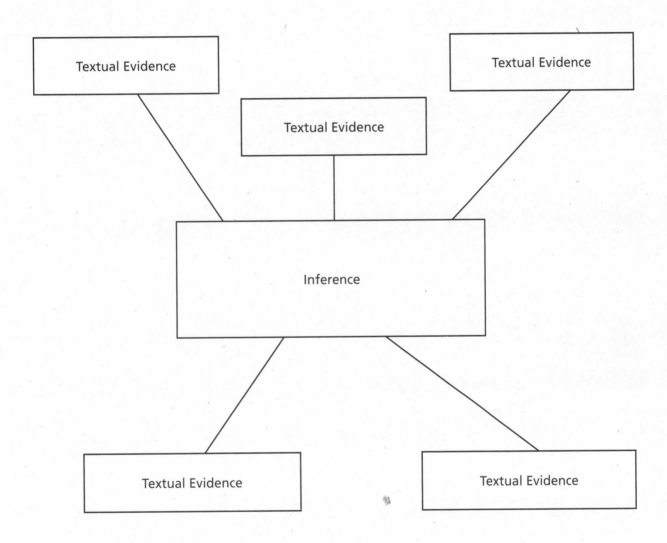

How well does the textual evidence cited provide strong, thorough support for your inference?

..........................................................................................................................
..........................................................................................................................
..........................................................................................................................
..........................................................................................................................
..........................................................................................................................

E

Name _____ Date _____ Assignment _____

# Making Inferences

Use this organizer to make an inference and cite textual evidence to support that inference. Write your inference in the center box. Then, in the outer boxes, write textual evidence that provides strong, thorough support. Finally, answer the question at the bottom of the page.

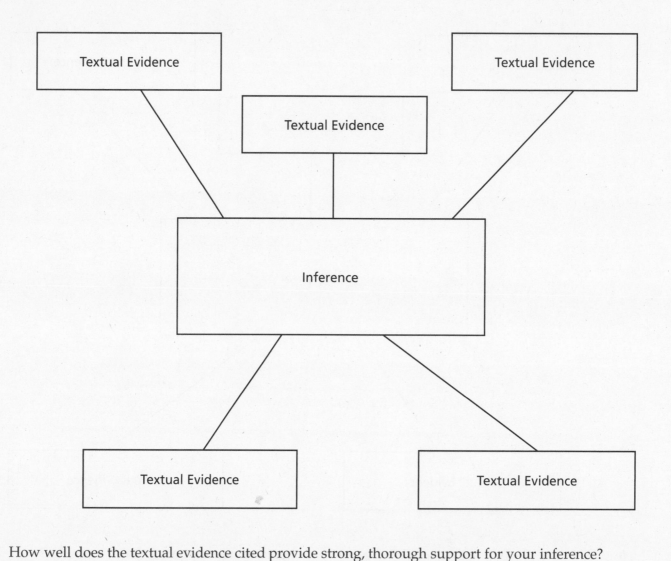

How well does the textual evidence cited provide strong, thorough support for your inference?

.....................................................................................................................................

.....................................................................................................................................

.....................................................................................................................................

.....................................................................................................................................

# Informational Text 2

> 2. **Determine a central idea of a text and analyze its development over the course of the text, including how it emerges and is shaped and refined by specific details; provide an objective summary of the text.**

## Explanation

An informational text may contain several ideas, but the text as a whole is usually organized around one **central idea.** This central idea, or thesis, is the main point that the author wants to make about the subject. An author usually presents the central idea in the opening paragraphs of the text. The author then develops the central idea in the remaining paragraphs by carefully selecting and arranging ideas and details that explain the thesis. Supporting details may include reasons, facts, examples, statistics, and statements from experts. Creating a summary is a good first step when analyzing a text. When you **summarize** a text, you briefly state in your own words its main idea and most important details.

## Examples

- The central idea of an informational text is often stated or implied in the opening paragraphs. For example, in the first paragraph of the essay "Making History with Vitamin C," the authors explain why the age of European naval exploration almost ended prematurely: Too many sailors were dying from scurvy, a disease caused by a lack of vitamin C in their diet. This paragraph suggests the essay's central idea that the age of exploration could not have continued without an improvement in the sailors' diets.

- The author then shapes and refines this thesis throughout the main body of the text by including specific facts and examples that support the thesis. In "Making History with Vitamin C," for example, the authors describe the devastating symptoms of scurvy, explaining that the disease is caused by a lack of vitamin C. They then describe how the disease affected European sailors on long ocean voyages. The authors next establish that once the sickness was diagnosed and the sailors' diet improved, efforts at eliminating scurvy were amazingly effective. The article concludes with an account of the discoveries Captain James Cook and his sailors were able to make, thanks to the health benefits of vitamin C.

## Academic Vocabulary

**central idea**  the main point the author wants to explain or prove; the thesis

**summarize**  to restate the main ideas and important details of a text in your own words

## Apply the Standard

Use the worksheets that follow to help you apply the standard as you read. Several copies of each worksheet have been provided for you for you to use with different informational texts.

- Summarizing the Text
- Analyzing the Central Idea

Name _____ Date _____ Assignment _____

# Summarizing the Text

Use the organizer below to briefly list only the most important ideas and details in the text. Then use the 3-4 main points from your organizer to write a summary. Remember, your summary should be objective. Tell only what was in the original source.

| Topic |
| --- |
| **Central idea** |
| **Most Important Details**<br><br>1.<br><br><br><br>2.<br><br><br><br>3. |

**Summary**

.................................................................................................................

.................................................................................................................

.................................................................................................................

.................................................................................................................

.................................................................................................................

.................................................................................................................

.................................................................................................................

.................................................................................................................

.................................................................................................................

A

Name _____ Date _____ Assignment _____

# Summarizing the Text

Use the organizer below to briefly list only the most important ideas and details in the text. Then use the 3-4 main points from your organizer to write a summary. Remember, your summary should be objective. Tell only what was in the original source.

| Topic |
|---|
| **Central idea** |
| **Most Important Details**<br><br>**1.**<br><br><br><br>**2.**<br><br><br><br>**3.** |

**Summary**

....................................................................................................................................

....................................................................................................................................

....................................................................................................................................

....................................................................................................................................

....................................................................................................................................

....................................................................................................................................

....................................................................................................................................

....................................................................................................................................

....................................................................................................................................

....................................................................................................................................

B

For use with Informational Text 2

Name _____  Date _____  Assignment _____

## Summarizing the Text

Use the organizer below to briefly list only the most important ideas and details in the text. Then use the 3-4 main points from your organizer to write a summary. Remember, your summary should be objective. Tell only what was in the original source.

| Topic |
| --- |
| Central idea |
| Most Important Details<br><br>1.<br><br><br><br>2.<br><br><br><br>3. |

## Summary

.................................................................................................................................

.................................................................................................................................

.................................................................................................................................

.................................................................................................................................

.................................................................................................................................

.................................................................................................................................

.................................................................................................................................

.................................................................................................................................

.................................................................................................................................

C

For use with Informational Text 2

Name _____ Date _____ Assignment _____

## Summarizing the Text

Use the organizer below to briefly list only the most important ideas and details in the text. Then use the 3-4 main points from your organizer to write a summary. Remember, your summary should be objective. Tell only what was in the original source.

| Topic |
| --- |
| **Central idea** |
| **Most Important Details**<br><br>1.<br><br><br><br>2.<br><br><br><br>3. |

## Summary

................................................................................................................

................................................................................................................

................................................................................................................

................................................................................................................

................................................................................................................

................................................................................................................

................................................................................................................

................................................................................................................

................................................................................................................

................................................................................................................

D

For use with Informational Text 2

Name _____ Date _____ Assignment _____

# Summarizing the Text

Use the organizer below to briefly list only the most important ideas and details in the text. Then use the 3-4 main points from your organizer to write a summary. Remember, your summary should be objective. Tell only what was in the original source.

| | |
|---|---|
| **Topic** | |
| **Central idea** | |
| **Most Important Details** <br><br>1.<br><br><br><br>2.<br><br><br><br>3. | |

**Summary**

..............................................................................................................................

..............................................................................................................................

..............................................................................................................................

..............................................................................................................................

..............................................................................................................................

..............................................................................................................................

..............................................................................................................................

..............................................................................................................................

..............................................................................................................................

E

For use with Informational Text 2

Name _____ Date _____ Assignment _____

# Summarizing the Text

Use the organizer below to briefly list only the most important ideas and details in the text. Then use the 3-4 main points from your organizer to write a summary. Remember, your summary should be objective. Tell only what was in the original source.

| Topic |
| --- |
| **Central idea** |
| **Most Important Details**<br><br>1.<br><br><br><br>2.<br><br><br><br>3. |

**Summary**

........................................................................................................................

........................................................................................................................

........................................................................................................................

........................................................................................................................

........................................................................................................................

........................................................................................................................

........................................................................................................................

........................................................................................................................

........................................................................................................................

........................................................................................................................

F

Name _____ Date _____ Assignment _____

## Analyzing the Central Idea

Use this organizer to analyze how an author develops the central idea of an informational text. Write the central idea (the thesis) in the top box. Write specific details from the text (reasons, facts, examples, statistics, and statements from experts) that help shape and develop the central idea in the other boxes. Then answer the question at the bottom of the page.

| Central Idea: |
|---|
| |

| Reasons | Facts | Examples | Statistics | Expert statements |
|---|---|---|---|---|
| | | | | |

How do the details listed above help develop the central idea?

......................................................................................................................

......................................................................................................................

......................................................................................................................

......................................................................................................................

......................................................................................................................

......................................................................................................................

A

Name _____ Date _____ Assignment _____

# Analyzing the Central Idea

Use this organizer to analyze how an author develops the central idea of an informational text. Write the central idea (the thesis) in the top box. Write specific details from the text (reasons, facts, examples, statistics, and statements from experts) that help shape and develop the central idea in the other boxes. Then answer the question at the bottom of the page.

**Central Idea:**

| Reasons | Facts | Examples | Statistics | Expert statements |
|---------|-------|----------|------------|-------------------|
|         |       |          |            |                   |

How do the details listed above help develop the central idea?

.......................................................................................................................

.......................................................................................................................

.......................................................................................................................

.......................................................................................................................

.......................................................................................................................

.......................................................................................................................

B          For use with Informational Text 2

Name _____ Date _____ Assignment _____

# Analyzing the Central Idea

Use this organizer to analyze how an author develops the central idea of an informational text. Write the central idea (the thesis) in the top box. Write specific details from the text (reasons, facts, examples, statistics, and statements from experts) that help shape and develop the central idea in the other boxes. Then answer the question at the bottom of the page.

**Central Idea:**

| Reasons | Facts | Examples | Statistics | Expert statements |
|---|---|---|---|---|
| | | | | |

How do the details listed above help develop the central idea?

......................................................................
......................................................................
......................................................................
......................................................................
......................................................................
......................................................................

Name _____ Date _____ Assignment _____

## Analyzing the Central Idea

Use this organizer to analyze how an author develops the central idea of an informational text. Write the central idea (the thesis) in the top box. Write specific details from the text (reasons, facts, examples, statistics, and statements from experts) that help shape and develop the central idea in the other boxes. Then answer the question at the bottom of the page.

**Central Idea:**

| Reasons | Facts | Examples | Statistics | Expert statements |
|---------|-------|----------|------------|-------------------|
|         |       |          |            |                   |

How do the details listed above help develop the central idea?

......................................................................................................

......................................................................................................

......................................................................................................

......................................................................................................

......................................................................................................

......................................................................................................

D

Name _____ Date _____ Assignment _____

# Analyzing the Central Idea

Use this organizer to analyze how an author develops the central idea of an informational text. Write the central idea (the thesis) in the top box. Write specific details from the text (reasons, facts, examples, statistics, and statements from experts) that help shape and develop the central idea in the other boxes. Then answer the question at the bottom of the page.

**Central Idea:**

| Reasons | Facts | Examples | Statistics | Expert statements |
|---|---|---|---|---|
|  |  |  |  |  |

How do the details listed above help develop the central idea?

...........................................................................................

...........................................................................................

...........................................................................................

...........................................................................................

...........................................................................................

E

**For use with Informational Text 2**

Name _____ Date _____ Assignment _____

## Analyzing the Central Idea

Use this organizer to analyze how an author develops the central idea of an informational text. Write the central idea (the thesis) in the top box. Write specific details from the text (reasons, facts, examples, statistics, and statements from experts) that help shape and develop the central idea in the other boxes. Then answer the question at the bottom of the page.

**Central Idea:**

| Reasons | Facts | Examples | Statistics | Expert statements |
|---------|-------|----------|------------|-------------------|
|         |       |          |            |                   |

How do the details listed above help develop the central idea?

........................................................................................

........................................................................................

........................................................................................

........................................................................................

........................................................................................

........................................................................................

F

# Informational Text 3

> 3. **Analyze how the author unfolds an analysis or series of ideas or events, including the order in which the points are made, how they are introduced and developed, and the connections that are drawn between them.**

## Explanation

To support their central ideas, authors present ideas and events in ways that will be easy and coherent for readers to follow. They introduce and develop ideas in **logical order,** using different text structures to make connections between the ideas and events clear to the reader. Among the text structures authors commonly use to make these connections are **chronological order, comparison-and-contrast,** and **cause-and-effect.**

## Examples

- Using **chronological order** allows authors to connect a number of events that happened over a period of time. For example, suppose that an author's central idea is that the Internet has changed the way that people relate to one another. To develop this idea, the author might relate a brief history of online social networking, with major events explained in chronological order—the order in which they actually happened. The author signals the order with such connecting words as *first, next, then, after that,* and *finally.*

- Using **cause-and-effect** order allows authors to develop and connect ideas by showing the consequences of related events—how and why one event led logically to another. For example, an author might use a cause-and-effect text structure to show that spending time on social networking sites causes people to spend less time interacting face-to-face with friends and family members. Words such as *because* and *as a result* signal cause-effect order.

- Using **comparison-and-contrast** allows authors to connect ideas by showing how they are alike and different. For example, an author might compare and contrast teenagers' and adults' usage of a variety of social networking sites. Words such as *similarly, in contrast,* and *on the other hand* signal comparison-contrast order.

## Academic Vocabulary

**cause-and-effect** a text structure used to explain how and why one event led to or influenced another

**chronological order** the arrangement of events in the order in which they actually occurred over a period of time

**comparison-and-contrast** a text structure used to explain how events or ideas are alike and different

**logical order** an order or sequence that makes sense and is easy for readers to follow

## Apply the Standard

Use the worksheet that follows to help you apply the standard as you read. Several copies of the worksheet have been provided for you to use with different informational texts.

- Analyzing the Development and Connection of Ideas

Name _____  Date _____  Assignment _____

# Analyzing the Development and Connection of Ideas

As you read informational texts, use this organizer to analyze how each author uses a particular text structure to develop and connect important details.

| Ideas Developed | Words Connecting the Ideas | Ideas Developed |
|---|---|---|
| | | |

Type of Connection Between Ideas

| Ideas Developed | Words Connecting the Ideas | Ideas Developed |
|---|---|---|
| | | |

Type of Connection Between Ideas

A

For use with Informational Text 3

Name _____ Date _____ Assignment _____

# Analyzing the Development and Connection of Ideas

As you read informational texts, use this organizer to analyze how each author uses a particular text structure to develop and connect important details.

| Ideas Developed | Words Connecting the Ideas | Ideas Developed |
|---|---|---|
| | | |

Type of Connection Between Ideas

| Ideas Developed | Words Connecting the Ideas | Ideas Developed |
|---|---|---|
| | | |

Type of Connection Between Ideas

B

Name _____ Date _____ Assignment _____

# Analyzing the Development and Connection of Ideas

As you read informational texts, use this organizer to analyze how each author uses a particular text structure to develop and connect important details.

| Ideas Developed | Words Connecting the Ideas | Ideas Developed |
|---|---|---|
|  |  |  |

| Type of Connection Between Ideas |
|---|
|  |

| Ideas Developed | Words Connecting the Ideas | Ideas Developed |
|---|---|---|
|  |  |  |

| Type of Connection Between Ideas |
|---|
|  |

C

For use with Informational Text 3

Name _____ Date _____ Assignment _____

# Analyzing the Development and Connection of Ideas

As you read informational texts, use this organizer to analyze how each author uses a particular text structure to develop and connect important details.

| Ideas Developed | Words Connecting the Ideas | Ideas Developed |
|---|---|---|
|  |  |  |

| Type of Connection Between Ideas |
|---|
|  |

| Ideas Developed | Words Connecting the Ideas | Ideas Developed |
|---|---|---|
|  |  |  |

| Type of Connection Between Ideas |
|---|
|  |

D

For use with Informational Text 3

Name _____ Date _____ Assignment _____

# Analyzing the Development and Connection of Ideas

As you read informational texts, use this organizer to analyze how each author uses a particular text structure to develop and connect important details.

| Ideas Developed | Words Connecting the Ideas | Ideas Developed |
|---|---|---|
|  |  |  |

Type of Connection Between Ideas

| Ideas Developed | Words Connecting the Ideas | Ideas Developed |
|---|---|---|
|  |  |  |

Type of Connection Between Ideas

E

Name _____ Date _____ Assignment _____

# Analyzing the Development and Connection of Ideas

As you read informational texts, use this organizer to analyze how each author uses a particular text structure to develop and connect important details.

| Ideas Developed | Words Connecting the Ideas | Ideas Developed |
|---|---|---|

| Type of Connection Between Ideas |
|---|

| Ideas Developed | Words Connecting the Ideas | Ideas Developed |
|---|---|---|

| Type of Connection Between Ideas |
|---|

F

# Informational Text 4

> **4. Determine the meaning of words and phrases as they are used in a text, including figurative, connotative, and technical meanings; analyze the cumulative impact of specific word choices on meaning and tone (e.g., how the language of a court opinion differs from that of a newspaper).**

## Explanation

Writers choose their words carefully because words convey both meanings and feelings. Two words may have similar dictionary meanings but different **connotations,** or positive or negative associations. Writers also convey meaning and emotion by using **figurative language,** such as similes and metaphors. Additionally, informational texts may include **technical terms,** words that have a special meaning in a particular field of study. By analyzing a writer's word choices, you can figure out the meaning of an informational text, as well as its **tone**—or the attitude it conveys about a subject.

## Examples

- Authors of different kinds of texts make specific word choices to convey different tones. For example, most legal documents include technical terms such as *pro bono* and convey a formal tone. A magazine article might use colloquial and figurative language, such as *spin* or *juice,* to convey a more casual, friendly tone.
- Many words with similar meanings have different connotations. A word's connotation can be positive, negative, or neutral. For example, *trusting* has a more positive connotation than *gullible.* Writers are aware of connotations and choose words specifically to convey different tones.
- Figurative language can also affect the meaning and tone of a piece of writing. For example, to describe an easygoing person as a "doormat" expresses disapproval.
- Informational texts may include common words with technical meanings (such as *current* in an article about electronics) or unfamiliar technical terms (such as *larva* in an article about insects).

## Academic Vocabulary

**connotation**  the positive, negative, or neutral feeling associated with a word

**figurative language**  writing or speech that is not meant to be taken literally

**technical term**  word that has a specialized meaning in a particular career or field of study

**tone**  the writer's attitude toward his or her audience and subject

## Apply the Standard

Use the worksheets that follow to help you apply the standard as you read. Several copies of each worksheet have been provided for you to use with different informational texts.

- Understanding Connotations, Figurative Language, and Technical Terms
- Analyzing Word Choice

Name _____ Date _____ Assignment _____

# Understanding Connotations, Figurative Language, and Technical Terms

Use this organizer to analyze important words and phrases in an informational text, particularly the author's use of technical terms, figurative language, and words with positive or negative connotations.

| Word with Connotation | What It Means | Tone It Conveys |
|---|---|---|
| | | |
| | | |
| | | |
| | | |
| | | |

+

| Figurative Language | What It Means | Tone It Conveys |
|---|---|---|
| | | |
| | | |
| | | |
| | | |
| | | |

+

| Technical Term | What It Means | Tone It Conveys |
|---|---|---|
| | | |
| | | |
| | | |
| | | |
| | | |

A

Name _____ Date _____ Assignment _____

# Understanding Connotations, Figurative Language, and Technical Terms

Use this organizer to analyze important words and phrases in an informational text, particularly the author's use of technical terms, figurative language, and words with positive or negative connotations.

| Word with Connotation | What It Means | Tone It Conveys |
|---|---|---|
|  |  |  |
|  |  |  |
|  |  |  |
|  |  |  |
|  |  |  |

+

| Figurative Language | What It Means | Tone It Conveys |
|---|---|---|
|  |  |  |
|  |  |  |
|  |  |  |
|  |  |  |
|  |  |  |

+

| Technical Term | What It Means | Tone It Conveys |
|---|---|---|
|  |  |  |
|  |  |  |
|  |  |  |
|  |  |  |
|  |  |  |

B                                      For use with Informational Text 4

Name _____  Date _____  Assignment _____

# Understanding Connotations, Figurative Language, and Technical Terms

Use this organizer to analyze important words and phrases in an informational text, particularly the author's use of technical terms, figurative language, and words with positive or negative connotations.

| Word with Connotation | What It Means | Tone It Conveys |
|---|---|---|
|  |  |  |
|  |  |  |
|  |  |  |
|  |  |  |
|  |  |  |

+

| Figurative Language | What It Means | Tone It Conveys |
|---|---|---|
|  |  |  |
|  |  |  |
|  |  |  |
|  |  |  |
|  |  |  |

+

| Technical Term | What It Means | Tone It Conveys |
|---|---|---|
|  |  |  |
|  |  |  |
|  |  |  |
|  |  |  |
|  |  |  |

C

For use with Informational Text 4

Name _____ Date _____ Assignment _____

# Understanding Connotations, Figurative Language, and Technical Terms

Use this organizer to analyze important words and phrases in an informational text, particularly the author's use of technical terms, figurative language, and words with positive or negative connotations.

| Word with Connotation | What It Means | Tone It Conveys |
|---|---|---|
| | | |
| | | |
| | | |
| | | |
| | | |

**+**

| Figurative Language | What It Means | Tone It Conveys |
|---|---|---|
| | | |
| | | |
| | | |
| | | |
| | | |

**+**

| Technical Term | What It Means | Tone It Conveys |
|---|---|---|
| | | |
| | | |
| | | |
| | | |
| | | |

D

For use with Informational Text 4

Name _____ Date _____ Assignment _____

# Understanding Connotations, Figurative Language, and Technical Terms

Use this organizer to analyze important words and phrases in an informational text, particularly the author's use of technical terms, figurative language, and words with positive or negative connotations.

| Word with Connotation | What It Means | Tone It Conveys |
|---|---|---|
| | | |
| | | |
| | | |
| | | |
| | | |

+

| Figurative Language | What It Means | Tone It Conveys |
|---|---|---|
| | | |
| | | |
| | | |
| | | |
| | | |

+

| Technical Term | What It Means | Tone It Conveys |
|---|---|---|
| | | |
| | | |
| | | |
| | | |
| | | |

E

For use with Informational Text 4

Name _____ Date _____ Assignment _____

# Understanding Connotations, Figurative Language, and Technical Terms

Use this organizer to analyze important words and phrases in an informational text, particularly the author's use of technical terms, figurative language, and words with positive or negative connotations.

| Word with Connotation | What It Means | Tone It Conveys |
|---|---|---|
|  |  |  |
|  |  |  |
|  |  |  |
|  |  |  |
|  |  |  |

+

| Figurative Language | What It Means | Tone It Conveys |
|---|---|---|
|  |  |  |
|  |  |  |
|  |  |  |
|  |  |  |
|  |  |  |

+

| Technical Term | What It Means | Tone It Conveys |
|---|---|---|
|  |  |  |
|  |  |  |
|  |  |  |
|  |  |  |
|  |  |  |

F

For use with Informational Text 4

Name _____ Date _____ Assignment _____

# Analyzing Word Choice

Use this organizer to analyze the overall meaning and tone of an informational text, based on important words and phrases the author uses in the text.

| Important Words and Phrases |
|---|
| |

| Overall Meaning | Overall Tone |
|---|---|
| | |

A

Name _____ Date _____ Assignment _____

# Analyzing Word Choice

Use this organizer to analyze the overall meaning and tone of an informational text, based on important words and phrases the author uses in the text.

Important Words and Phrases

........................................................................................................................

........................................................................................................................

........................................................................................................................

........................................................................................................................

........................................................................................................................

........................................................................................................................

........................................................................................................................

........................................................................................................................

........................................................................................................................

........................................................................................................................

| Overall Meaning | Overall Tone |
|---|---|

Name _____ Date _____ Assignment _____

# Analyzing Word Choice

Use this organizer to analyze the overall meaning and tone of an informational text, based on important words and phrases the author uses in the text.

Important Words and Phrases

................................................................................................
................................................................................................
................................................................................................
................................................................................................
................................................................................................
................................................................................................
................................................................................................
................................................................................................
................................................................................................
................................................................................................

Overall Meaning

..........................................................
..........................................................
..........................................................
..........................................................
..........................................................
..........................................................
..........................................................
..........................................................
..........................................................
..........................................................

Overall Tone

..........................................................
..........................................................
..........................................................
..........................................................
..........................................................
..........................................................
..........................................................
..........................................................
..........................................................
..........................................................

C

For use with Informational Text 4

Name _____ Date _____ Assignment _____

# Analyzing Word Choice

Use this organizer to analyze the overall meaning and tone of an informational text, based on important words and phrases the author uses in the text.

Important Words and Phrases

Overall Meaning

Overall Tone

D

Name _____ Date _____ Assignment _____

# Analyzing Word Choice

Use this organizer to analyze the overall meaning and tone of an informational text, based on important words and phrases the author uses in the text.

| Important Words and Phrases |
|---|
| |

| Overall Meaning | Overall Tone |
|---|---|
| | |

E

Name _____ Date _____ Assignment _____

## Analyzing Word Choice

Use this organizer to analyze the overall meaning and tone of an informational text, based on important words and phrases the author uses in the text.

| Important Words and Phrases |
| --- |
| .................................................................................................. |
| .................................................................................................. |
| .................................................................................................. |
| .................................................................................................. |
| .................................................................................................. |
| .................................................................................................. |
| .................................................................................................. |
| .................................................................................................. |
| .................................................................................................. |

| Overall Meaning | Overall Tone |
| --- | --- |
| ........................................... | ........................................... |
| ........................................... | ........................................... |
| ........................................... | ........................................... |
| ........................................... | ........................................... |
| ........................................... | ........................................... |
| ........................................... | ........................................... |
| ........................................... | ........................................... |
| ........................................... | ........................................... |

F

For use with Informational Text 4

# Informational Text 5

> **5. Analyze in detail how an author's ideas or claims are developed and refined by particular sentences, paragraphs, or larger portions of text (e.g., a section or chapter).**

## Explanation

Authors use **text structures** such as chronological order, cause and effect, and comparison and contrast to develop and refine their ideas. These structures are often important in persuasive texts, in which an author makes a **claim,** or assertion, to support a main point. To identify sentences and paragraphs that develop an idea or claim, look for key words, such as *before, after, because, since, as a result, more,* and *less.* **Text features** such as titles, headings, and subheadings can also help identify which key ideas are developed in larger portions of texts, such as sections or chapters.

## Examples

- Writers develop a claim by supporting it with numerous reasons and examples. You can identify sentences with reasons by scanning for key words, such as *because, since,* and *why.* Examples, on the other hand, often include dates or statistical data with numbers. For instance, an author might give the following reason for supporting her opinion that a town needs to put a stoplight at a certain corner: *We should put a stoplight at the corner of Oak and Third because stoplights at busy intersections dramatically reduce traffic accidents.* The writer might then support this reason with an example: *A stoplight at Main and Elm reduced the annual number of traffic accidents there from 10 to just 1.*

- **Text features** can help identify larger portions of a text that develop and refine key ideas. A title usually tells the topic of a text or chapter. For example, the title "The History of the Guitar" shows what kind of information the text contains. Headings and subheadings within the text indicate which main ideas are developed in different sections. For example, the heading "Ancient Beginnings" shows that this section tells about how guitars began to evolve long ago.

## Academic Vocabulary

**claim**  a supporting point or idea in a persuasive text

**text features**  titles, headings, and subheadings that identify key ideas in a text

**text structures**  ways of organizing textual support in sentences and paragraphs

## Apply the Standard

Use the worksheet that follows to help you apply the standard as you read. Several copies have been provided for you to use with different informational texts.

- Analyzing the Development of an Idea or Claim

Name _____ Date _____ Assignment _____

# Analyzing the Development of an Idea or Claim

Use this organizer to analyze particular sentences, paragraphs, and sections of a text that develop and refine an author's ideas or claims. Identify the sentence or part of the text on the left. Next to it, explain how that part of the text develops the idea or claim.

| Portion of the Text | How It Develops an Idea or Claim |
|---|---|
| Sentence: | |
| Paragraph: | |
| Section and Heading: | |

Name _____ Date _____ Assignment _____

## Analyzing the Development of an Idea or Claim

Use this organizer to analyze particular sentences, paragraphs, and sections of a text that develop and refine an author's ideas or claims. Identify the sentence or part of the text on the left. Next to it, explain how that part of the text develops the idea or claim.

| Portion of the Text | How It Develops an Idea or Claim |
|---|---|
| Sentence: | |
| Paragraph: | |
| Section and Heading: | |

Name _____ Date _____ Assignment _____

# Analyzing the Development of an Idea or Claim

Use this organizer to analyze particular sentences, paragraphs, and sections of a text that develop and refine an author's ideas or claims. Identify the sentence or part of the text on the left. Next to it, explain how that part of the text develops the idea or claim.

| Portion of the Text | How It Develops an Idea or Claim |
|---|---|
| Sentence: | |
| Paragraph: | |
| Section and Heading: | |

C

Name _____ Date _____ Assignment _____

# Analyzing the Development of an Idea or Claim

Use this organizer to analyze particular sentences, paragraphs, and sections of a text that develop and refine an author's ideas or claims. Identify the sentence or part of the text on the left. Next to it, explain how that part of the text develops the idea or claim.

| Portion of the Text | How It Develops an Idea or Claim |
|---|---|
| Sentence: | |
| Paragraph: | |
| Section and Heading: | |

D

Name _____ Date _____ Assignment _____

# Analyzing the Development of an Idea or Claim

Use this organizer to analyze particular sentences, paragraphs, and sections of a text that develop and refine an author's ideas or claims. Identify the sentence or part of the text on the left. Next to it, explain how that part of the text develops the idea or claim.

| Portion of the Text | How It Develops an Idea or Claim |
|---|---|
| Sentence: | |
| Paragraph: | |
| Section and Heading: | |

E

Name _____ Date _____ Assignment _____

# Analyzing the Development of an Idea or Claim

Use this organizer to analyze particular sentences, paragraphs, and sections of a text that develop and refine an author's ideas or claims. Identify the sentence or part of the text on the left. Next to it, explain how that part of the text develops the idea or claim.

| Portion of the Text | How It Develops an Idea or Claim |
|---|---|
| Sentence: | |
| Paragraph: | |
| Section and Heading: | |

F

# Informational Text 6

> 6. Determine an author's point of view or purpose in a text and analyze how an author uses rhetoric to advance that point of view or purpose.

## Explanation

An **author's purpose** is his or her main reason for writing—to inform, explain, describe, persuade, or entertain. An author's perspective or **point of view** refers to beliefs, attitudes, and experiences relating to a subject. Writers advance their point of view by using **rhetoric**. Four of the more common rhetorical devices include repetition, parallelism, slogans, and rhetorical questions.

## Examples

- **Purpose and Point of View:** To determine purpose and point of view, analyze the kinds of details an author uses. For example, if the purpose is to inform or explain, the details will mostly focus on facts. To describe, the author will focus on sensory details. To persuade, the author will focus on reasons and examples. Also analyze the kinds of words and sentences the author uses. For example, if an author uses the words *should* and *because* in an article about exercise, the purpose is to persuade. If she includes facts about the benefits of exercise, including benefits she has noticed in herself, her point of view toward exercise is positive and reflects firsthand experience.

- **Rhetoric:** Authors use rhetoric to advance their purpose and point of view. Repetition of key words or phrases is a rhetorical device that emphasizes important ideas. Parallelism uses similar grammatical structures to express related ideas. For example, *Exercise tones the body, sharpens the mind, and refreshes the spirit*. Note the three present-tense verbs (*tones, sharpens, refreshes*) that are parallel. Slogans are short, catchy phrases that help readers remember the author's point of view. For example, *No pain, no gain* is a commonly heard slogan. Finally, authors might also ask rhetorical questions with obvious answers for dramatic effect. For example, *Don't we all want to be fitter, more alert, and more attractive?*

## Academic Vocabulary

**author's point of view**  the author's beliefs, attitudes, and experiences relating to a subject

**author's purpose**  the author's main reason for writing a text

**rhetoric**  verbal techniques that advance a point of view by creating emphasis and emotional appeal

## Apply the Standard

Use the worksheets that follow to help you apply the standard as you read. Several copies of each worksheet have been provided for you to use with different informational texts.

- Determining Author's Purpose and Point of View
- Analyzing Author's Rhetoric

Name _____ Date _____ Assignment _____

# Determining Author's Purpose and Point of View

Use this organizer to determine the author's purpose for writing a text and the point of view the author expresses about the topic.

**Kinds of Details**
- ❏ Facts
- ❏ Reasons
- ❏ Examples
- ❏ Sensory details
- ❏ Other (Explain.) ................................................................

**Important Words and Sentences**

**Author's Purpose and Perspective**

**Purpose:**
- ❏ to inform or explain
- ❏ to persuade
- ❏ to describe
- ❏ to entertain

**Perspective:**

Name _____ Date _____ Assignment _____

# Determining Author's Purpose and Point of View

Use this organizer to determine the author's purpose for writing a text and the point of view the author expresses about the topic.

---

**Kinds of Details**

❏ Facts
❏ Reasons
❏ Examples
❏ Sensory details
❏ Other (Explain.) ................................................................................................

---

**Important Words and Sentences**

---

**Author's Purpose and Perspective**

**Purpose:**

❏ to inform or explain
❏ to persuade
❏ to describe
❏ to entertain

**Perspective:**

---

B

Name _____ Date _____ Assignment _____

# Determining Author's Purpose and Point of View

Use this organizer to determine the author's purpose for writing a text and the point of view the author expresses about the topic.

---

**Kinds of Details**

❏ Facts
❏ Reasons
❏ Examples
❏ Sensory details
❏ Other (Explain.) ............................................................................................

---

**Important Words and Sentences**

---

**Author's Purpose and Perspective**

**Purpose:**

❏ to inform or explain
❏ to persuade
❏ to describe
❏ to entertain

**Perspective:**

---

C

For use with Informational Text 6

Name _____ Date _____ Assignment _____

# Determining Author's Purpose and Point of View

Use this organizer to determine the author's purpose for writing a text and the point of view the author expresses about the topic.

---

**Kinds of Details**

❏ Facts
❏ Reasons
❏ Examples
❏ Sensory details
❏ Other (Explain.) ...........................................................................................................

---

**Important Words and Sentences**

---

**Author's Purpose and Perspective**

**Purpose:**
❏ to inform or explain
❏ to persuade
❏ to describe
❏ to entertain

**Perspective:**

---

D

For use with Informational Text 6

Name _____ Date _____ Assignment _____

# Determining Author's Purpose and Point of View

Use this organizer to determine the author's purpose for writing a text and the point of view the author expresses about the topic.

---

**Kinds of Details**

❑ Facts
❑ Reasons
❑ Examples
❑ Sensory details
❑ Other (Explain.) ................................................................................................................

---

**Important Words and Sentences**

---

**Author's Purpose and Perspective**

**Purpose:**
❑ to inform or explain
❑ to persuade
❑ to describe
❑ to entertain

**Perspective:**

---

E

Name _____  Date _____  Assignment _____

# Determining Author's Purpose and Point of View

Use this organizer to determine the author's purpose for writing a text and the point of view the author expresses about the topic.

### Kinds of Details

❏ Facts
❏ Reasons
❏ Examples
❏ Sensory details
❏ Other (Explain.) ............................................................................................................

### Important Words and Sentences

### Author's Purpose and Perspective

**Purpose:**

❏ to inform or explain
❏ to persuade
❏ to describe
❏ to entertain

**Perspective:**

Name _____ Date _____ Assignment _____

# Analyzing Author's Rhetoric

Use this organizer to identify the rhetorical devices used in a text and to explain how they advance the author's purpose and point of view.

| Rhetorical Device | Example | Effect |
|---|---|---|
| repetition | | |
| parallelism | | |
| slogan | | |
| rhetorical question | | |

A

For use with Informational Text 6

Name _____ Date _____ Assignment _____

# Analyzing Author's Rhetoric

Use this organizer to identify the rhetorical devices used in a text and to explain how they advance the author's purpose and point of view.

| Rhetorical Device | Example | Effect |
|---|---|---|
| repetition | | |
| parallelism | | |
| slogan | | |
| rhetorical question | | |

B

Name _____ Date _____ Assignment _____

## Analyzing Author's Rhetoric

Use this organizer to identify the rhetorical devices used in a text and to explain how they advance the author's purpose and point of view.

| Rhetorical Device | Example | Effect |
| --- | --- | --- |
| repetition | | |
| parallelism | | |
| slogan | | |
| rhetorical question | | |

For use with Informational Text 6

Name _____ Date _____ Assignment _____

## Analyzing Author's Rhetoric

Use this organizer to identify the rhetorical devices used in a text and to explain how they advance the author's purpose and point of view.

| Rhetorical Device | Example | Effect |
|---|---|---|
| repetition | | |
| parallelism | | |
| slogan | | |
| rhetorical question | | |

For use with Informational Text 6

Name _____ Date _____ Assignment _____

# Analyzing Author's Rhetoric

Use this organizer to identify the rhetorical devices used in a text and to explain how they advance the author's purpose and point of view.

| Rhetorical Device | Example | Effect |
|---|---|---|
| repetition | | |
| parallelism | | |
| slogan | | |
| rhetorical question | | |

E

Name _____ Date _____ Assignment _____

# Analyzing Author's Rhetoric

Use this organizer to identify the rhetorical devices used in a text and to explain how they advance the author's purpose and point of view.

| Rhetorical Device | Example | Effect |
|---|---|---|
| repetition | | |
| parallelism | | |
| slogan | | |
| rhetorical question | | |

F

# Informational Text 7

> 7. **Analyze various accounts of a subject told in different mediums (e.g., a person's life story in both print and multimedia), determining which details are emphasized in each account.**

## Explanation

Now people can find information available in many different **mediums**, or forms of communication, including print, audio CD, DVD, podcast, Internet text, and online video. The format of a specific medium can influence which details about the subject an author might choose to include, omit, or emphasize. Reading or viewing several accounts of a subject will help you become both better informed and a more critical consumer of media. Analyze which details are emphasized in each account to determine the author's purpose and any possible biases. Evaluate which sources are reliable and which are not.

## Examples

- The format of a specific medium has its own range of possibilities. The format can influence which details of the subject an author might choose to include, leave out, or emphasize. In a written text, authors depend primarily on words to describe a person, topic, or event. A multimedia account of a subject may emphasize details that can be presented dramatically through music, the spoken word, sound effects, still pictures, or video. For example, a written biography of the African American opera singer Marian Anderson might focus on her family background, vocal training, and how she overcame racial prejudice. A multimedia biography might emphasize dramatic newsreel images of Anderson's concerts and include audio clips of her singing.

- To analyze a subject presented in two or more different mediums, study each work and note which details are emphasized, shared, or absent in each. Synthesize information from the accounts to gain a deeper understanding of the subject. Compare and contrast the ideas and attitudes of the works and your own response to them. Ask: Does this account include useful information? Does it add to my understanding? Does it leave out important details? Is the author biased?

## Academic Vocabulary

**medium** a particular means or format of communication, such as text, audio, video, or multimedia

## Apply the Standard

Use the worksheet that follows to help you apply the standard as you read. Several copies have been provided for you to use with different informational texts and multimedia accounts.

- Analyzing Accounts in Different Mediums

Name _____ Date _____ Assignment _____

# Analyzing Accounts in Different Mediums

Use this organizer to analyze and compare accounts of the same subject in two different mediums, detailing what information is shared or exclusive to each. Then answer the questions.

TITLE:

MEDIUM:

TITLE:

MEDIUM:

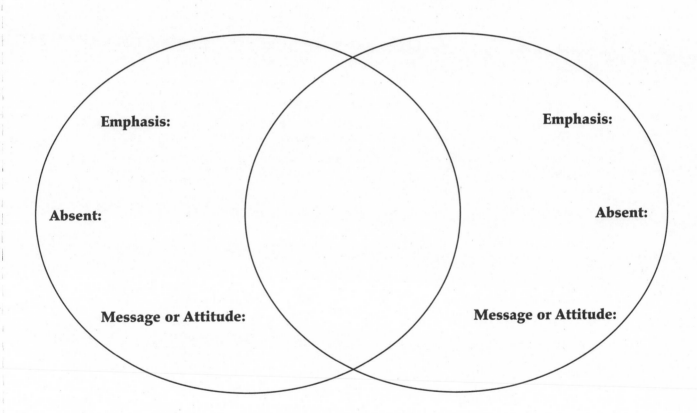

Emphasis:

Absent:

Message or Attitude:

Emphasis:

Absent:

Message or Attitude:

How did each account add to your understanding? .........................................................................

Were both accounts trustworthy and useful? Explain. .................................................................

A

For use with Informational Text 7

Name _____ Date _____ Assignment _____

# Analyzing Accounts in Different Mediums

Use this organizer to analyze and compare accounts of the same subject in two different mediums, detailing what information is shared or exclusive to each. Then answer the questions.

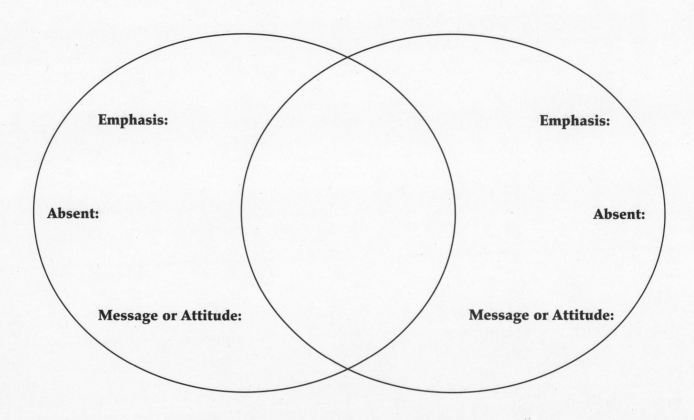

TITLE:

MEDIUM:

TITLE:

MEDIUM:

Emphasis:

Absent:

Message or Attitude:

Emphasis:

Absent:

Message or Attitude:

How did each account add to your understanding? .....................................................................

Were both accounts trustworthy and useful? Explain. ...............................................................

Name _____ Date _____ Assignment _____

# Analyzing Accounts in Different Mediums

Use this organizer to analyze and compare accounts of the same subject in two different mediums, detailing what information is shared or exclusive to each. Then answer the questions.

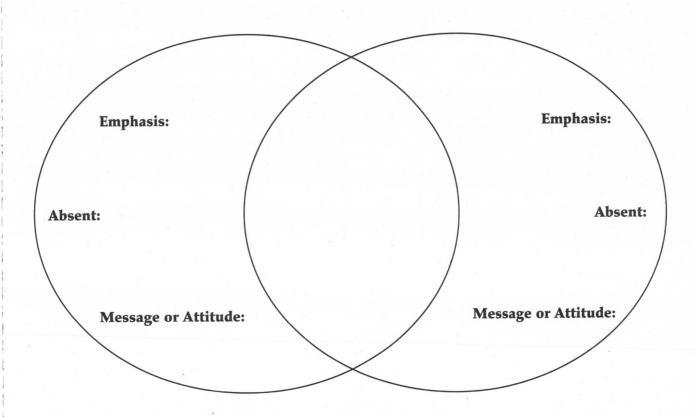

TITLE:

MEDIUM:

TITLE:

MEDIUM:

Emphasis:

Absent:

Message or Attitude:

Emphasis:

Absent:

Message or Attitude:

How did each account add to your understanding? ................................................................

Were both accounts trustworthy and useful? Explain. ................................................................

C

Name _____ Date _____ Assignment _____

# Analyzing Accounts in Different Mediums

Use this organizer to analyze and compare accounts of the same subject in two different mediums, detailing what information is shared or exclusive to each. Then answer the questions.

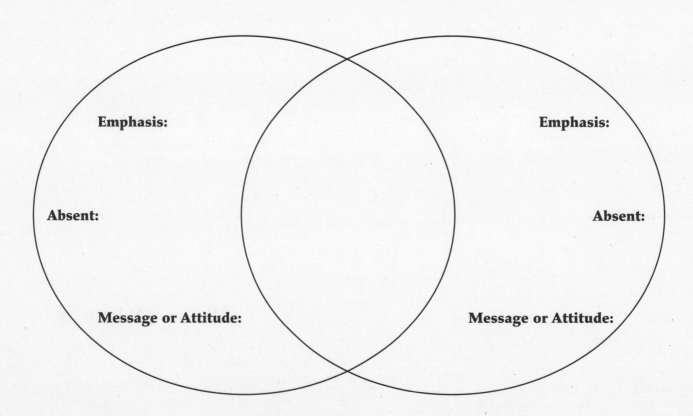

TITLE:

MEDIUM:

TITLE:

MEDIUM:

Emphasis:

Absent:

Message or Attitude:

Emphasis:

Absent:

Message or Attitude:

How did each account add to your understanding? ...................................................................................

Were both accounts trustworthy and useful? Explain. ...................................................................................

Name _____ Date _____ Assignment _____

# Analyzing Accounts in Different Mediums

Use this organizer to analyze and compare accounts of the same subject in two different mediums, detailing what information is shared or exclusive to each. Then answer the questions.

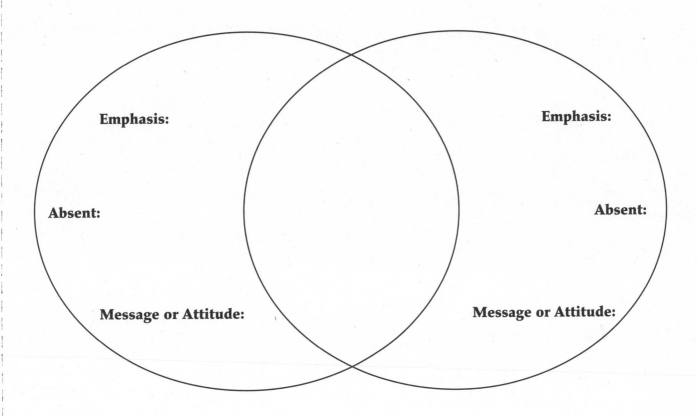

TITLE:

MEDIUM:

TITLE:

MEDIUM:

Emphasis:

Absent:

Message or Attitude:

Emphasis:

Absent:

Message or Attitude:

How did each account add to your understanding? ................................................................

Were both accounts trustworthy and useful? Explain. ................................................................

Name _____ Date _____ Assignment _____

# Analyzing Accounts in Different Mediums

Use this organizer to analyze and compare accounts of the same subject in two different mediums, detailing what information is shared or exclusive to each. Then answer the questions.

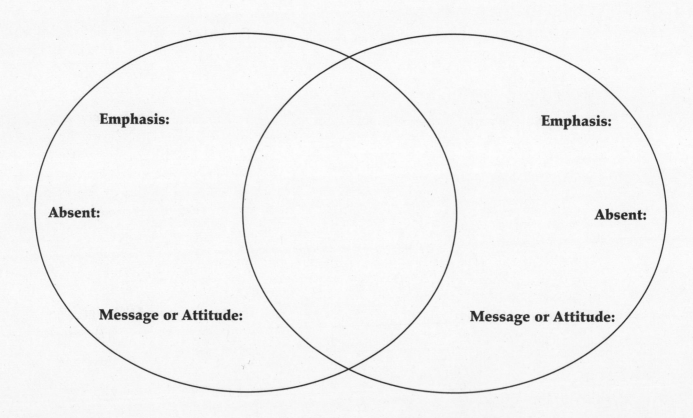

TITLE:

MEDIUM:

TITLE:

MEDIUM:

Emphasis:

Absent:

Message or Attitude:

Emphasis:

Absent:

Message or Attitude:

How did each account add to your understanding? .................................................................................

Were both accounts trustworthy and useful? Explain. .........................................................................

F

For use with Informational Text 7

# Informational Text 8

8. **Delineate and evaluate the argument and specific claims in a text, assessing whether the reasoning is valid and the evidence is relevant and sufficient; identify false statements and fallacious reasoning.**

## Explanation

A persuasive text presents an author's **argument**—a claim or position on an issue that the author asks readers to accept. To evaluate an argument and its specific claims, you must assess both the author's supporting evidence and the author's reasoning, or logical thinking, and determine if the argument is valid and realistic.

## Examples

- Every claim in an argument must be supported by **factual evidence,** statements that can be proven to be true. Identifying false statements may lead you to conclude that an argument is not valid or reliable. For example, suppose an author makes this claim: *Ice cream is the most nutritious food you can eat.* The author supports the claim with this faulty evidence: *Ice cream contains protein and calcium, and it is low in fat and cholesterol.* Therefore, the author's claim is not reliable.

- Make sure that the author presents enough facts to support each claim and that every fact is actually relevant to the issue. For example, suppose the author supported the claim about ice cream being nutritious with this fact: *Eighty percent of Americans prefer ice cream to yogurt.* Whether this statement is true or false, it has no relevance to the claim that ice cream is nutritious.

- You also need to evaluate the author's reasoning, or logic, to see if the argument makes sense. **Fallacious reasoning,** or false logic, is a critical flaw in an argument. Carefully evaluate the author's generalizations—broad statements or inferences that an author might make. For example, in the argument about ice cream, the author might write: *Eating ice cream every day will help most people lose weight. I proved this by trying it myself, and I lost five pounds.* The author tries to support a generalization about "most people" with a fact about his own limited experience. This logic does not make sense.

## Academic Vocabulary

**argument**  a claim or position on an issue

**factual**  evidence statements than can be proven to be true

**fallacious reasoning**  false or faulty logic

## Apply the Standard

Use the worksheet that follows to help you apply the standard as you read persuasive texts. Several copies of the worksheet have been provided for you.

- Evaluating an Argument

Name _____ Date _____ Selection _____

## Evaluating an Argument

Use this organizer to evaluate the argument and claims made in a persuasive text. Consider the evidence the author uses to support his or her argument and why it is or isn't reliable or logical.

| Argument or Position | Claim | Factual Evidence | Is the Reasoning Logical? |
|---|---|---|---|
| | | true? ..........................<br><br>relevant? ...................... | Yes, because ....................<br>..............................................<br>No, because ....................<br>.............................................. |
| | | true? ..........................<br><br>relevant? ...................... | Yes, because ....................<br>..............................................<br>No, because ....................<br>.............................................. |
| | | true? ..........................<br><br>relevant? ...................... | Yes, because ....................<br>..............................................<br>No, because ....................<br>.............................................. |

Name _____  Date _____  Selection _____

# Evaluating an Argument

Use this organizer to evaluate the argument and claims made in a persuasive text. Consider the evidence the author uses to support his or her argument and why it is or isn't reliable or logical.

| Argument or Position | Claim | Factual Evidence | Is the Reasoning Logical? |
|---|---|---|---|
| | | true? ............................<br><br>relevant? ...................... | Yes, because ...................<br>................................<br>No, because ....................<br>................................ |
| | | true? ............................<br><br>relevant? ...................... | Yes, because ...................<br>................................<br>No, because ....................<br>................................ |
| | | true? ............................<br><br>relevant? ...................... | Yes, because ...................<br>................................<br>No, because ....................<br>................................ |

For use with Informational Texts 8

Name _____ Date _____ Selection _____

# Evaluating an Argument

Use this organizer to evaluate the argument and claims made in a persuasive text. Consider the evidence the author uses to support his or her argument and why it is or isn't reliable or logical.

| Argument or Position | Claim | Factual Evidence | Is the Reasoning Logical? |
|---|---|---|---|
| | | true? ..................... <br><br> relevant? ................ | Yes, because ................ <br> ............................. <br> No, because ................ <br> ............................. |
| | | true? ..................... <br><br> relevant? ................ | Yes, because ................ <br> ............................. <br> No, because ................ <br> ............................. |
| | | true? ..................... <br><br> relevant? ................ | Yes, because ................ <br> ............................. <br> No, because ................ <br> ............................. |

Name _____ Date _____ Selection _____

# Evaluating an Argument

Use this organizer to evaluate the argument and claims made in a persuasive text. Consider the evidence the author uses to support his or her argument and why it is or isn't reliable or logical.

| Argument or Position | Claim | Factual Evidence | Is the Reasoning Logical? |
|---|---|---|---|
| | | true? ........................... <br><br> relevant? ...................... | Yes, because ................... <br> ................................... <br> No, because .................... <br> ................................... |
| | | true? ........................... <br><br> relevant? ...................... | Yes, because ................... <br> ................................... <br> No, because .................... <br> ................................... |
| | | true? ........................... <br><br> relevant? ...................... | Yes, because ................... <br> ................................... <br> No, because .................... <br> ................................... |

D

Name _____ Date _____ Selection _____

# Evaluating an Argument

Use this organizer to evaluate the argument and claims made in a persuasive text. Consider the evidence the author uses to support his or her argument and why it is or isn't reliable or logical.

| Argument or Position | Claim | Factual Evidence | Is the Reasoning Logical? |
|---|---|---|---|
| | | true? ......................<br><br>relevant? ................ | Yes, because ...................<br>.............................................<br>No, because ....................<br>............................................. |
| | | true? ...........................<br><br>relevant? ................ | Yes, because ...................<br>.............................................<br>No, because ....................<br>............................................. |
| | | true? ...........................<br><br>relevant? ................ | Yes, because ...................<br>.............................................<br>No, because ....................<br>............................................. |

E

Name _____ Date _____ Selection _____

# Evaluating an Argument

Use this organizer to evaluate the argument and claims made in a persuasive text. Consider the evidence the author uses to support his or her argument and why it is or isn't reliable or logical.

| Argument or Position | Claim | Factual Evidence | Is the Reasoning Logical? |
|---|---|---|---|
| | | true? ........................... relevant? ...................... | Yes, because .................. ........................................ No, because ................... ........................................ |
| | | true? ........................... relevant? ...................... | Yes, because .................. ........................................ No, because ................... ........................................ |
| | | true? ........................... relevant? ...................... | Yes, because .................. ........................................ No, because ................... ........................................ |

F

# Informational Text 9

> **9. Analyze seminal U.S. documents of historical and literary significance (e.g., Washington's Farewell Address, the Gettysburg Address, Roosevelt's Four Freedoms speech, King's "Letter from Birmingham Jail"), including how they address related themes and concepts.**

## Explanation

Many documents and speeches in U.S. history present political arguments, positions on important issues and American ideals. A good political argument uses both logical appeals and emotional appeals to persuade its audience. Many historic U.S. documents address related themes and concepts. By analyzing and comparing these documents, you can gain a better understanding of the key ideas that have contributed to American values throughout the nation's history.

## Examples

- Historical documents include **logical appeals** when the author uses facts to build a logical argument. For example, part of the Declaration of Independence lists facts about wrongs committed by England in order to explain why the colonies must declare independence.

- Historical documents include **emotional appeals** when they include words with strong positive or negative connotations to stir people's feelings. For example, before presenting the facts about England's actions, the Declaration uses words with strong negative connotations to describe England's intent: "a long train of abuses and usurpations" and "absolute Tyranny." In *The Crisis,* also written during the American Revolution, Thomas Paine compares England's King George III to "a common murderer, a highwayman, or a housebreaker."

- While many historical documents address similar **themes** and concepts, their authors may use different kinds of language. These documents often include memorable quotations and images that help people remember the authors' key ideas. For example, most Americans remember this key clause in the Declaration: "We hold these truths to be self-evident, that all men are created equal." They may also remember Thomas Paine's criticism of "the summer soldier" and the "sunshine patriot" in *The Crisis.*

## Academic Vocabulary

**logical appeal**  using facts and reasons to persuade an audience

**emotional appeal**  using words with strong positive or negative connotations to persuade

**theme**  central idea or message of a text

## Apply the Standard

Use the worksheet that follows to help you apply the standard as you read important documents from U.S. history. Several copies of the worksheet have been provided for you.

- Analyzing Historical Documents

Name _____ Date _____ Selection _____

# Analyzing Historical Documents

Use this organizer to analyze and compare two historic U.S documents or speeches. Focus on the authors' use of different types of appeals or memorable language to address an important theme or ideas.

|  | **Document 1** | **Document 2** |
|---|---|---|
| Title |  |  |
| Author |  |  |
| Theme |  |  |
| Logical Appeals |  |  |
| Emotional Appeals |  |  |
| Important Concepts |  |  |
| Memorable Quotations |  |  |

A

Name _____ Date _____ Selection _____

# Analyzing Historical Documents

Use this organizer to analyze and compare two historic U.S documents or speeches. Focus on the authors' use of different types of appeals or memorable language to address an important theme or ideas.

|  | **Document 1** | **Document 2** |
|---|---|---|
| Title |  |  |
| Author |  |  |
| Theme |  |  |
| Logical Appeals |  |  |
| Emotional Appeals |  |  |
| Important Concepts |  |  |
| Memorable Quotations |  |  |

Name _____ Date _____ Selection _____

# Analyzing Historical Documents

Use this organizer to analyze and compare two historic U.S documents or speeches. Focus on the authors' use of different types of appeals or memorable language to address an important theme or ideas.

|  | Document 1 | Document 2 |
|---|---|---|
| Title |  |  |
| Author |  |  |
| Theme |  |  |
| Logical Appeals |  |  |
| Emotional Appeals |  |  |
| Important Concepts |  |  |
| Memorable Quotations |  |  |

C

Name _____ Date _____ Selection _____

## Analyzing Historical Documents

Use this organizer to analyze and compare two historic U.S documents or speeches. Focus on the authors' use of different types of appeals or memorable language to address an important theme or ideas.

|  | Document 1 | Document 2 |
|---|---|---|
| Title |  |  |
| Author |  |  |
| Theme |  |  |
| Logical Appeals |  |  |
| Emotional Appeals |  |  |
| Important Concepts |  |  |
| Memorable Quotations |  |  |

D

Name _____ Date _____ Selection _____

# Analyzing Historical Documents

Use this organizer to analyze and compare two historic U.S documents or speeches. Focus on the authors' use of different types of appeals or memorable language to address an important theme or ideas.

|  | Document 1 | Document 2 |
|---|---|---|
| Title |  |  |
| Author |  |  |
| Theme |  |  |
| Logical Appeals |  |  |
| Emotional Appeals |  |  |
| Important Concepts |  |  |
| Memorable Quotations |  |  |

E

Name _____ Date _____ Selection _____

# Analyzing Historical Documents

Use this organizer to analyze and compare two historic U.S documents or speeches. Focus on the authors' use of different types of appeals or memorable language to address an important theme or ideas.

| | Document 1 | Document 2 |
|---|---|---|
| Title | | |
| Author | | |
| Theme | | |
| Logical Appeals | | |
| Emotional Appeals | | |
| Important Concepts | | |
| Memorable Quotations | | |

F

# Informational Text 10

> 10. By the end of grade 10, read and comprehend literary nonfiction at the high end of the grades 9–10 text complexity band independently and proficiently.

## Explanation

Literary nonfiction varies in **complexity,** or how difficult it is to understand and analyze. Some nonfiction texts have familiar subjects and present a clearly stated thesis and main ideas. They use a simple style, with conventional vocabulary and short sentences. Other nonfiction texts present unfamiliar concepts, contain main ideas that are merely implied, and include advanced vocabulary and long sentences.

In grade 10, you will be expected to read complex literary nonfiction independently and proficiently. You will be asked to demonstrate that you **comprehend**, or understand, the meaning and importance of many kinds of essays, articles, and texts. Reading strategies such as previewing, skimming, asking questions, taking notes, and summarizing can help you understand complex texts.

## Examples

- Previewing a nonfiction text can help give you an idea of what you are about to read. Before you read, scan the title; text features, such as headings and bulleted text; and graphic aids, such as photos, diagrams, and maps. For example, the title "Tides" prepares you for an article about ocean tides. The headings "What Causes Tides" and "The Monthly Tide Cycle" tell you about two main ideas in the text. The table and diagram in the article show that you will learn about different kinds of tides and what causes them.

- Then skim the text, quickly reading a paragraph or two, looking for key words to determine the kind of text structure the author uses. Is the text organized in chronological order, by cause-and-effect, by comparison and contrast? Is the author's purpose to inform, to persuade, or simply to discuss a topic? Skimming the first section of "What Causes Tides," you see that the author presents information about causes and effects. The author's purpose is clearly to inform.

- As you read, take notes on the main ideas and details. Ask yourself questions about parts you don't understand. Then reread or read ahead to find the answers. Finally, use your notes to summarize the author's perspective and main ideas in your own words.

## Academic Vocabulary

**complexity** the degree to which a text is difficult to understand and analyze

**comprehend** understand the meaning and importance of something

## Apply the Standard

Use the worksheet that follows to help you apply the standard as you read nonfiction texts. Several copies of the worksheet have been provided for you.

- Comprehending Complex Texts

Name _____ Date _____ Selection _____

# Comprehending Complex Texts

Explain what makes the nonfiction text you are reading complex. Then, use the table to explain which reading strategies help you to better comprehend the selection.

**What makes this selection challenging?**

....................................................................................................

| Strategy | How I Used It | How it Helped |
|---|---|---|
| Previewing | | |
| Skimming | | |
| Asking questions | | |
| Taking notes | | |
| Summarizing | | |

A

Name _____ Date _____ Selection _____

# Comprehending Complex Texts

Explain what makes the nonfiction text you are reading complex. Then, use the table to explain which reading strategies help you to better comprehend the selection.

**What makes this selection challenging?**

.......................................................................................................................................

| Strategy | How I Used It | How it Helped |
|---|---|---|
| Previewing | | |
| Skimming | | |
| Asking questions | | |
| Taking notes | | |
| Summarizing | | |

B

Name _____ Date _____ Selection _____

# Comprehending Complex Texts

Explain what makes the nonfiction text you are reading complex. Then, use the table to explain which reading strategies help you to better comprehend the selection.

**What makes this selection challenging?**

........................................................................................

| Strategy | How I Used It | How it Helped |
|---|---|---|
| Previewing | | |
| Skimming | | |
| Asking questions | | |
| Taking notes | | |
| Summarizing | | |

C

Name _____  Date _____  Selection _____

# Comprehending Complex Texts

Explain what makes the nonfiction text you are reading complex. Then, use the table to explain which reading strategies help you to better comprehend the selection.

**What makes this selection challenging?**

..............................................................................................................................................

| Strategy | How I Used It | How it Helped |
|---|---|---|
| Previewing | | |
| Skimming | | |
| Asking questions | | |
| Taking notes | | |
| Summarizing | | |

D

Name _____ Date _____ Selection _____

# Comprehending Complex Texts

Explain what makes the nonfiction text you are reading complex. Then, use the table to explain which reading strategies help you to better comprehend the selection.

**What makes this selection challenging?**

......................................................................................................................

| Strategy | How I Used It | How it Helped |
|---|---|---|
| Previewing | | |
| Skimming | | |
| Asking questions | | |
| Taking notes | | |
| Summarizing | | |

E

Name _____ Date _____ Selection _____

# Comprehending Complex Texts

Explain what makes the nonfiction text you are reading complex. Then, use the table to explain which reading strategies help you to better comprehend the selection.

**What makes this selection challenging?**

..................................................................................................................

| Strategy | How I Used It | How it Helped |
|---|---|---|
| Previewing | | |
| Skimming | | |
| Asking questions | | |
| Taking notes | | |
| Summarizing | | |

F

# Writing Standards

# Writing 1

> 1. **Write arguments to support claims in an analysis of substantive topics or texts, using valid reasoning and relevant and sufficient evidence.**

## Writing Workshop: Argument

When you develop an argument in writing, you present a claim, and then support your claim. An argument is not just your opinion on an issue. Sound arguments are supported with relevant, sufficient evidence. For example, a letter to the editor of your local newspaper might present a claim such as, "Our community does not need a new shopping center." Evidence and valid reasoning that support the claim form the heart of the argument. Strong arguments are made more persuasive by the careful use of persuasive techniques, including appeals to logic and to emotion. Remember, though, emotional appeals alone will not make an unsupported, poorly-reasoned argument effective.

## Assignment

Write a letter to the editor of your local newspaper about an issue of concern in your community. Include these elements:

✓ a claim that clearly states your position on the issue

✓ evidence, reasoning, and persuasive techniques to support your position or claim

✓ acknowledgement of opposing positions or claims, recognizing their strengths as well as pointing out their limitations

✓ standard business letter format and an effective and coherent organization

✓ use of rhetorical technique, such as phrases and clauses to convey meaning and add interest

✓ an appropriately formal style and objective tone

✓ correct use of language conventions

## Additional Standards

**Writing**
**1.** Write arguments to support claims in an analysis of substantive topics or texts, using valid reasoning and relevant and sufficient evidence.

**1.a.** Introduce precise claim(s), distinguish the claim(s) from alternate or opposing claims, and create an organization that establishes clear relationships among claim(s), counterclaims, reasons, and evidence.

**1.b.** Develop claim(s) and counterclaims fairly, supplying evidence for each while pointing out the strengths and limitations of both in a manner that

anticipates the audience's knowledge level and concerns.

**1.c.** Use words, phrases, and clauses to link the major sections of the text, create cohesion, and clarify the relationships between claim(s) and reasons, between reasons and evidence, and between claim(s) and counterclaims.

**1.d.** Establish and maintain a formal style and objective tone while attending to the norms and conventions of the discipline in which they are writing.

**1.e.** Provide a concluding statement or section that follows from and supports the argument presented.

**4.** Produce clear and coherent writing in which the development, organization, and style are appropriate to task, purpose, and audience. (Grade-specific expectations for writing types are defined in standards 1–3 above.)

**5.** Develop and strengthen writing as needed by planning, revising, editing, rewriting, or trying a new approach, focusing on addressing what is most significant for a specific purpose and audience.

**6.** Use technology, including the Internet, to produce, publish, and update individual or shared writing products, taking advantage

of technology's capacity to link to other information and to display information flexibly and dynamically.

**Language**
**1.b.** Use various types of phrases (noun, verb, adjectival, adverbial, participial, prepositional, absolute) and clauses (independent, dependent; noun, relative, adverbial) to convey specific meanings and add variety and interest to writing or presentations.

**2.** Demonstrate command of the conventions of standard English capitalization, punctuation, and spelling when writing.

Name _____ Date _____ Assignment _____

# Prewriting/Planning Strategies

**Choose a topic.** Scan through your local newspaper to find an issue facing your community. You may also find issues by talking with neighbors, family members, and classmates. Look for issues on which you could take two or more positions. For example, if your community's planning board is considering a proposal to develop a new shopping center, you could take a position in favor of the proposal or against it.

**Identify your claim.** After choosing a topic, decide what position you will take on the issue. If you are not certain what position you wish to take, research to learn more about the issue. For example, read additional articles about the proposed shopping center to learn more about how it might affect your community. You can also pair up with a classmate to discuss the issue, noting where you agree and where you disagree. When you've chosen a position, write it in a sentence. That sentence is your claim.

| My Issue: |  |
|---|---|
| **Possible Position #1:** | **Possible Position #2:** |
| **Where I agree/disagree:** | **Where I agree/disagree:** |
| **My Claim:** | |

**Define task, purpose, and audience.** At all points of the writing process, consider your **task,** or what specifically you are writing; your **purpose,** or the effect you want your writing to have; and your **audience,** or the people you want to persuade—in this case, the newspaper's editors and readers.

Name _____ Date _____ Assignment _____

# Supporting a Claim

**Use reasoning, evidence, and persuasive techniques.** Support your claim with valid reasoning and with relevant, sufficient evidence. In addition, use persuasive techniques such as appeals to logic and emotion. For example, if you oppose a new shopping center because stores in your community will lose business, appeal to your audience's emotions by describing a store that has been part of your community for many years but might close if the new shopping center opens.

In the chart below, write the reasons you will use to support your claim. Below each reason, include:

- enough relevant **evidence** to back up the reason

- one or more **persuasive techniques** to make your reason more convincing.

| My Claim: |  |
|---|---|
| **Reason #1:** |  |
| **Evidence:** | **Persuasive Techniques:** |
| **Reason #2:** |  |
| **Evidence:** | **Persuasive Techniques:** |

Name _____ Date _____ Assignment _____

# Drafting Strategies

**Create a structure for your draft.** Plan a strategy for presenting your ideas. Be sure to structure your letter to the editor in a way that is both persuasive and easy to follow.

- Evaluate your reasoning, evidence, and persuasive techniques. Are your reasons valid? Are they supported by relevant, sufficient evidence? Will your persuasive techniques appeal to your audience's logic and emotions?
- Use the organizer below to plan the structure of your argument. Consider starting with your strongest, most logical reason and ending with a reason that appeals to your audience's emotions.

Introduction/Claim

Reason #1

    Evidence

    Persuasive Technique(s)

Reason #2

    Evidence

    Persuasive Technique(s)

Reason #3

    Evidence

    Persuasive Technique(s)

Counterclaims/Conclusion

Name _____  Date _____  Assignment _____

**Develop your claim.** Use the organizer below to develop your claim and to anticipate and respond to counterclaims.

1. Write your claim, using precise wording to state your position on the issue accurately.

2. Evaluate your claim, being sure to:

   • distinguish it from other claims that take different positions on the issue,

   • consider your task and purpose for writing, and

   • anticipate your audience's knowledge of the issue.

3. Revise your claim as necessary.

4. Anticipate counterclaims and plan your responses. Strive to be fair as you respond to counterclaims, pointing out their strengths as well as their limitations.

| **My Claim:** |
|---|

| | |
|---|---|
| **Evaluating my Claim** | ❑ Does my claim take a clear position on the issue? |
| | ❑ Is my claim easily distinguished from other claims on the issue? |
| | ❑ Is my claim suited to my writing task and my purpose for writing? |
| | ❑ Does my claim anticipate my audience's knowledge about the issue? |
| | ❑ Is my claim supported with valid reasoning and relevant, sufficient evidence? |
| | Additional notes: |
| | ................................................................................. |
| | ................................................................................. |
| | ................................................................................. |

| **My Revised Claim:** |
|---|

| **Counterclaim #1:** | **Counterclaim #2:** |
|---|---|
| **Addressing this counterclaim:** | **Addressing this counterclaim:** |

Name _____ Date _____ Assignment _____

# Style and Tone

**Establish an appropriately formal style and tone.** A formal style is appropriate for a written piece that will be read by a variety of people. However, your letter to the editor should not be as formal as an essay or a research report. An objective tone will encourage readers to keep an open mind, while a subjective tone may repel readers who do not already agree with your position.

## Examples:

**Informal Style:** Since folks in our town have a ton of great stores to choose from already, we don't need a new place to go shopping.

**Overly Formal Style:** A number of stores are already well established in this community, making it unnecessary to construct an additional shopping center.

**Appropriately Formal Style:** Because our community already has a wide variety of stores, we do not actually need a new shopping center.

**Subjective Tone:** If they open this new shopping center, our friends and neighbors who own stores will be forced out of business.

**Objective Tone:** A new shopping center will take business away from stores that have been part of our community.

As you draft your letter to the editor, choose words and phrases to maintain an appropriately formal style and an objective tone.

**Use words, phrases, and clauses to create cohesion.** Link the sections of your letter to the editor by using appropriate words, phrases, and clauses. Include transitions to help your audience follow your claim, reasoning, and evidence.

- Linking your claim to your reasoning: *because, for these reasons*

- Linking reasons to each other: *first, also, in addition, more importantly*

- Linking reasoning to evidence: *for example, for instance, specifically*

- Linking your claim to counterclaims: *however, on the other hand*

By including transitions, you can clarify the relationships between your claim and your reasoning, between your reasons and your evidence, and between your claim and any counterclaims.

- Building a new shopping center in our community is a bad idea for a number of reasons. *First of all*, the proposed center will increase traffic congestion dramatically.

- The land on which the proposed center would be developed can be used in ways that benefit our town. *For example*, it could be turned into a much-needed new public park.

- *Although I believe the proposal should be rejected*, a new shopping center would offer some benefits for our community.

Name _____  Date _____  Assignment _____

# Conclusion

**Provide a persuasive conclusion.** Your conclusion is your last opportunity to convince your audience. A persuasive conclusion follows from and supports the argument you make in your letter to the editor. The examples below illustrate different strategies for writing a persuasive conclusion.

- Use a memorable analogy that supports your claim and reasoning: *A new shopping center may seem appealing. However, the center as it is currently proposed would be an expensive luxury we cannot afford. We do not need it, and the costs that come with it would hurt our community.*

- Restate your claim and offer one final reason: *I believe the proposed shopping center is a bad idea for our community. If the center is built, traffic will increase and local businesses may close. More importantly, the character of our town will change forever.*

- Return to your most persuasive reason and examples: *As you consider the proposal to build a new shopping center, think about the Rosa Sanchez, the owner and operator of the Main Street Flower Shop. Think also about the Robert Miller and his family, who have run Miller's Groceries for thirty years. They are an important part of our community that could be lost if the new center opens.*

Use the organizer below to plan and evaluate your conclusion.

| My Conclusion |
|---|
| ............................................................................................................ <br> ............................................................................................................ <br> ............................................................................................................ <br> ............................................................................................................ |

| Evaluating My Conclusion | |
|---|---|
| ❑ Does my conclusion follow from my argument? <br><br> ❑ Does it support my claim, reasoning, and evidence? <br><br> ❑ Did I maintain an appropriately formal style and objective tone? <br><br> ❑ Does it offer a memorable analogy or final reason? <br><br> ❑ Does it return to and reinforce my most persuasive reason and examples? | ❑ Does it use a different strategy? If so, describe your strategy: <br><br> .................................................... <br><br> .................................................... <br><br> .................................................... <br><br> ❑ Is my conclusion persuasive? Explain. <br><br> .................................................... <br><br> .................................................... <br><br> .................................................... <br><br> .................................................... |

Name _____ Date _____ Assignment _____

# Revising Strategies

Put a checkmark beside each question as you address it in your revision.

| | **Questions To Ask as You Revise** |
|---|---|
| **Writing Task** | ❏ Have I fulfilled my task?<br><br>❏ Does my writing contain the elements of a letter to the editor?<br><br>❏ Did I use a standard business letter format?<br><br>❏ Did I begin with a claim that takes a clear position on an issue facing my community?<br><br>❏ Did I include valid reasoning and relevant, sufficient evidence? |
| **Purpose** | ❏ Is my letter to the editor persuasive?<br><br>❏ What reasons and evidence in my letter helped me achieve my purpose?<br><br>❏ Is there enough evidence to support my claim and reasons?<br><br>❏ Should I add more support to my argument? If so, list below:<br><br>...................................................................<br><br>...................................................................<br><br>❏ What evidence, if any, is irrelevant and detracts from my argument?<br><br>...................................................................<br><br>...................................................................<br><br>❏ Have I used persuasive techniques effectively?<br><br>❏ Should I include additional persuasive techniques? If so, list below:<br><br>...................................................................<br><br>...................................................................<br><br>❏ Have I provided a strong conclusion that follows from and supports my argument? |
| **Audience** | ❏ Have I addressed my audience's knowledge of my issue? Have I addressed their concerns?<br><br>❏ Is my style of writing and tone suited to my audience? If not, what words and phrases need revision?<br><br>...................................................................<br><br>...................................................................<br><br>❏ Will my audience be able to follow my letter to the editor?<br><br>❏ What words, phrases, and clauses should be added to link sections of my letter, create cohesion, and clarify relationships between ideas?<br><br>...................................................................<br><br>...................................................................<br><br>................................................................... |

For use with Writing 1

Name _____ Date _____ Assignment _____

# Revising

**Use phrases and clauses to convey meaning and add interest.** A phrase is a group of words that is used in a sentence as a single part of speech and that doesn't contain both a subject and a verb. A clause is a group of words that includes both a subject and a verb. Independent clauses can be used as sentences; dependent clauses are used in sentences as a single part of speech.

| Sample Phrases and Dependent Clauses | |
|---|---|
| Noun phrase | *The proposed shopping center* is unnecessary. |
| Verb phrase | Nevertheless, there is a good chance the center *will be built.* |
| Adjectival phrase | I have serious concerns *about the new center.* |
| Adverbial phrase | It could create a serious traffic problem *in our neighborhood.* |
| Participial phrase | *Living near the proposed site,* I am especially worried about parking. |
| Noun clause | *Whether the benefits outweigh the costs* is the central question. |
| Relative clause | The center, *which would open in sixteen months,* may have hidden costs. |
| Adverbial clause | *If the new center is built,* our community will change in important ways. |

As you revise your letter to the editor, include phrases and dependent clauses to convey specific meaning. You can also use phrases and clauses to add variety to your writing or to make details more interesting.

**Convey specific meaning.** Identify sentences that are vague or unclear and rewrite them, adding phrases or clauses that clarify or build on the sentences' meanings.

> **Original:** The new center would create problems for local businesses.
>
> **Revised:** The new center, **which would include large discount stores,** would create problems for local businesses.
>
> **Original:** Local stores will have trouble competing.
>
> **Revised:** Local stores will have trouble competing **with the proposed shopping center.**

**Add variety and interest.** Identify paragraphs with repetitive sentences and rewrite them, varying sentence structures by adding phrases and clauses.

> **Original:** Traffic downtown is already heavy. The traffic will get much worse, however. Many more people will drive into town. Traffic jams may become a daily event.
>
> **Revised:** Traffic downtown is already heavy. The traffic will get much worse **when the new shopping center opens,** however. Many more people will drive into town **every day to shop.** Traffic jams may become a daily event.

### Revision Checklist

❑ Have I used phrases and clauses to convey specific meaning?

❑ Are there vague or unclear sentences that could be clarified by including a phrase or dependent clause?

❑ Have I used phrases and clauses to add variety or interest to my letter?

Name _____ Date _____ Assignment _____

# Editing and Proofreading

Review your draft to correct errors in capitalization, spelling, and punctuation.

**Focus on Capitalization:** Review your draft carefully to find and correct capitalization errors. If your letter to the editor includes geographical names, such as the names of states, counties, towns, and streets, be sure that you have capitalized the names.

| **Incorrect capitalization:** | **Correct capitalization:** |
|---|---|
| Highland county | Highland County |
| county road 589 | County Road 589 |

**Focus on Spelling:** An argumentative essay that includes spelling errors loses its authority to convince. Check the spelling of each word. Look for words that you frequently misspell and make sure they are correct. If you have typed your draft on a computer, use the spell-check feature to double-check for errors. Carefully review each suggested change before accepting the spell-check's suggestions. Also note that spell-check features will not catch all errors. Proofread carefully even after running a spell-check.

**Focus on Punctuation: Semicolons and Colons** Proofread your writing to find and address punctuation errors. In particular, look for places in your letter where you link independent clauses or introduce statements, quotations, or lists. Be sure that you have used semicolons and colons correctly.

**Rule: Use semicolons to link closely related independent clauses.** Use semicolons alone or with a conjunctive adverb or transitional phrase.

*Traffic on County Road 589 is already congested; the new shopping center will make the problem worse. The new center means we will have new stores; however, older stores in our town may lose business.*

**Rule: Use colons to introduce lists or before statements.** Use colons before lists that do not serve as direct objects or objects of prepositions.

*A new shopping center offers several benefits for our community: new jobs, increased revenue, and easy access to discount stores.*

*After researching the proposal, I have come to this conclusion: The benefits the new center offers are outweighed by the costs.*

## Revision Checklist

❑ Have you reviewed your letter to the editor for geographical names that should be capitalized?

❑ Have you read each sentence and checked that all of the words are spelled correctly?

❑ Do you have sentences composed of two independent clauses that should be linked with semicolons?

❑ Do you have lists or statements that should be introduced with colons?

❑ Have you used semicolons in places where colons are needed? Have you used colons where semicolons are needed?

Name _____  Date _____  Assignment _____

# Publishing and Presenting

Consider one of the following ways to present your writing:

**Deliver a multimedia presentation.** Use your letter to the editor as the basis for a multimedia presentation. Using presentation software, create charts, graphs, and images to illustrate points in your argument. Consider including audio or video clips. Before delivering your presentation, rehearse with a peer to ensure that media elements are incorporated smoothly into your argument.

**Hold a debate.** Team up with one or more of your classmates to write letters that make different claims on the same issue. Then, use your letters as the basis for a public debate. Prepare opening statements based on your letters, and use your reasoning and evidence to respond to each other's arguments. Hold the debate in class, and be prepared to take questions from your audience.

## Rubric for Self-Assessment

Find evidence in your writing to address each category. Then, use the rating scale to grade your work. Circle the score that best applies for each category.

| Evaluating Your Argument | not very | | | very | |
|---|---|---|---|---|---|
| **Focus:** How clearly has your claim been stated? | 1 | 2 | 3 | 5 | 6 |
| **Organization:** How effectively and coherently have you organized your argument? | 1 | 2 | 3 | 5 | 6 |
| **Style:** How well have you maintained a formal, objective tone throughout your argument? | 1 | 2 | 3 | 5 | 6 |
| **Support/Elaboration:** How valid, sufficient, and suited to your audience is your evidence? | 1 | 2 | 3 | 5 | 6 |
| **Conventions:** How free of errors in grammar, usage, spelling, and punctuation is your argument? | 1 | 2 | 3 | 5 | 6 |

For use with Writing 1

# Writing 2

> 2. Write informative/explanatory texts to examine and convey complex ideas, concepts, and information clearly and accurately through the effective selection, organization, and analysis of content.

## Writing Workshop: Expository Essay

When you write an **expository essay,** your task is to inform or explain something to your audience. Doing so might involve explaining something in detail, describing steps in a process, comparing or contrasting ideas, or presenting a problem and its solution. When you present a problem and a solution, you must explain the problem using concrete and relevant details to your readers. A clear description of the problem and its solution should appear as your thesis in your opening paragraph, followed by an organized and detailed explanation of the problem and the solution (or solutions) that you are proposing.

## Assignment

Write an expository essay about a problem and solution in your school or neighborhood. Include these elements:

- ✓ a clear statement of the problem and the recommended solution(s)
- ✓ an organization, formatted as useful, that helps make the problem and its solution(s) clear
- ✓ graphics or multimedia
- ✓ explanation, sufficient facts, quotations, concrete details, and other development specific to the purpose and audience
- ✓ appropriate transitional words and phrases
- ✓ precise language, including words that are specific to your topic, as needed
- ✓ a logical and effective conclusion
- ✓ correct use of language conventions and formal style and objective tone

## Additional Standards

**2.a.** Introduce a topic; organize complex ideas, concepts, and information to make important connections and distinctions; include formatting (e.g., headings), graphics (e.g., figures, tables), and multimedia when useful to aiding comprehension.

**2.b.** Develop the topic with well-chosen, relevant, and sufficient facts, extended definitions, concrete details, quotations, or

other information and examples appropriate to the audience's knowledge of the topic.

**2.c.** Use appropriate and varied transitions to link the major sections of the text, create cohesion, and clarify the relationships among complex ideas and concepts.

**2.d.** Use precise language and domain-specific vocabulary to manage the complexity of the topic.

**2.e.** Establish and maintain a formal style and objective tone while attending to the norms and conventions of the discipline in which students are writing.

**2.f.** Provide a concluding statement or section that follows from and supports the information or explanation presented (e.g., articulating implications or the significance of the topic).

**Language**

**1.** Demonstrate command of the conventions of standard English grammar and usage when writing or speaking.

**2.** Demonstrate command of the conventions of standard English capitalization, punctuation, and spelling when writing.

Name _____  Date _____  Assignment _____

# Prewriting/Planning Strategies

**Browse media sources to find a topic.** Look through newspapers, magazines, Internet publications, or your school Web site for recent stories that mention or discuss a current problem. Write down any problems for which you think you can propose a workable solution. Choose your essay topic from this list of ideas.

**Discuss ideas to find a topic.** Begin with an audience in mind. For example, if you're writing for a group of your peers, ask them what troubles them—what needs fixing at your school, in the athletics department, or in a social group or club. If your audience is your neighbors, ask about a problem that needs solving in your neighborhood. Make notes of these problems and of any solutions that come to mind. Choose a topic from these ideas.

**Evaluate your topic.** Record and test your problem and solution(s) before you begin.

| Problem: | Appropriate to my audience because— |
| | Interesting to my audience because— |
| | Can be explained with these details: |
| Solution(s): | Solution(s) workable because— |
| | Can be explained with these details: |

Name _____  Date _____  Assignment _____

# Developing a Topic

**Explore the problem.** Once you have chosen your topic, you should explore it in detail. One way to do this is to create a problem profile. Then, list any facts, examples or supporting information that relates to the problem and its solution. The more fully you complete this profile beforehand, the easier it will be to draft your essay later. Use the chart below to list and organize this information.

| |
|---|
| **Problem:** |
| **Who is affected?** |
| **What causes the problem?** |
| **Why is this problem significant?** |
| **What will happen if the problem goes unsolved?** |

Name _____ Date _____ Assignment _____

**Evaluate the solution(s).** In addition to making sure that you can fully and clearly explain a problem to your audience in an informative and interesting way, you must make sure that you present one or more workable and convincing solutions. To organize and test how workable your solution or solutions are, record them. List facts, details, and other possible support for each solution. Then, list the pros and cons of putting each solution into action.

| Solution 1: | Pros—<br><br><br>Cons— | **Facts, Details, and Other Support**<br>•<br><br>•<br><br>•<br><br>•<br><br>• |
| --- | --- | --- |
| Solution 2: | Pros—<br><br><br>Cons— | **Facts, Details, and Other Support**<br>•<br><br>•<br><br>•<br><br>•<br><br>• |

Name _____ Date _____ Assignment _____

**Develop body paragraphs.** Develop the body paragraphs of your essay by using various types of support, such as:

- **Quotations.** Quote people who are affected by the problem, as well as information and opinions from experts on your topic.

- **Extended definitions.** Make sure that you define the problem or the solution(s) in depth, when necessary. Keep in mind that it may require more than one paragraph to fully explain a complex issue or problem.

- **Relevant facts.** When explaining your topic, present specific facts and information over general statements. Statistics and other facts are more likely to make your audience take notice and give your essay serious thought. For example, "109 colleges and universities added the study of Mandarin to their offerings last year" is much more concrete than "Many colleges and universities now offer classes in Mandarin."

- **Concrete details.** General statements, such as "The current drop-off area is a problem," are always less effective than providing concrete details. Instead, it is much more helpful for your readers if you say, "Because the drop-off area rarely accommodates more than two vehicles at a time, traffic is backed up onto State Road, and wait times can be up to 9 minutes."

| Problem |
|---|
| **Topic sentence:** |
| **Support:** |
| • |
| • |
| • |

| Solution |
|---|
| **Topic sentence:** |
| **Support:** |
| • |
| • |
| • |

**Include formatting, graphics, or multimedia.** If and when it is useful, use bulleted points to break large chunks of information into smaller, more manageable bits. You can also use headings to highlight the problem and its solutions. Make sure that you don't overuse boldface text and other formatting choices when you add headings. Keep in mind that your task is to produce an explanatory essay—not an ad, e-mail, or social networking page.

If you need them to make your information clearer or more compelling, you might also include photos or other illustrations that are relevant to your topic. Think about adding tables, graphs, or other graphic displays to showcase data you have gathered or researched. Another option is to embed a hyperlink to the photo, illustration, or video that shows the problem or the solution that you are addressing.

# Using Transitions

**Use appropriate and varied transitions.** Link the sentences and paragraphs in your essay by using transitional words, phrases, and clauses. Below are some examples:

- To introduce support: *according to, as ___ notes/says/writes, for example, for instance, in one survey, the data show*

- To introduce the solution or to conclude: *as a result, because (of), for the best results, for our future, for these reasons, in summary, on the whole, in the final analysis, therefore*

To make smooth transitions from one paragraph to the next, use repetition to connect the last line of the previous paragraph and the first line of the next.

**Paragraph 1 ends:** . . . the school library needs fewer books and <u>more databases</u>.

**Paragraph 2 begins:** To make the shift to <u>more databases</u>, . . .

**Create coherence.** Good writing is coherent and easy to follow. That means that all ideas lead smoothly from one to the next. Linking ideas by using transitional words and phrases, repeating key words, and maintaining clear pronoun reference helps the reader comprehend your message. To create coherence in a problem-solution essay, use words such as the following to link ideas in sentences:

- To show when the problem occurs: *after, before, during, prior to, when, whenever*

- To show where the problem occurs: *above, across, beneath, here, in front of, inside, throughout, under*

Use words such as the following to lead from one sentence or paragraph to the next:

- To classify issues related to the problem: *one group, one kind, other types, other sorts, the first issue, the last effect*

- To emphasize the significance of the problem or its solution: *as can be plainly seen, even, indeed, in fact, without a doubt*

Name _____ Date _____ Assignment _____

# Drafting a Conclusion

**Write an effective conclusion.** An expository essay with a problem-solution purpose should end with a formal conclusion. In your conclusion, avoid repeating your original topic sentence word for word. Restate your main points and stress the importance of your solution in a different and more emphatic way. Try to leave your reader with a new and thought-provoking final thought, prediction, or question.

| **Transition or other link from previous point:** |
|---|
| |
| **Fresh, interesting restatement of your main points:** |
| |
| **Final thought, prediction, or question:** |
| |

# Evaluating Language

**Check for precise language.** If you describe the problem by saying that the school library is out of date, you might be accurate, but you are not being precise. To be precise, you must be more specific and concrete. Instead, you might add details such as the following: *there are only two PCs available, there are no history databases, and there are only six plugs that can be used by students who have their own laptops.* In addition, you should aim to replace every general, imprecise, or overused word and phrase. That means eliminating clichés, preferring action verbs to state-of-being verbs, and eliminating tired modifiers such as *really, awesome,* and *unbelievable.*

**Check for technological or topic-specific language.** If you are addressing the need for greener heating and cooling systems in your school, it is appropriate to integrate technical terms, such as *geothermal heat pumps* or *HVAC systems.* If your audience consists of heating and cooling experts, you will not need to explain these terms. But if this is not the case, then you may need to explain such terms briefly and concisely the first time you use them. You may also consider including an illustration to help convey meaning more effectively.

For use with Writing 2

Name _____  Date _____  Assignment _____

# Evaluating Your Writing Style and Tone

**Evaluate your tone.** A goal of expository writing is almost always objectivity—or at least a tone that makes the writer sound as if he or she is being objective. To create an objective tone, stick to the third person. Using *I,* or any other form of the first person, such as *me, my, mine,* or *we, our, ours* will almost always undercut the appearance of objectivity. Similarly, avoid the second person: *you, your, yours.* Also, avoid casual and personal choices—such as contractions, slang, and chatty or friendly language.

**Evaluate your style.** Tone is just one element of your style, and it should reflect your task, your purpose, and your audience. If you have a serious purpose such as updating the school library, and your audience consists of faculty members, the school board, and community members, you will want your style to be both direct and formal. This means avoiding slang, personal asides, unneeded exclamation points, and other choices that might make your writing sound too casual. Additionally, sarcastic or biting remarks are never an appropriate choice, so always maintain a serious and respectful tone.

In the writing example below, decide why the tone and style choices in bold below do not match the expository task, purpose, and the audience. Suggest replacements in the blanks that follow the example.

**(1) You (2) wouldn't** believe our school library if **(3) you** walked in there today. **(4) It's** a **(5) pathetic** place to do research **(6)!** Instead of offering up-to-date databases and online resources, the library has reference shelves filled with dusty encyclopedias, some of which were published in the 1980s and 1990s. That may be **(7) okay** if **(8) you're** looking for a (9) Shakespeare bio, but **(10) it sure doesn't** work for lasers or augmented reality. **(11) I propose we** stop buying all hardbound books immediately and put all the library funds into hardware such as workstations and e-readers, software, and databases instead.

1. ................................................  6. ................................................

2. ................................................  7. ................................................

3. ................................................  8. ................................................

4. ................................................  9. ................................................

5. ................................................  10. ...............................................

# Revising Strategies

Using the checklist below, put a checkmark beside each question as you address it in your revision.

| | **Questions To Ask as You Revise** |
|---|---|
| **Writing Task** | ❏ Have I written a problem-solution essay?<br>❏ Have I fully explained the problem and its solution(s)? |
| **Purpose** | ❏ Have I set forth a clear problem and a workable solution?<br>❏ Have I used relevant facts, statistics, quotations, concrete details, expert opinions, and other forms of development?<br>❏ Have I sufficiently supported my ideas?<br>❏ Which details detract from my purpose and should be deleted?<br>❏ Have I provided an effective conclusion? |
| **Audience** | ❏ Do I create interest in my opening paragraph?<br>❏ Have I used transitions, repeated words, and clear pronoun references so that my audience can easily follow my ideas?<br>❏ Do I need to add, delete, or adjust any details to suit them more effectively to my audience's knowledge and experience?<br>❏ Have I explained technical or topic-specific language?<br>❏ Will my audience think I am objective?<br>❏ Have I included graphics, headings, or multimedia when they might be needed to help my audience understand the problem or solution? |

# Revising

**Revise for subject-verb agreement.** For a subject and its verb to agree, both must be in either singular or plural form, depending on whether the subject is singular or plural.

## Identifying Errors in Subject-Verb Agreement

Errors in agreement often occur when the subject and verb are separated by other words, phrases, or clauses. In the examples below, subjects are underlined, and the verbs are set in italic type.

**Singular Subject and Verb**

**Incorrect:** The copyright <u>date</u> of the encyclopedias *are* 1994.

**Correct:** The copyright <u>date</u> of the encyclopedias *is* 1994.

**Plural Subject and Verb**

**Incorrect:** Library <u>users</u> who need up-to-date information *is* out of luck.

**Correct:** Library <u>users</u> who need up-to-date information *are* out of luck.

## Identifying Indefinite Pronouns

These are the most common indefinite pronouns categorized by number:

**Singular:** *anybody, anyone, each, either, everybody, everything, neither, nobody, nothing, somebody, something*

**Plural:** *both, few, many, others, several*

**Singular or Plural:** *all, any, more, most, none, some*

## Fixing Errors

To correct mismatched subjects and verbs, follow these steps:

**1.** Identify the subject and determine whether it is singular or plural.

**2.** Select the verb that matches the subject.

For compound subjects joined by *and*, use the plural form.

For singular subjects joined by *or* or *nor*, use the singular form.

When the subject is an indefinite pronoun, use the appropriate form of the verb.

## Revision Checklist

❏ Have I used the plural form of the verb for compound subjects joined by *and?*

❏ Have I used the singular form of the verb for compound subjects joined by *or* or *nor?*

❏ Have I used the singular form of the verb with subjects that are singular indefinite pronouns?

❏ Have I used the plural form of the verb with subjects that are plural indefinite pronouns?

# Editing and Proofreading

Review your draft to correct errors in capitalization, spelling, and punctuation.

**Focus on Clear References:** Make sure that you have used *that* and *which* correctly. Use *that* to introduce clauses that are essential to the meaning of the noun and *which* to introduce clauses that are not essential to the meaning of the noun.

**Focus on Capitalization:** Review your draft carefully to find and correct capitalization errors. Capitalize the first word and all other key words in the titles of books.

**Incorrect capitalization:** The latest edition of the *encyclopedia of computer science and technology* in the school library is from 2000.

**Correct capitalization:** The latest edition of the *Encyclopedia of Computer Science and Technology* in the school library is from 2000.

**Focus on Spelling:** As you read, circle any words that you are not sure how to spell, frequently misspell, or seldom use. Then, use reference resources, such as a dictionary or thesaurus, to confirm the correct spelling. Follow these steps to find spellings in a dictionary:

- **Check the first letters of a word.** Think of homophones for that sound.

- **Check the other letters.** Once you spell the first sound correctly, try sounding out the rest of the word. Look for likely spellings in the dictionary. If you do not find your word, look for more unusual spellings of the sound.

**Focus on Punctuation: Commas in Places and Dates.** Proofread your writing to find and address punctuation errors. In particular, look for places in your writing where you name places or dates. Be sure you use commas correctly.

**Rule: Use commas with places.** *Public transit systems in Blacksburg, Virginia, and Salt Lake City, Utah, offer free wireless.*

**Rule: Use commas with dates.** *It may be possible to launch free wireless on Springfield buses as early as January 1, 2013.*

For use with Writing 2

Name _____ Date _____ Assignment _____

# Publishing and Presenting

Consider one of the following ways to present your writing:

**Launch a discussion.** Send an email, electronic invitation, or text message to classmates with whom you can form a discussion group. Set a date and time, and note your problem and solution as the discussion topic. At a meeting, read your essay, and then invite comments on your solution and other possible solutions.

**Make an audio recording.** Practice reading your essay aloud. Once you are comfortable with reading it aloud, make an audio recording of yourself reading your essay. Integrate headings such as "Problem," "Solution," and "Significance" to provide additional audio signals or guideposts for your listeners.

## Rubric for Self-Assessment

Find evidence in your writing to address each category listed below. Then, use the rating scale to grade your work. Circle the score that best applies for each category.

| Evaluating Your Expository Essay | not very        very |
|---|---|
| **Focus:** How clearly did you describe the nature of the problem and what needs to be done to solve it? | 1  2  3  4  5  6 |
| **Organization:** How effectively have you structured your essay? Did you include an interesting introduction, a clear and developed statement of the problem and its solution(s), and a conclusion? | 1  2  3  4  5  6 |
| **Support/Elaboration:** How good is your evidence? Is it well chosen, relevant, and concrete? Does it include quotations or other information and examples that are appropriate to your audience and purpose? | 1  2  3  4  5  6 |
| **Style:** How effective have you been in creating a formal style and objective tone that are appropriate to your task, purpose, and audience? | 1  2  3  4  5  6 |
| **Conventions:** How free is your essay from errors in grammar, spelling, and punctuation? | 1  2  3  4  5  6 |

# Writing 3

3. **Write narratives to develop real or imagined experiences or events using effective technique, well-chosen details, and well-structured event sequences.**

## Writing Workshop: Narrative

When you write a narrative, your task is to tell a story, and your purpose is to engage your audience. Short stories are a type of narrative writing that springs in part or in full from the writer's imagination. To fulfill the purpose of entertaining the reader, a short story must grab and hold its readers' attention from the first sentence to the last. To create this power over your audience, you must create vivid characters, a problem or conflict that lures readers in and keeps them reading, events that create increasing narrative tension and lead smoothly to a climax, and a satisfying ending.

## Assignment

Write a realistic or purely imaginative short story. Include these elements:

✓ a clear, consistent, single point of view, or clear, effective multiple points of view

✓ characters, a setting, and an inciting incident

✓ a conflict that focuses the story and helps determine the rising action, climax, and resolution

✓ a clear sequence of events

✓ narrative techniques, including natural dialogue, reflection or interior monologue, multiple plot lines, and effective pacing

✓ precise language and sensory details

✓ a satisfying conclusion that arises from the conflict and events

✓ correct use of language conventions

## Additional Standards

**3.a.** Engage and orient the reader by setting out a problem, situation, or observation, establishing one or multiple point(s) of view, and introducing a narrator and/or characters; create a smooth progression of experiences or events.

**3.b.** Use narrative techniques, such as dialogue,

pacing, description, reflection, and multiple plot lines, to develop experiences, events, and/or characters.

**3.c.** Use a variety of techniques to sequence events so that they build on one another to create a coherent whole.

**3.d.** Use precise words and phrases, telling details,

and sensory language to convey a vivid picture of the experiences, events, setting, and/or characters.

**3.e.** Provide a conclusion that follows from and reflects on what is experienced, observed, or resolved over the course of the narrative.

**Language**

**1.d.** Recognize and correct inappropriate shifts in verb tense.

**2.** Demonstrate command of the conventions of standard English capitalization, punctuation, and spelling when writing.

Name _____ Date _____ Selection _____

# Prewriting/Planning Strategies

**Come up with characters, setting, and events.** The organization of a story includes several elements, which are often presented in a particular order. The major building blocks of a story's plot include the following:

- **Exposition.** Introduce the characters, setting, and basic situation.

- **Inciting incident.** Introduce the main conflict.

- **Rising action.** Develop the conflict.

- **Climax.** Bring the conflict to a high point of interest or suspense.

- **Falling action.** Wind down the conflict.

- **Resolution.** Provide a general insight or change in the characters.

Jot down ideas for a plot in this organizer.

| Exposition: Characters | Exposition: Setting |
| --- | --- |
| | |

| Beginning: Conflict and Inciting Incident |
| --- |
| |

| Middle: Main Events |
| --- |
| |

| Ending/Resolution |
| --- |
| |

Name _____ Date _____ Selection _____

# Introducing Characters, Conflict, and Setting

**Develop the main character and the conflict.** Make a character chart for your main character. Strive to make the details about appearance, habits, and other traits consistent with the character's goal or main problem.

| **Name:** |
|---|
| **Appearance:** |
| **Three Key Adjectives:** |
| **Habits or quirks:** |
| **Likes:** |
| **Dislikes:** |

| **Main goal or problem:** | **Conflict with:** |
|---|---|
| | |

Name _____ Date _____ Selection _____

**Determine the setting.** Establish a time, such as a time of day or season of the year. Consider future time or historical times as well. Next, select a place, such as a crowded studio apartment, a rugged mountain range, a sports stadium, or an isolated cabin. Also, determine the environment, such as wind, rain, or burning heat; silence or noise; darkness or light.

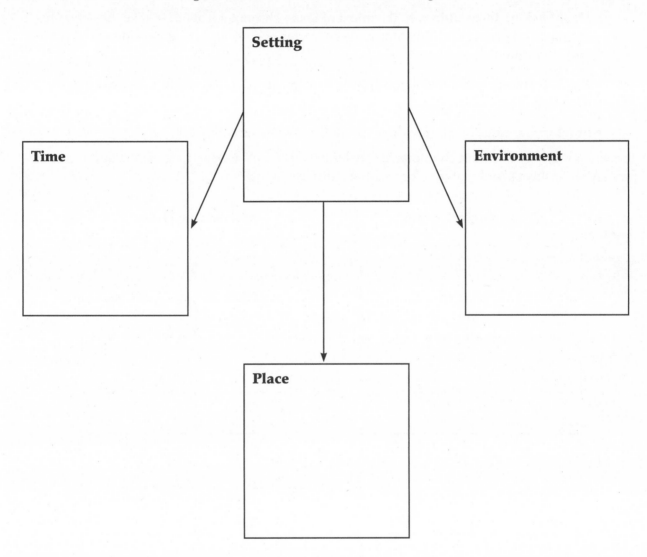

## Creating Point of View

**Select a point of view.** Choose a narrator, or the person who will relate the events of the story from start to finish. If your narrator is a character who takes part in the action of the story, you will introduce him or her at the very beginning. If your narrator is someone who simply reports on the action, the readers will hear his or her voice from the very beginning. Your narrator can be anything you want: sympathetic, nonjudgmental, or biased toward one character or outcome. Whoever you choose, your narrator must use a consistent voice and person (most often first person or third person) to express the events of the story.

Name _____ Date _____ Selection _____

## Organizing the Narrative

**Use different techniques.** You can organize your story completely with predictable, chronological order, or you can use one or more of these narrative techniques:

- **Flashback or foreshadow.** In the midst of using chronological order, take the action back in time to an event that helped form the character or contribute to the conflict, or layer in hints to future events.

- **Flash-forward.** In the midst of using chronological order, insert a future event into the narrative.

- **Start in the middle.** Start with an event that shows the conflict already under way.

Try arranging your events in chronological order first. Then try mixing them up by adding a flash-forward or flashback, or by otherwise creating a different sequence.

| **Chronological Order** | **Alternative Order** |
|:---:|:---:|
| | |
| ↓ | ↓ |
| | |
| ↓ | ↓ |
| | |
| ↓ | ↓ |
| | |
| ↓ | ↓ |
| | |

Name _____ Date _____ Selection _____

# Using Narrative Techniques

**Create realistic dialogue.** Your goal in writing dialogue is to move the plot along. Dialogue is one of the best ways of communicating events to the reader. You can and should use it to create rising action and to increase narrative tension.

Follow these guidelines for writing effective dialogue:

- **Make it natural.** People use informal, everyday language in real-life conversation. Do the same by including contractions, fragments, and informal word choices in the dialogue you write.

- **Use dialect if appropriate.** If your characters have a background or come from a region with specific and unique patterns of spoken language, incorporate them.

- **Combine dialogue with other techniques.** Don't give away the whole story in the dialogue or rely on dialogue to tell everything that happens.

- **Vary your speaker tags.** Do not follow every bit of dialogue with "he said" or "she said." After you identify the first speaker and the respondent, it may be clear who is saying what. Also, when you do repeat speaker tags, strive for variety in the verbs, such as *considered, whispered, assented, begged,* and *demanded.*

**Use reflection or interior monologue.** You can also move the plot along by revealing the inner thoughts and feelings of a character. In a reflection or interior monologue, a character reacts to events and other characters. He or she may offer a commentary on his or her own actions—or inaction. This reflection or monologue is often extended so that the reader knows exactly how the character interprets what just happened or what another character said.

**Pace your narrative.** Don't race to the climax. Instead, create narrative tension by introducing the characters, the setting, and the inciting incident with care. Then lead slowly from the exposition and the inciting incident to the climax by developing the characters and the conflict through a series of related events. Once you reach the climax, then you can move at a much faster pace toward the ending.

**Craft multiple plot lines.** You can increase interest and excitement in your story by using more than one plot line. For example, two antagonists may be preparing for the same high-stakes race or contest. A multiple plot line might follow a sequence of events that each character experiences separately before the story converges, most likely at the climax.

Name _____ Date _____ Selection _____

# Using Descriptive and Sensory Language

**Use sensory language.** Sensory details are words that appeal to the senses: sight, smell, taste, hearing, and touch. Sensory details are a key to developing the setting and mood of your story. They can also help you build suspense.

Remember, however, that a few well-chosen details can be better than a suitcase full. "A blaring horn" is preferable to "a loud, blaring, insistent, noisy, bothersome horn." Similarly, there is no need to engage every sense if the context doesn't work. If the sights, colors, and sounds are enough to describe a visit to racetrack, do not throw in imagery related to smell or taste.

**Use descriptive language.** Because your purpose is to entertain or engage your reader, your language must be constantly "on," creating images, rousing feelings, and drawing your reader into the story. To add descriptive depth, try these techniques:

- **Observe closely.** For example, see your main character in your mind's eye. How does he or she move? What are some characteristic gestures? Overall, what is there about the character's posture or look that makes him or her appear confident, frightened, excited, embarrassed, or cowed?

- **Be concrete and specific.** Don't choose an abstract noun when you can choose a concrete one. For example, "He showed her his trust" is far better as "He gave her the money to hold for him until Wednesday." Don't be general when you can be specific. For example, "She felt great," is far better as, "She could not hold back the whoop of joy that rushed off her tongue."

# Writing and Evaluating a Conclusion

**Resolve the conflict.** Your conclusion must relate to the inciting incident and conflict. For example, if your character is trying out for a team in a brave effort that is a stretch for her and that in conflict with her own sense of what she can do or achieve, the ending should be about making—or not making—that team. You must also create a satisfying sense of closure. This can often be achieved simply through the resonance created by the main character's final words or thoughts (*Lisa never stepped foot in Jade's house again.*) or external action (*A crack severed the earth, and, before Nichita could even scream, the house disappeared inside it.*).

**Evaluate the ending.** On your own, or with the help of a peer reader, decide whether the ending of your story truly resolves the conflict. Similarly, determine whether you have left any loose ends hanging, perhaps by forgetting to tell what became of a minor character or failing to make a clear enough transition between the rising action and the climax of the story.

Name _____  Date _____  Selection _____

# Revising Strategies

Put a checkmark beside each question as you address it in your revision.

| | **Questions To Ask as You Revise** |
|---|---|
| **Task** | ❑ Have I written a short story? |
| | ❑ Have I included the following elements of a short story: characters, setting, and inciting incident; conflict; rising action; climax; and resolution? |
| **Purpose** | ❑ Have I created an effective and consistent point of view, or have I effectively and clearly used multiple points of view? |
| | ❑ Have I included natural sounding dialogue? |
| | ❑ Have I paced my story to lead slowly to the climax and more quickly from the climax to the end? |
| | ❑ Have I varied narrative techniques, such as by including reflection or interior monologue? |
| | ❑ Have I sequenced events effectively? |
| **Audience** | ❑ Have I kept my reader interested from start to finish? |
| | ❑ Have I used sensory and descriptive language to create interest? |
| | ❑ Do I need to add, delete, or adjust any details to make the characters or setting more interesting, more convincing, or more appropriate to the conflict and events? |
| | ❑ Do I need to add, delete, or adjust any details to make the events clearer, more interesting, or easier to follow in sequence? |
| | ❑ Have I provided my readers with a satisfying ending? |

**For use with Writing 3**

Name _____ Date _____ Selection _____

# Revising

**Revise for inconsistent verb tenses.** Correct use of verb tenses indicates when an event occurs. Depending on the relationship of ideas in time, you will sometimes need to shift tense. Other times, you should avoid shifting tense.

| Six Basic Verb Tenses | |
|---|---|
| Present | Elena draws the curtain. |
| Past | Elena drew the curtain. |
| Future | Elena will draw the curtain. |
| Present Perfect | Elena has drawn the curtain. |
| Past Perfect | Elena had drawn the curtain. |
| Future Perfect | Elena will have drawn the curtain. |

Keep tense consistent when the action takes place at the same time:

> **Incorrect:** Mr. Chang *has approached* the child slowly. He *extends* a hand in greeting and *had said* hello.

> **Correct:** Mr. Chang *approached* the child slowly. He *extended* a hand in greeting and *said* hello.

## Identifying Inconsistent Verb Tenses

Inconsistent verb tense occurs when a sentence begins in one verb tense and incorrectly switches to another. Shifts in tense should always reflect a logical sequence.

> **Incorrect:** Peeking from behind the curtain, Elena has noticed that the man *is* still *standing* at the corner. He *will have been* standing there all morning.

> **Correct:** Peeking from behind the curtain, Elena *noticed* that the man *was* still *standing* at the corner. He *had been standing* there all morning.

Mixing tenses is necessary when you refer to two different times.

> **Incorrect:** Doug *had pleaded* with his mother for hours before she *had given* in.

> **Correct:** Doug *had pleaded* with his mother for hours before she *gave* in.

## Fixing Inconsistent Verb Tense

To correct inconsistent verb tense, find each verb in your narrative.

1. Identify your overall verb tense as past, present, or future.
2. Review the verbs in your writing, circling each one.
3. If you find a verb that is not in your overall verb tense, make sure the shift in tense is necessary.
4. Revise the verb if the shift is unnecessary.

### Revision Checklist

❑ Have I kept tense consistent when the action occurs at the same time?
❑ Have I shifted tense correctly when one action occurs earlier in a related series of actions?

**For use with Writing 3**

Name _____ Date _____ Selection _____

# Editing and Proofreading

Review your draft to correct errors in capitalization, spelling, and punctuation.

**Focus on Capitalization:** Review your draft carefully to find and correct capitalization errors. Capitalize the first word in each new bit of dialogue.

> **Incorrect capitalization:** "that man is watching this house," Elena said.

> **Correct capitalization:** "That man is watching this house," Elena said.

Capitalize the first word in dialogue that is interrupted by a speaker tag if the words that follow form a complete sentence.

> **Incorrect capitalization:** "Okay," Elena said, "let's be careful, though."

> **Correct capitalization:** "Okay," Elena said, "Let's be careful, though."

**Focus on Spelling:** Check for the correct spelling of words with doubled consonants. These words include words whose base forms include double consonants, such as *terrify*. They also include words whose final consonant is doubled when you add a suffix, such as *occurred* and *committing*.

**Focus on Punctuation:** Proofread your writing to find and address punctuation errors. In particular, look at the dialogue. Be sure you have used commas, end marks, and quotation marks correctly.

**Rule: Use quotation marks to enclose a person's exact speech or thoughts.**

*Elena's mother said, "Don't let your imagination run away with you."*

**Rule: Always place a comma inside the final quotation mark.**

*"I know what I see," Leah replied.*

**Rule: Place a question mark or an exclamation mark inside the final quotation mark if the end mark is part of the quotation.**

*"But do you know what it means?" her mother answered.*

For use with Writing 3

Name _____ Date _____ Selection _____

# Publishing and Presenting

Consider one of the following ways to present your writing:

**Give a dramatic reading.** Practice reading your story aloud, experimenting with pace, emphasis, and tone. Then read your story to a group of classmates. After your presentation, discuss which of your story's elements were especially effective when read dramatically.

**Illustrate and design your story.** Use desktop publishing and downloaded or original illustrations to create a professional looking magazine treatment of your story. Share your designed and formatted story with family members or friends.

## Rubric for Self-Assessment

Find evidence in your writing to address each category. Then, use the rating scale to grade your work. Circle the score that best applies for each category.

| Evaluating Your Narrative | not very          very |
|---|---|
| **Focus:** How clear are the characters, the setting, the inciting incident, and the conflict? | 1  2  3  4  5  6 |
| **Organization:** How clearly have you presented the sequence of events? Have you used appropriate pacing, dialogue, and other narrative techniques to help move the plot along and reach an effective ending? | 1  2  3  4  5  6 |
| **Support/Elaboration:** How sufficient and well-chosen are the details to make the characters, setting, and action clear and entertaining? | 1  2  3  4  5  6 |
| **Style:** How well have you engaged the reader with a compelling conflict, a consistent or effective point of view, and precise words that create a vivid picture of the characters? | 1  2  3  4  5  6 |
| **Conventions:** How free is your essay from errors in grammar, spelling, and punctuation? | 1  2  3  4  5  6 |

# Writing 4

> **4. Produce clear and coherent writing in which the development, organization, and style are appropriate to task, purpose, and audience.**

## Explanation

Producing clear, coherent writing is an important goal for writers. Because every writer writes for different reasons and readers, however, producing writing that is appropriate to your task, purpose, and audience is just as critical.

- Your **task** is the specific reason you are writing.
- Your **purpose** is the goal you want your writing to achieve, such as presenting an argument, explaining a topic, or telling a story.
- Your **audience** is the person or people who will read your writing.

In making choices as a writer, consider these elements as you develop and organize your ideas and select an appropriate writing style.

**Development** The information, evidence, and details you use to present and build ideas in your writing should be appropriate to your task, purpose, and audience. For example, if you are writing an essay to explain how peer pressure affects high school students, support your ideas with examples that everyone in your audience—including teachers and your fellow students—will find familiar and easy to understand.

**Organization** Use appropriate words, phrases, and clauses to show how your ideas are related to each other. In a letter to the editor of a newspaper, for example, use *because* to link your claim that young people should volunteer in their communities and your reason that volunteering is a valuable experience. *For example* can be used to introduce supporting details. Sequence your ideas and information—or events in a narrative—appropriately for your task, purpose, and audience.

**Style** Choosing appropriate language and the right tone for your task, purpose, and audience is also important. An essay on peer pressure, which will be read by your teacher, requires a formal style and an objective tone. A letter to the editor should remain objective but use less formal language than an essay. A humorous short story should have a comic tone and precise, descriptive language to engage readers.

## Academic Vocabulary

**development** the use of information, evidence, and details in writing to present and build an argument, a topic, or a narrative

**organization** the way ideas, information, and other elements are arranged and connected in writing

**style** the language and tone used by a writer to communicate clearly and engage readers

## Apply the Standard

Use the worksheet that follows to help you apply the standard as you write. Several copies of the worksheet have been provided for you to use with different assignments.

- Writing to a Specific Task, Purpose, and Audience

Name _____ Date _____ Assignment _____

# Writing to a Specific Task, Purpose, and Audience

Identify your writing task, your purpose for writing, and your audience. Then use the organizer to describe appropriate development, organization, and style for your writing.

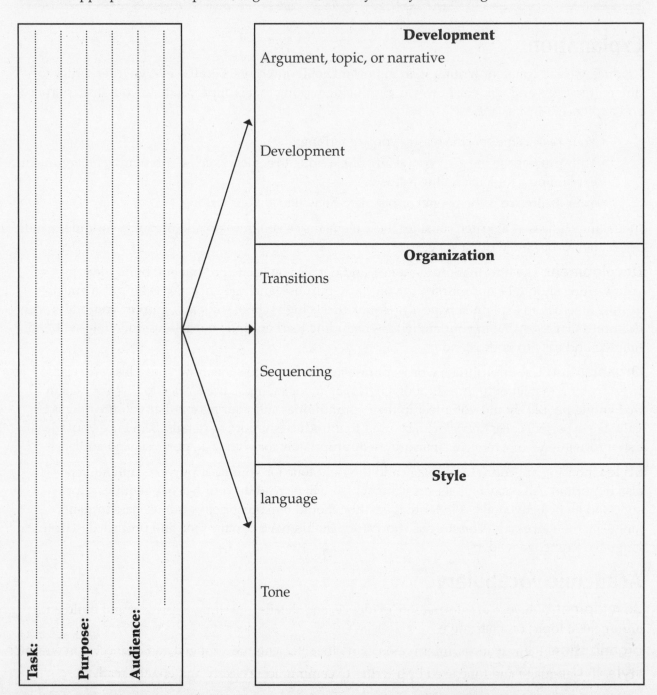

Task:

Purpose:

Audience:

**Development**

Argument, topic, or narrative

Development

**Organization**

Transitions

Sequencing

**Style**

language

Tone

**In what ways will your writing be appropriate to your task, purpose, and audience?**

_____

_____

A

Name _____ Date _____ Assignment _____

# Writing to a Specific Task, Purpose, and Audience

Identify your writing task, your purpose for writing, and your audience. Then use the organizer to describe appropriate development, organization, and style for your writing.

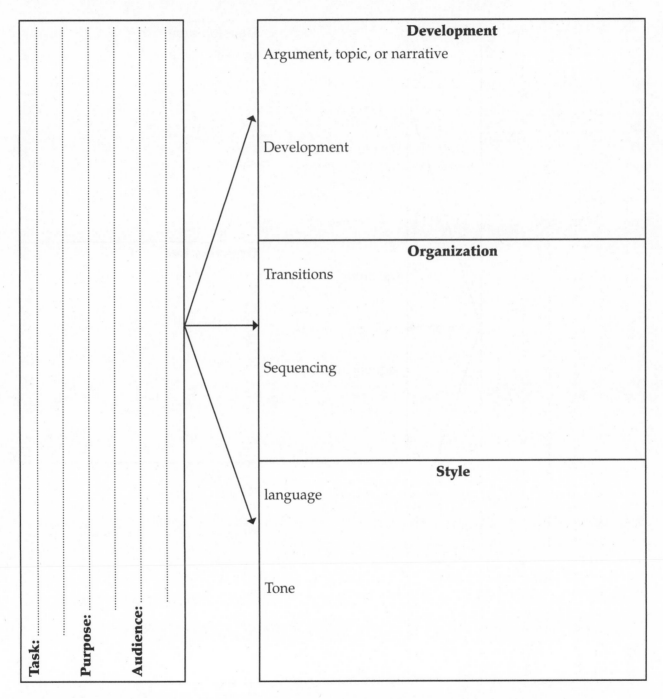

**Task:**

**Purpose:**

**Audience:**

**Development**

Argument, topic, or narrative

Development

**Organization**

Transitions

Sequencing

**Style**

language

Tone

**In what ways will your writing be appropriate to your task, purpose, and audience?**

..................................................................................................

..................................................................................................

B

For use with Writing 4

Name _____ Date _____ Assignment _____

# Writing to a Specific Task, Purpose, and Audience

Identify your writing task, your purpose for writing, and your audience. Then use the organizer to describe appropriate development, organization, and style for your writing.

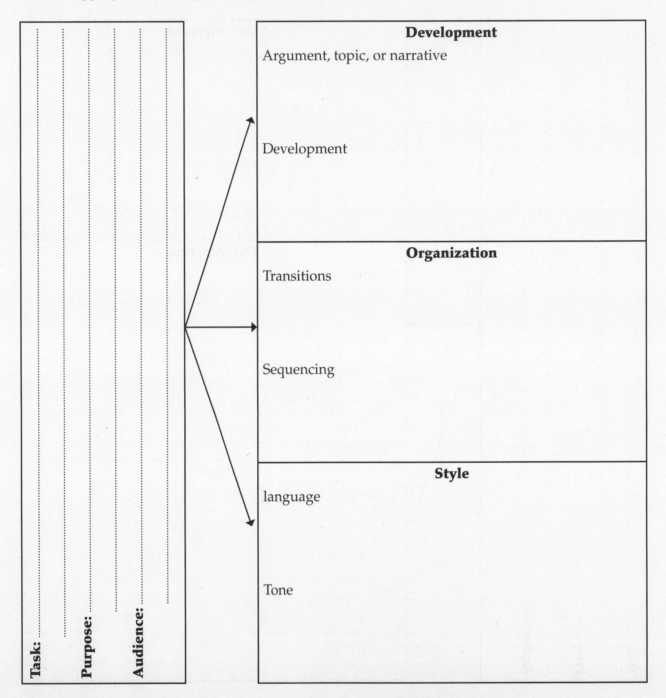

**Task:**

**Purpose:**

**Audience:**

**Development**

Argument, topic, or narrative

Development

**Organization**

Transitions

Sequencing

**Style**

language

Tone

**In what ways will your writing be appropriate to your task, purpose, and audience?**

....................................................................................................................

....................................................................................................................

C

Name _____ Date _____ Assignment _____

# Writing to a Specific Task, Purpose, and Audience

Identify your writing task, your purpose for writing, and your audience. Then use the organizer to describe appropriate development, organization, and style for your writing.

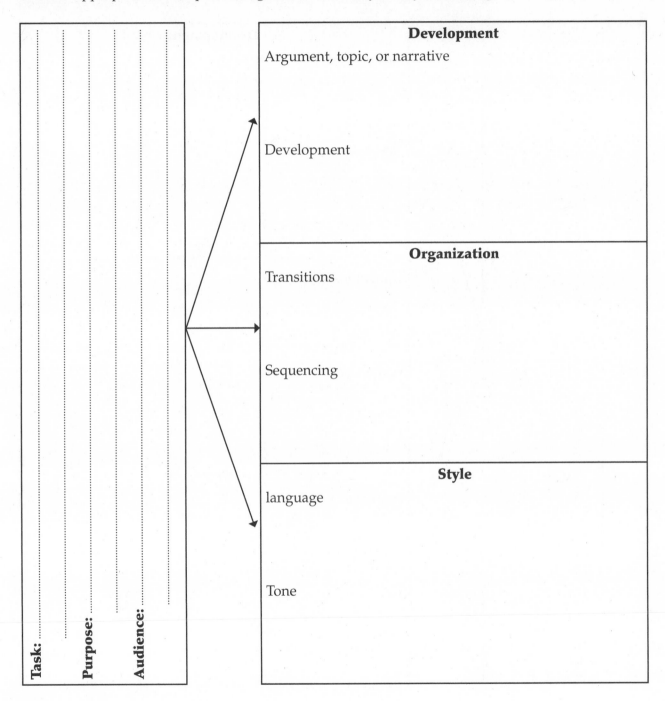

Task:

Purpose:

Audience:

**Development**

Argument, topic, or narrative

Development

**Organization**

Transitions

Sequencing

**Style**

language

Tone

**In what ways will your writing be appropriate to your task, purpose, and audience?**

_____

_____

D

Name _____  Date _____  Assignment _____

# Writing to a Specific Task, Purpose, and Audience

Identify your writing task, your purpose for writing, and your audience. Then use the organizer to describe appropriate development, organization, and style for your writing.

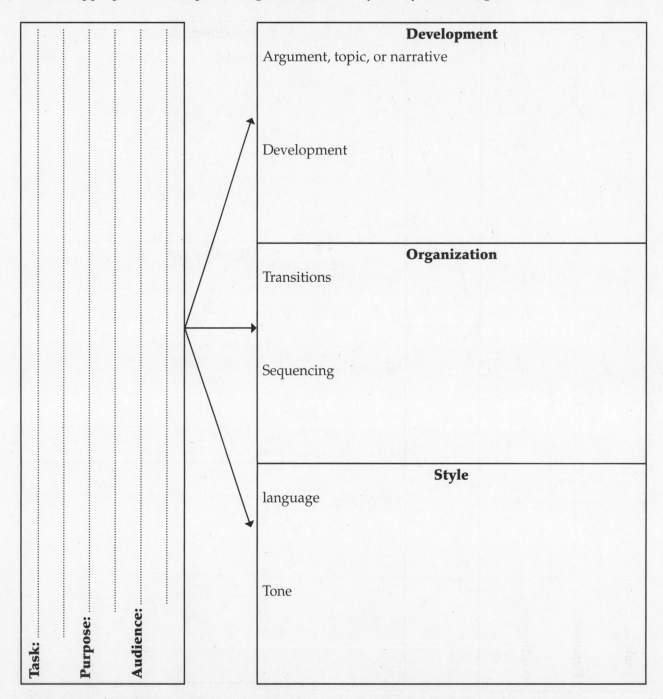

**Task:**

**Purpose:**

**Audience:**

**Development**

Argument, topic, or narrative

Development

**Organization**

Transitions

Sequencing

**Style**

language

Tone

**In what ways will your writing be appropriate to your task, purpose, and audience?**

...............................................................................................................................

...............................................................................................................................

E

For use with Writing 4

Name _____ Date _____ Assignment _____

# Writing to a Specific Task, Purpose, and Audience

Identify your writing task, your purpose for writing, and your audience. Then use the organizer to describe appropriate development, organization, and style for your writing.

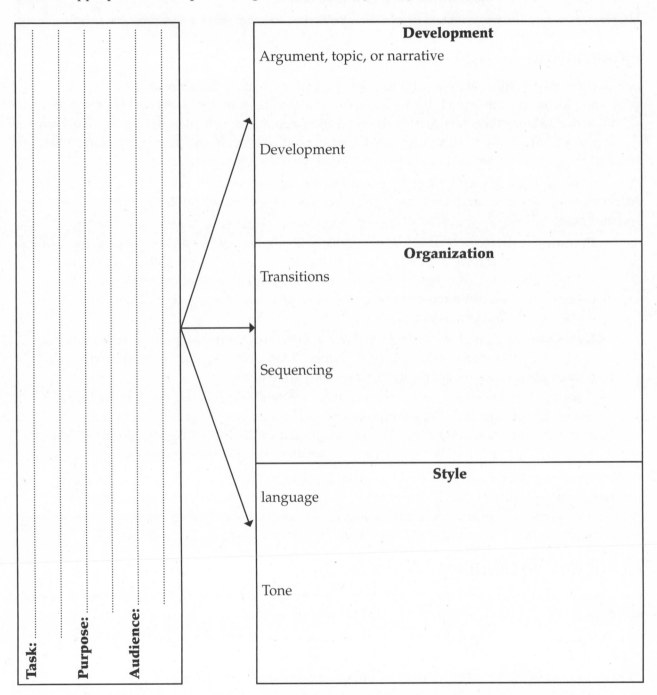

**Task:**

**Purpose:**

**Audience:**

### Development
Argument, topic, or narrative

Development

### Organization
Transitions

Sequencing

### Style
language

Tone

**In what ways will your writing be appropriate to your task, purpose, and audience?**

_____

_____

F

For use with Writing 4

# Writing 5

> **5. Develop and strengthen writing as needed by planning, revising, editing, rewriting, or trying a new approach, focusing on addressing what is most significant for a specific purpose and audience.**

## Explanation

Finished pieces of writing are not produced without effort. Writers **develop** their writing by generating ideas and gathering information about their issues, topics, or subjects. After finishing a draft, writers **strengthen** their writing by reviewing and making changes to improve it. Careful revising of a draft allows writers to achieve their purpose, or goal. It also helps writers meet the needs of their audience, or the people who will read what they have written.

Develop and strengthen your writing by **planning** before you begin to write and by **revising** and **editing** after you finish a first draft. Keep your focus on what is most significant for your purpose and audience.

- **Planning:** Select ideas and information that will help you achieve your purpose for writing. For example, if you are planning a letter to the editor of a newspaper about a proposal to build a new shopping center in your community, choose a position on the issue, and generate several sound reasons to support your position. Then, gather evidence that your audience will find persuasive.

- **Revising:** Carefully review what you have written and keep your purpose and audience in mind. Be prepared to add, delete, or change ideas, details, sentences, and even whole paragraphs to address your purpose and audience effectively.

- **Editing:** After revising, check what you have written for errors in grammar, spelling, usage, and punctuation. For example, keep your audience engaged by fixing any sentence fragments, run-ons, and awkward sentences that may distract readers. Correcting these errors will help your audience read and understand what you have written.

Even when you plan, revise, and edit, your writing might not address what is most significant for your purpose and audience. Be prepared to rewrite what you have written and to try new approaches. Writers make choices as they write, revise, and edit that strengthen and further develop their writing, usually by refining the purpose and by better addressing the audience.

## Academic Vocabulary

**develop**  present and build an argument, topic, or narrative in writing with information, evidence, and details

**edit**  prepare material for publication by correcting errors in grammar, spelling, usage, and punctuation

**revise**  reviewing and making changes to a piece of writing in order to improve it

## Apply the Standard

Use the worksheet that follows to help you apply the standard as you write. Several copies of the worksheet have been provided for you to use with different assignments.

- Developing and Strengthening Your Writing

Name _____ Date _____ Assignment _____

# Developing and Strengthening Your Writing

Use the organizer to describe how you plan, revise, and edit your writing.

**Your Purpose for Writing:** ............................................................................................................

**Your Audience:** ........................................................................................................................................

| | **PLANNING** |
|---|---|
| **BEFORE YOU WRITE** | Issue, Topic, or Subject:<br><br>Ideas:<br><br>Information: |

**WRITE YOUR FIRST DRAFT**

| | **REVISING** |
|---|---|
| **AFTER WRITING YOUR FIRST DRAFT** | Most significant for purpose and audience:<br><br>Add:<br><br>Delete:<br><br>Change: |
| | **EDITING** |
| | Grammar:<br><br>Spelling:<br><br>Usage:<br><br>Punctuation: |

A

Name _____ Date _____ Assignment _____

# Developing and Strengthening Your Writing

Use the organizer to describe how you plan, revise, and edit your writing.

**Your Purpose for Writing:** ..................................................................................................................

**Your Audience:** ........................................................................................................................................

<table>
<tr><td rowspan="2">BEFORE YOU WRITE</td><td colspan="1">PLANNING</td></tr>
<tr><td>

Issue, Topic, or Subject:


Ideas:


Information:

</td></tr>
</table>

## WRITE YOUR FIRST DRAFT

<table>
<tr><td rowspan="2">AFTER WRITING YOUR FIRST DRAFT</td><td>REVISING</td></tr>
<tr><td>

Most significant for purpose and audience:

Add:

Delete:

Change:

</td></tr>
<tr><td></td><td>

EDITING

Grammar:

Spelling:

Usage:

Punctuation:

</td></tr>
</table>

B

Name _____ Date _____ Assignment _____

# Developing and Strengthening Your Writing

Use the organizer to describe how you plan, revise, and edit your writing.

**Your Purpose for Writing:** ............................................................................................

**Your Audience:** ....................................................................................................................

<table>
<tr><td rowspan="4">BEFORE YOU WRITE</td><td align="center">**PLANNING**</td></tr>
<tr><td>Issue, Topic, or Subject:</td></tr>
<tr><td>Ideas:</td></tr>
<tr><td>Information:</td></tr>
</table>

## WRITE YOUR FIRST DRAFT

<table>
<tr><td rowspan="8">AFTER WRITING YOUR FIRST DRAFT</td><td align="center">**REVISING**</td></tr>
<tr><td>Most significant for purpose and audience:</td></tr>
<tr><td>Add:</td></tr>
<tr><td>Delete:</td></tr>
<tr><td>Change:</td></tr>
<tr><td align="center">**EDITING**</td></tr>
<tr><td>Grammar:</td></tr>
<tr><td>Spelling:</td></tr>
<tr><td>Usage:</td></tr>
<tr><td>Punctuation:</td></tr>
</table>

C

For use with Writing 5

Name _____ Date _____ Assignment _____

# Developing and Strengthening Your Writing

Use the organizer to describe how you plan, revise, and edit your writing.

**Your Purpose for Writing:** ................................................................................................................

**Your Audience:** ..............................................................................................................................

<table>
<tr><td rowspan="2" style="writing-mode:vertical">BEFORE YOU WRITE</td><td style="text-align:center">**PLANNING**</td></tr>
<tr><td>
Issue, Topic, or Subject:

Ideas:

Information:
</td></tr>
</table>

**WRITE YOUR FIRST DRAFT**

<table>
<tr><td rowspan="2" style="writing-mode:vertical">AFTER WRITING YOUR FIRST DRAFT</td><td style="text-align:center">**REVISING**</td></tr>
<tr><td>
Most significant for purpose and audience:

Add:

Delete:

Change:
</td></tr>
<tr><td></td><td style="text-align:center">**EDITING**</td></tr>
<tr><td></td><td>
Grammar:

Spelling:

Usage:

Punctuation:
</td></tr>
</table>

D

For use with Writing 5

Name _____ Date _____ Assignment _____

# Developing and Strengthening Your Writing

Use the organizer to describe how you plan, revise, and edit your writing.

**Your Purpose for Writing:** ...........................................................................................................

**Your Audience:** ...........................................................................................................................

<table>
<tr><td rowspan="4" style="writing-mode: vertical-lr;">BEFORE YOU WRITE</td><td colspan="1">PLANNING</td></tr>
<tr><td>Issue, Topic, or Subject:</td></tr>
<tr><td>Ideas:</td></tr>
<tr><td>Information:</td></tr>
</table>

## WRITE YOUR FIRST DRAFT

<table>
<tr><td rowspan="8" style="writing-mode: vertical-lr;">AFTER WRITING YOUR FIRST DRAFT</td><td>REVISING</td></tr>
<tr><td>Most significant for purpose and audience:</td></tr>
<tr><td>Add:</td></tr>
<tr><td>Delete:</td></tr>
<tr><td>Change:</td></tr>
<tr><td>EDITING</td></tr>
<tr><td>Grammar:</td></tr>
<tr><td>Spelling:</td></tr>
<tr><td>Usage:</td></tr>
<tr><td>Punctuation:</td></tr>
</table>

E

Name _____ Date _____ Assignment _____

# Developing and Strengthening Your Writing

Use the organizer to describe how you plan, revise, and edit your writing.

**Your Purpose for Writing:** ......................................................................................................................

**Your Audience:** ..........................................................................................................................................

<table>
<tr><td rowspan="4" style="writing-mode: vertical">BEFORE YOU WRITE</td><td colspan="1" align="center">PLANNING</td></tr>
<tr><td>Issue, Topic, or Subject:</td></tr>
<tr><td>Ideas:</td></tr>
<tr><td>Information:</td></tr>
</table>

**WRITE YOUR FIRST DRAFT**

<table>
<tr><td rowspan="8" style="writing-mode: vertical">AFTER WRITING YOUR FIRST DRAFT</td><td align="center">REVISING</td></tr>
<tr><td>Most significant for purpose and audience:</td></tr>
<tr><td>Add:</td></tr>
<tr><td>Delete:</td></tr>
<tr><td>Change:</td></tr>
<tr><td align="center">EDITING</td></tr>
<tr><td>Grammar:</td></tr>
<tr><td>Spelling:</td></tr>
<tr><td>Usage:</td></tr>
<tr><td>Punctuation:</td></tr>
</table>

F

For use with Writing 5

# Writing 6

> 6. Use technology, including the Internet, to produce, publish, and update individual or shared writing products, taking advantage of technology's capacity to link to other information and to display information flexibly and dynamically.

## Explanation

Technology provides today's writers with many powerful tools. The Internet offers access to the information they need to develop ideas and topics. Word processing software simplifies writing, revising, and editing. Writers can present information in a range of formats and create links readers can follow to other sources. As you produce, publish, and update your writing, use technology—including the Internet—to link to and display information.

- **Link to other information:** Use **links** to connect your writing with other sources of information. Links usually appear as underlined words or phrases in blue type. You can create links in any document in an electronic format. For example, in an expository essay about how scientists work on the ocean floor, create a link to a reliable Web page on the history of underwater exploration.

- **Display information:** Display information in flexible and dynamic ways using **word processing software**. For example, if you are writing an argumentative essay that calls for healthier choices in your school's cafeteria, create a pie chart that displays the types of food the cafeteria currently serves. Add color to make your chart, graph, or table more dynamic.

- **Multimedia information:** Use technology and the Internet to include **multimedia** information in essays, reports, and other writing products. For example, if you are writing a short story that you will post on a class Web site, look for downloadable illustrations on the Internet. You can also find audio clips for your audience to hear as they read your story.

## Academic Vocabulary

**link**  a word, phrase, or other segment of text in a document that lets readers jump to a Web page or to another document on the Internet

**multimedia**  information in more than one medium, such as photographs, audio recordings, and videos

**word processing software**  a computer program used to create, modify, and print documents

## Apply the Standard

Use the worksheet that follows to help you apply the standard as you write. Several copies have been provided for you to use with different assignments.

- Using Technology

Name _____ Date _____ Assignment _____

# Using Technology

Use the organizer to plan how you will use technology to link to and display information.

**What You Are Writing:** ..................................................................................................................

**Electronic Format:** ........................................................................................................................

| Use technology and the Internet to link to other information |
|---|
| Information to which you want to link: ................................................................................................ |
| Where you will create link(s): ........................................................................................................... |
| How will linking to other information improve your writing product? ............................................... |

| Use technology and the Internet to display information flexibly and dynamically |
|---|
| Information you want to display flexibly and dynamically: ............................................................... |
| Format(s) you will use to display the information: ........................................................................... |
| How will using these formats make the information stand out for your readers? ............................. |

| Use technology and the Internet to incorporate multimedia information |
|---|
| Multimedia information you want to incorporate: ............................................................................. |
| What will the multimedia information add to your writing product? ................................................ |

**List any other ways you will use technology to link to and display information.**

..................................................................................................................................................

..................................................................................................................................................

A

Name _____ Date _____ Assignment _____

# Using Technology

Use the organizer to plan how you will use technology to link to and display information.

**What You Are Writing:** ................................................................................................

**Electronic Format:** ....................................................................................................

| Use technology and the Internet to link to other information |
|---|
| Information to which you want to link: ........................................................................ |
| Where you will create link(s): .................................................................................... |
| How will linking to other information improve your writing product? ................................. |

| Use technology and the Internet to display information flexibly and dynamically |
|---|
| Information you want to display flexibly and dynamically: ............................................... |
| Format(s) you will use to display the information: ......................................................... |
| How will using these formats make the information stand out for your readers? ................. |

| Use technology and the Internet to incorporate multimedia information |
|---|
| Multimedia information you want to incorporate: .......................................................... |
| What will the multimedia information add to your writing product? ................................. |

**List any other ways you will use technology to link to and display information.**

................................................................................................................................

................................................................................................................................

Name _____ Date _____ Assignment _____

# Using Technology

Use the organizer to plan how you will use technology to link to and display information.

**What You Are Writing:** ...................................................................................................................

**Electronic Format:** .........................................................................................................................

| **Use technology and the Internet to link to other information** |
|---|
| Information to which you want to link: .................................................................................... |
| Where you will create link(s): .................................................................................................. |
| How will linking to other information improve your writing product? ...................................... |

| **Use technology and the Internet to display information flexibly and dynamically** |
|---|
| Information you want to display flexibly and dynamically: ........................................................ |
| Format(s) you will use to display the information: ................................................................... |
| How will using these formats make the information stand out for your readers? ...................... |

| **Use technology and the Internet to incorporate multimedia information** |
|---|
| Multimedia information you want to incorporate: ..................................................................... |
| What will the multimedia information add to your writing product? ......................................... |

**List any other ways you will use technology to link to and display information.**

...............................................................................................................................................

...............................................................................................................................................

C

Name _____ Date _____ Assignment _____

# Using Technology

Use the organizer to plan how you will use technology to link to and display information.

**What You Are Writing:** .........................................................................................................................................

**Electronic Format:** ...............................................................................................................................................

| Use technology and the Internet to link to other information |
|---|
| Information to which you want to link: ......................................................................................................... |
| Where you will create link(s): ...................................................................................................................... |
| How will linking to other information improve your writing product? ...................................................... |

| Use technology and the Internet to display information flexibly and dynamically |
|---|
| Information you want to display flexibly and dynamically: ......................................................................... |
| Format(s) you will use to display the information: ..................................................................................... |
| How will using these formats make the information stand out for your readers? ................................... |

| Use technology and the Internet to incorporate multimedia information |
|---|
| Multimedia information you want to incorporate: ...................................................................................... |
| What will the multimedia information add to your writing product? ....................................................... |

**List any other ways you will use technology to link to and display information.**

.................................................................................................................................................................................

.................................................................................................................................................................................

D

For use with Writing 6

Name _____ Date _____ Assignment _____

# Using Technology

Use the organizer to plan how you will use technology to link to and display information.

**What You Are Writing:** ...............................................................................................................

**Electronic Format:** ...................................................................................................................

| Use technology and the Internet to link to other information |
| --- |
| Information to which you want to link: ....................................................................................... |
| Where you will create link(s): ................................................................................................... |
| How will linking to other information improve your writing product? .............................................. |

| Use technology and the Internet to display information flexibly and dynamically |
| --- |
| Information you want to display flexibly and dynamically: ............................................................. |
| Format(s) you will use to display the information: ....................................................................... |
| How will using these formats make the information stand out for your readers? .............................. |

| Use technology and the Internet to incorporate multimedia information |
| --- |
| Multimedia information you want to incorporate: ........................................................................ |
| What will the multimedia information add to your writing product? ................................................ |

**List any other ways you will use technology to link to and display information.**

....................................................................................................................................

....................................................................................................................................

E

For use with Writing 6

Name _____ Date _____ Assignment _____

# Using Technology

Use the organizer to plan how you will use technology to link to and display information.

**What You Are Writing:** ...........................................................................................................................

**Electronic Format:** ...............................................................................................................................

| **Use technology and the Internet to link to other information** |
|---|
| Information to which you want to link: ........................................................................................... |
| Where you will create link(s): ........................................................................................................ |
| How will linking to other information improve your writing product? ........................................... |

| **Use technology and the Internet to display information flexibly and dynamically** |
|---|
| Information you want to display flexibly and dynamically: ............................................................ |
| Format(s) you will use to display the information: ........................................................................ |
| How will using these formats make the information stand out for your readers? ........................... |

| **Use technology and the Internet to incorporate multimedia information** |
|---|
| Multimedia information you want to incorporate: .......................................................................... |
| What will the multimedia information add to your writing product? ............................................. |

**List any other ways you will use technology to link to and display information.**

...................................................................................................................................................

...................................................................................................................................................

F

# Writing 7

> 7. Conduct short as well as more sustained research projects to answer a question (including a self-generated question) or solve a problem; narrow or broaden the inquiry when appropriate; synthesize multiple sources on the subject, demonstrating understanding of the subject under investigation.

## Explanation

Research projects vary in their scope and can have different goals. Short research projects focus on very narrow topics. Complex subjects require more **sustained research** involving in-depth investigation and multiple sources. As you conduct research, you may need to narrow or broaden your **inquiry**. Narrowing an inquiry is appropriate for short research projects, and broadening an inquiry is appropriate for more sustained projects.

- **Narrowing an Inquiry:** Narrow a broad question or problem for a short research project. For example, if you are researching Arthurian legends, the question "How has the legend of King Arthur developed over time?" is too broad. Narrow your inquiry by focusing on one telling of King Arthur's story: "How did T.H. White adapt the legend of King Arthur in *The Once and Future King?*"

- **Broadening an Inquiry:** Broaden a narrow question or problem for a more sustained research project. For example, putting a paper recycling bin in your classroom is too narrow a problem for a sustained project. Broaden your inquiry to focus on establishing a paper recycling program for your school or a comprehensive recycling program for your community.

To better understand the subject you are investigating, gather ideas and information from multiple sources, rather than relying on only one or two. Then **synthesize,** or creatively combine multiple sources, and draw your own conclusion about the question or problem. When you present the results of your research project, demonstrate your understanding of the subject by supporting your answer or your solution with relevant information from several different sources.

## Academic Vocabulary

**inquiry**  the process of looking for information to answer questions about a topic or to solve a problem

**sustained research**  in-depth investigation or inquiry involving multiple sources

**synthesize**  bring together information from different sources to present a new answer or solution

## Apply the Standard

Use the worksheets that follow to help you apply the standard as you write. Several copies of each worksheet have been provided for you to use with different assignments.

- Researching to Answer Questions or Solve Problems

- Synthesizing Information from Different Sources

Name _____ Date _____ Assignment _____

# Researching to Answer Questions or Solve Problems

Narrow or broaden a research inquiry. Then, use the organizer to gather ideas and information from multiple sources.

**Subject:** ....................................................................................................................................

**Scope of Research Project:** .......................................................................................................

| **Initial Question or Problem:** | Narrow Inquiry    Broaden Inquiry | **Narrowed/Broadened Question or Problem:** |
|---|---|---|

| **Source 1:** |
|---|
| Ideas and Information: |

| **Source 2:** |
|---|
| Ideas and Information: |

| **Source 3:** |
|---|
| Ideas and Information: |

| **Source 4:** |
|---|
| Ideas and Information: |

A

For use with Writing 7

Name _____ Date _____ Assignment _____

# Researching to Answer Questions or Solve Problems

Narrow or broaden a research inquiry. Then, use the organizer to gather ideas and information from multiple sources.

**Subject:** ...................................................................................................................................

**Scope of Research Project:** ..............................................................................................

| **Initial Question or Problem:** | | **Narrowed/Broadened Question or Problem:** |
|---|---|---|
| | Narrow Inquiry → | |
| | Broaden Inquiry | |

| **Source 1:** |
|---|
| Ideas and Information: |
| **Source 2:** |
| Ideas and Information: |
| **Source 3:** |
| Ideas and Information: |
| **Source 4:** |
| Ideas and Information: |

Name _____ Date _____ Assignment _____

# Researching to Answer Questions or Solve Problems

Narrow or broaden a research inquiry. Then, use the organizer to gather ideas and information from multiple sources.

**Subject:** ...........................................................................................................................

**Scope of Research Project:** .............................................................................................

| Initial Question or Problem: | | Narrowed/Broadened Question or Problem: |
|---|---|---|
| | Narrow Inquiry → Broaden Inquiry → | |

| Source 1: |
|---|
| Ideas and Information: |

| Source 2: |
|---|
| Ideas and Information: |

| Source 3: |
|---|
| Ideas and Information: |

| Source 4: |
|---|
| Ideas and Information: |

Name _____ Date _____ Assignment _____

# Synthesizing Information from Different Sources

Use the organizer below to synthesize information from your sources. Support your answer or solution with information from multiple sources.

**Subject:** ......................................................................................................................

**Question or Problem:** ...................................................................................................

| INFORMATION FROM DIFFERENT SOURCES | | | |
|---|---|---|---|
| **Source 1** | **Source 2** | **Source 3** | **Source 4** |
| | | | |

| SYNTHESIS |
|---|
| Your Answer/Solution: ............................................................................................ ............................................................................................................................ |
| Support 1: ........................................................................................................... ............................................................................................................................ |
| Support 2: ........................................................................................................... ............................................................................................................................ |
| Support 3: ........................................................................................................... ............................................................................................................................ |

A

For use with Writing 7

Name _____  Date _____  Assignment _____

# Synthesizing Information from Different Sources

Use the organizer below to synthesize information from your sources. Support your answer or solution with information from multiple sources.

**Subject:** ..............................................................................................................................

**Question or Problem:** ....................................................................................................

| INFORMATION FROM DIFFERENT SOURCES | | | |
|---|---|---|---|
| **Source 1** | **Source 2** | **Source 3** | **Source 4** |
| | | | |

| SYNTHESIS |
|---|
| Your Answer/Solution: .......................................................................................... <br> .......................................................................................................................... |
| Support 1: ........................................................................................................... <br> .......................................................................................................................... |
| Support 2: ........................................................................................................... <br> .......................................................................................................................... |
| Support 3: ........................................................................................................... <br> .......................................................................................................................... |

Name _____ Date _____ Assignment _____

# Synthesizing Information from Different Sources

Use the organizer below to synthesize information from your sources. Support your answer or solution with information from multiple sources.

**Subject:** ................................................................................................................

**Question or Problem:** ...........................................................................................

| INFORMATION FROM DIFFERENT SOURCES | | | |
|---|---|---|---|
| **Source 1** | **Source 2** | **Source 3** | **Source 4** |
| | | | |

| SYNTHESIS |
|---|
| Your Answer/Solution: .......................................................................................... ........................................................................................................................ |
| Support 1: ........................................................................................................ ........................................................................................................................ |
| Support 2: ........................................................................................................ ........................................................................................................................ |
| Support 3: ........................................................................................................ ........................................................................................................................ |

C

# Writing 8

8. **Gather information from multiple print and digital sources, using advanced searches effectively; assess the usefulness of each source in answering the research question; integrate information into the text selectively to maintain the flow of ideas, avoiding plagiarism and following a standard format for citation.**

## Writing Workshop: Research Report

When you write a **research report,** your task is to present and interpret information that you have gathered through extensive reading and study. The process begins with deciding on a topic, reading about it in several sources, and narrowing it down to an appropriate scope and focus in order to arrive at a thesis. Then, once again using multiple and reliable sources, you must gather information to develop, refine, and support that thesis. Smooth integration of source material, an effective method of organization, and an appropriate tone and style also underpin the effective research report.

Furthermore, a successful research depends in large part on the notetaking process. Care at this stage not only ensures relevant and ample support for your thesis but also the responsible and ethical use of source material.

## Assignment

Write a research report about an event or development in history. You do not have to limit yourself to political or cultural history. Consider the history of science, math, technology, art, music, business, architecture, and other disciplines. Include these elements:

- ✓ a topic whose scope is appropriate to the length of your paper
- ✓ a clear, specific thesis that functions as the controlling idea for your entire paper
- ✓ body paragraphs that clearly relate to and develop that thesis
- ✓ substantial and smoothly integrated support for the thesis
- ✓ quoted, paraphrased, or summarized information from a variety of credible sources
- ✓ consistent, correct use of a style manual for citations within the paper and an accurate, correctly formatted Works Cited list or bibliography at the end of the paper
- ✓ correct manuscript conventions and correct use of language conventions

## Additional Standards

**Language**
**1.b.** Use various types of phrases (nouns, verb, adjectival, adverbial, participial, prepositional, absolute) and clauses (independent, dependent; noun, relative, adverbial) to convey

specific meanings and add variety and interest to writing or presentations.

**2.a.** Use a semicolon (and perhaps a conjunctive adverb) to link two or more closely related independent clauses.

**3.a.** Write and edit work so that it conforms to the guidelines in a style manual (e.g., *MLA Handbook, Turabian's Manual for Writers*) appropriate for the discipline and writing type.

Name _____ Date _____ Selection _____

# Prewriting/Planning Strategies

**Scan your notebooks.** Follow your instincts and interests when looking for a topic. Review the notes you have taken in any subject—from history to math to drama. Use a marker or self-sticking notes to highlight ideas that interest you. Then, choose one that you want to investigate further.

**Look through periodicals.** Flip through newspaper and magazine articles for topics that you find intriguing. For example, you might consider researching the history of a conflict, product, or debate that is currently in the news. Determine what you already know about the topic and what you would like to learn. Use a chart like this one to organize your thoughts:

| Item from the news: | |
|---|---|
| **What I Already Know About This** | **What I Want to Know About the History of This Event/Issue/Conflict** |
| | |

**Ask research questions.** Next, compose specific questions to focus your search for information. For example, if the event you want to investigate is the release of the latest smart phone, you might ask about the beginning of that technology, including when and where it started, or issues related to who got credit for it.

**Questions:**

1. .........................................................................................................................

2. .........................................................................................................................

3. .........................................................................................................................

Name _____ Date _____ Selection _____

**Jot down a working thesis and ideas about your audience.** Because the thesis is central to a research report, you need to make it a centerpiece of the writing process from beginning to end. Even though you cannot write a specific thesis before you have begun your research, jotting down a first attempt will help you focus your research. Next, record ideas about who would be most interested by your topic or most likely to benefit by learning about it, and consider what they know about your topic.

| |
|---|
| **Working Thesis:** |
| **Audience's Interest in and Knowledge of Topic:** |

# Researching from Print and Digital Sources

**Read extensively.** A research report relies on information—fact-based, appropriate, carefully selected information—and plenty of it. Therefore, the task of writing a report requires extensive reading. Prepare for two separate reading phases: first, to develop a general sense of your topic and to begin narrowing it down to a specific focus and thesis; and second, to find additional information in support of that specific thesis. Throughout this reading process, you will be choosing and evaluating sources, taking notes from them, and documenting them.

**Use reference sources.** Encyclopedias, especially specialized encyclopedias, such as encyclopedias of science, ecology, inventions, World War II, the Renaissance, the 20th century, and so on, are good places to begin. Articles in these volumes will often divide or narrow your topic for you, by offering you specific subheadings. You will find some of these resources online and accessible with a public library card. You may have to visit the library to find others on the shelves of the reference section.

**Use primary and secondary sources.** Consult primary sources, original or firsthand accounts of events. Primary sources include interview transcripts, journals, letters, eyewitness accounts, and speeches. Also consult secondary sources, such as books, encyclopedia entries, magazine articles, and newspaper articles that present a report, a retelling, or an analysis of primary sources.

Name _____ Date _____ Selection _____

**Use a variety of other sources.** Web sites provide plenty of information, but they are not the only source of information—and they are not always the best source. Do not neglect to use books, which you may access on the shelves of your library or online. Also use sources such as the following:

- **Almanacs.** These reference works offer social, political, and economic statistics.

- **Atlases.** You will find maps, tables, charts, and illustrations in these general or specialized works.

- **Databases.** There are specialized database topics ranging from economics and social sciences to business and science. Databases index magazines, newspapers, general and specialized encyclopedias, and scholarly journals. You can access databases from terminals in your local library. To access them from home, you usually need a library card number.

- **Government publications.** These documents provide information on laws, government programs, and topics such as agriculture and economics.

- **Microfiche.** Use this electronic storage method for back issues of periodicals that you cannot access online.

- **Consumer, workplace, and other public documents.** Consumer documents include instructions for using a product, guarantees, and warranties. Workplace documents include instructions for carrying out tasks on the job as well items such a task force reports. Public documents include anything in the public domain, such as the annual reports prepared by your town, city, or state government, or anything else intended for public use.

**Opt for advanced searches.** Advanced searches can save you time and lead you to better source material. Look for a link called "Advanced Search" on the home page of your favorite search engine. Once you have selected that link, fill in the options for limiting your search. For example, you can limit your search to documents with some words but not others. You might be able to limit your search strictly to a specific domain such as .gov or .org. In a library catalog, look for an advanced search on the catalog home page. By means of it, you might be able to limit your results to the material type (book, CD, periodical, software, and so on); to the collection type (adult or children's); and to the publication date. You might also be able to order your search results by relevance or by date.

**Re-evaluate your topic.** After you have gathered a variety of sources and begun to read with a specific thesis in mind, make sure the topic you have chosen is appropriate for your task, your purpose, and your audience. Ask yourself these questions:

❏ Am I still curious about or intrigued by this topic?

❏ Is this an appropriate topic for meeting the requirements of the assignment?

❏ Have I sufficiently narrowed my topic?

❏ Will I find enough information on this topic?

Name _____ Date _____ Selection _____

# Evaluating Credibility and Usefulness of Your Sources

**Evaluate Web sites.** Because almost anyone can create a Web site for almost any reason, the job of establishing credibility of a Web site is up to you. Use this form to record information about Web sites and to make decisions about their credibility and usefulness to you.

| Web site name and URL: | |
|---|---|
| | **My Evaluation** |
| **Author or Sponsor**<br>• Is the author or sponsor named? Who or what is it?<br>• What are the author's or sponsor's credentials?<br>• Is the author or sponsor a respected authority on this topic? | |
| **Documentation**<br>• Are there footnotes, endnotes, or other source documentation?<br>• Is there a bibliography or list of works cited?<br>• Where does the information come from? | |
| **Date**<br>• Is the information current?<br>• When was the site created?<br>• When was the site last updated? | |
| **Bias**<br>• Does this site want to sell things or sway thinking in any way?<br>• Does bias affect the quality of the information on the site? | |

Name _____ Date _____ Selection _____

**Evaluate Other Sources.** You must also subject your other sources to an evaluation that includes these criteria:

- **Publisher.** The work should be published by a respected publisher. This offers some guarantee that the work has been fact-checked and edited. Avoid self-published materials and popular presses.

- **Publication date.** If you are researching a current topic, you want up-to-date information. Remember that scholarship changes, too. The best insights into the life of a Renaissance woman may have built on earlier research and been published last year, not in 1960. This does not mean all older works are not useful; some, however, are out of date.

- **Respected publications.** Some magazines and newspapers are not intended as the basis for research. For example, *Myself* magazine is not meant to offer scholarly insights on, for example, the topic of depression. Prefer a journal of psychology for such information. If you are not sure about how respected a publication is, ask a teacher or librarian.

## Taking Notes

**Create electronic or print source cards.** Record every source you use by creating a print card, electronic file, or column on a spreadsheet for it. Assign a number or letter to each source, beginning with 1 or A.

- **Books.** If your source is a book, your source card should list the title, the author, the publisher, the city, and the copyright date.

- **Web sites.** If your source is a Web site, your source card should list the name and Web address of the site, the author and sponsoring institution if available, and the date you accessed the site.

**Make notecards.** Create a separate notecard, a listing, or an electronic file listing every bit of information you take from your sources. Number or letter each source card or listing in the upper right hand corner with the number or letter you assigned to the source on your source card. Then record any useful or interesting information.

**Revisit your thesis.** New information will help you adjust your thesis or make it more specific. Remember that the crafting of your thesis is ongoing: evaluate yours as you prewrite, draft, and revise.

For use with Writing 8

Name _____ Date _____ Selection _____

# Avoiding Plagiarism

**Credit your sources.** From the moment you lay eyes on your first source, you must be thinking about how you will document, or cite, your sources. This is not only a requirement your teacher will set but an ethical condition of research writing. Keeping careful records of your sources can also save you time and trouble. For example, it will help you avoid a last-minute scramble to find the source of a particularly apt quotation or paraphrased information that is crucial to supporting your thesis.

**Paraphrase.** Never copy and paste from Web sites and other online sources. Instead, take notes that paraphrase the source material as much as possible. An effective strategy for doing this is to read the entire source or source part, and then write down your understanding of what you read without looking directly at the source. You can also try this method with smaller chunks of the text, such as information covered under just one subheading or in just one paragraph. When you paraphrase, you may copy words such as *the* and *and,* as well as core vocabulary that is essential to your topic. For example, if you are writing about the development of smart phones, you can copy words such as *technology, Web access, data package, mobile,* and so on. Nevertheless, translate all the surrounding concepts into your own words. If you think few uncommon but exact words from the source are indispensable, include them in your paraphrase, but enclose them in quotation marks.

**Summarize.** Sometimes, you will want to compress a paragraph, a web page, a book page, or another large portion of text into a much briefer version. Because you are doing the work of distilling main ideas, you may think you do not have to credit those ideas. That's incorrect. If the idea came from your source, even if in a far different form, you must credit the source.

**Make judgments about facts.** There are some facts you do not have to document. These include facts everyone knows, such as the Declaration of Independence being signed on July 4, 1776. With your specific topic, when the same facts appear in every source, you need not credit them. If, however, a fact is available in only one source, you must credit it. Likewise, credit all opinions.

**Quote directly.** Record the author's exact words when they are especially interesting, particularly well-phrased, unique, or persuasive. Be sure to enclose those words in quotation marks on your notecard. Indicate any omissions with ellipsis points. Keep in mind, however, that your finished paper should not be a patchwork of quotations. Instead, the majority of the writing, even if it is paraphrasing, should be your own. Also, keep long quotations to a minimum. In a short paper, one long quotation may be more than enough.

Name _____ Date _____ Selection _____

# Developing a Structure

**Make your thesis more specific.** Your thesis should take a position and be supported by most of your research. Make your thesis as specific as possible: it will serve as the controlling idea of your report.

**Map out body paragraphs.** Record your specific thesis. Then develop main idea sentences or topic sentences that reflect your research and relate specifically back to your thesis:

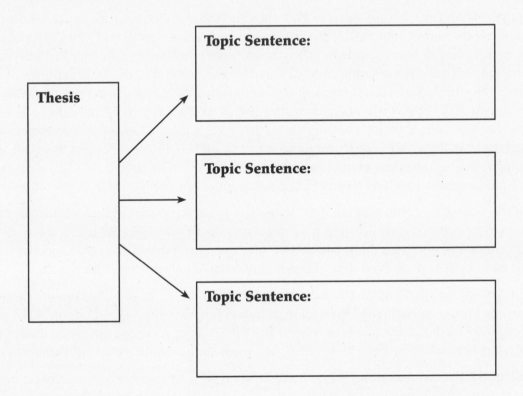

**Choose a text structure.** Use your thesis statement, your possible topic sentences, and knowledge of your audience to choose an organizational structure. Consider these options, as well as any logical order that fits your purpose and your information:

- **Chronological order.** Offer information in the sequence in which it occurred.

- **Part-to-whole order.** Examine how categories affect a larger subject.

- **Order of importance.** Present information in order of increasing or decreasing significance.

- **Comparison and contrast.** Present similarities and differences.

**Incorporate graphic aids and visuals.** Consider using illustrations, photographs, maps, graphs, or charts to clarify facts, highlight trends, or add dramatic impact. You may include visuals you discover in your research process. You must, of course, cite the sources of them; similarly, you must cite information you use to construct a table, graph, or other visual.

**For use with Writing 8**

Name _____ Date _____ Selection _____

# Organizing and Drafting Your Report

**Support your ideas.** Group your notes together into chunks of support that are related to specific topic sentences or to a specific aspect of your thesis. Refer to them as you draft each paragraph.

## Drafting

**Lead into and out of your information.** After your draft your topic sentences, remember that your quoted, paraphrased, or summarized information does not create its own links to your thesis or to surrounding ideas in your paper. One way to create unity and coherence in your paper is to introduce quoted and paraphrased material with a transitional word or phrase, such as "[Author's name] notes," "According to…," or "In [title of work]." Of course, you should also use other transitional words and phrases, such as *furthermore, therefore, as a result,* and *on the other hand* to link ideas within sentences, to link sentences, and to link paragraphs. Similarly, keep in mind that whatever you quote or paraphrase may not only need explanation to relate it to your topic sentence and thesis, but it may also need to be clearly connected to the ideas that follow it. You may also need to insert a sentence or more in your own words to explain the significance of the cited information.

**Structure your body paragraphs.** Begin each body paragraph in one of the following ways:

- **A transitional sentence.** Create a transitional sentence that repeats a key word or phrase from the sentence that ended the previous paragraph or otherwise creates a link to ideas that preceded it.

- **A topic sentence.** Write a topic sentence that provides an overview of the facts, explanation, and support you will include in the paragraph. Be sure that topic sentence provides an echo of your thesis statement or otherwise relates to your thesis.

Next, introduce and explain the information you have researched. Present that information clearly and objectively. Use your own words as much as possible, but cite every idea that came from your sources. If needed to sum up the paragraph, to help your audience follow your ideas, or to create emphasis, close each body paragraph with a summary or clincher statement.

**Use an objective tone from start to finish.** Sound as reasonable and objective as you can. Even if you are writing on a timely topic such as smart phones or writing for an audience of your peers, choose formal words and phrases and standard usages.

Name _____ Date _____ Selection _____

# Citing Sources

**Use a style manual.** To cite your sources, use the manual of style specified by your teacher, such as the MLA (Modern Language Association) handbook for research papers or APA (American Psychological Association) style manual. Make consistent use of the same manual style for all your documentation.

**Cite sources in the body of your report.** Responsible writers are thorough and accurate in citing all of their sources. Giving proper credit to the people whose ideas and words you have borrowed ensures that you will meet key requirements of research report writing. It is also necessary to obey copyright law.

- **Print works.** Provide the author's or editor's name followed by a page number. If the work does not have an author, use a key word or short phrase from the title.

- **Web sources.** Provide the author's name, if given, title of the article, if any, or title of the site.

- **Other works.** For variations within books and Web sources, such as multiple authors, multivolume works, translations, and so on, do not guess. Consult your style manual. Similarly, use your style manual to find the correct way to cite sound recordings, interviews, or other less common sources.

**Create a Works Cited list or bibliography.** Publication information for each source you cite must appear in a separate list at the end of your report. Sources on the list should be arranged alphabetically by author's or editor's last name. If the author or editor's last name is not given, then alphabetize by the first word of the title.

- **Books.** Give the author's name (last name first), the title of the work, the city of publication, the name of the publisher, and the year of publication. This information usually appears on the title and copyright pages.

- **Periodicals.** Give the author's last name, first name, title of the article, the name of the magazine, the date of the issue, the volume and issue number, and the pages of the article. For any month with more than four letters, abbreviate the month by using the first three letters followed by a period. You may have to search the cover, as well as several opening pages or final pages, for this information.

- **Web sites.** Use this order, depending on the information that is available: the author's name, the title of the page, the title of the site, the date of last update, and the name of the sponsoring organization. Give the date you accessed the Web site and its full URL, or Web address.

Name _____ Date _____ Selection _____

# Revising Strategies

Put a checkmark beside each question as you address it in your revision.

| | **Questions To Ask as You Revise** |
|---|---|
| **Task** | ❏ Does my research report inform?<br><br>❏ Is my research report based on a topic that answers or is appropriate to the assignment requirements?<br><br>❏ Have I used the correct format to cite every source I consulted?<br><br>❏ Have I consistently used one style manual for all citations?<br><br>❏ Have I formatted my paper according to the assignment specifications or according to standard conventions for a research report? |
| **Purpose** | ❏ Have I set forth a clear and specific thesis?<br><br>❏ Have I fully developed that thesis by presenting a great deal of supporting information?<br><br>❏ Have I supported my thesis?<br><br>❏ What details, if any, do not relate to my purpose and should be deleted?<br><br>❏ Where do I need to add more details or explanation to achieve my purpose? |
| **Audience** | ❏ Will my audience be interested in my topic?<br><br>❏ Will my audience be able to identify my thesis and follow my support and explanation?<br><br>❏ Have I provided enough support for my thesis?<br><br>❏ Have I led smoothly into and out of my support and clearly linked it to my thesis?<br><br>❏ Have I limited myself to formal and standard word choices and created an objective tone throughout my paper?<br><br>❏ Can my audience follow the sources of all my ideas? |

For use with Writing 8

Name _____ Date _____ Selection _____

**Revise to combine sentences using adverb clauses.** Avoid choppy writing by combining some sentences using adverb clauses. You can also make the relationship of some ideas clearer when you combine sentences to create adverb clauses.

**Two sentences:** There was a need for a highly advanced mobile phone. The smart phone was developed.

**Combined:** Because there was a need for a highly advanced mobile phone, the smart phone was developed.

## Identifying Adverb Clauses

A clause is a group of words with a subject and a verb. An independent clause can stand alone as a complete sentence, but a subordinate clause cannot stand alone because it does not express a complete thought. An adverb clause is a subordinate clause that begins with a subordinating conjunction that tells where, when, in what way, to what extent, under what condition, or why. It modifies a verb, an adjective, or another adverb in the sentence.

## Subordinating Conjunctions

| | | | |
|---|---|---|---|
| *after* | *although* | *as* | *as if* |
| *as long as* | *because* | *before* | *even though* |
| *if* | *since* | *so that* | *than* |
| *though* | *unless* | *until* | *when* |
| *whenever* | *where* | *wherever* | *while* |

**When:** *Before* the first phone was introduced in 1993, there were no phones with calendars, notes, address books, and other similar features.

**Under what condition:** *If* you want to combine the functions of a phone and a computer, a smart phone is the answer.

**In what way:** That phone provides advanced connectivity *as if* it were a laptop.

**Why:** Many companies are competing in the smart phone business *because* it is so profitable.

## Combining Sentences with Adverb Clauses

When using adverb clauses to combine sentences, follow these steps:

1. Identify the relationship between the ideas in the sentences.
2. Choose a subordinating conjunction that clarifies that relationship. Use the conjunction to begin an adverb clause, and put the clause at the beginning or end of the combined sentence.
3. When a subordinate clause begins the sentence, use a comma to separate it from the rest of the sentence.

### Revision Checklist

❑ Where have I used short sentences that could be effectively combined with adverb clauses?

❑ Do the sentences I have combined more clearly accurately convey my intended meaning than the original, shorter sentences do?

For use with Writing 8

Name _____ Date _____ Selection _____

# Editing and Proofreading

Review your draft to correct errors in format, capitalization, spelling, and punctuation.

**Focus on Format:** Include an appropriate title page, pagination, spacing and margins, and citations; use your style manual for guidelines. Also make certain that you have used the preferred manual or set of guidelines for crediting sources in your paper and for bibliographical sources at the end. Double-check all punctuation and capitalization within your citations. If you are using MLA style, follow these rules for your Works Cited page:

- Begin a new page with the centered title "Works Cited."

- Double space all the entries; do not add extra lines of space between them.

- Create a hanging indent for entries that are more than one line long.

- Use the same one-inch margins on all sides that you used in the rest of the paper.

**Focus on Spelling:** Some words are difficult to spell because they are commonly mispronounced. In some cases, a common mispronunciation results in the loss of sounds, as in *accidentally*, *environment*, *government*, *mathematics*, *probably*, and *sophomore*. Other times, a common mispronunciation results in the addition of sounds, as in *athletics* (**not** *atheletics*), *disastrous* (**not** *disasterous*), and *grievous* (**not** *grievious*).

**Focus on Punctuation: Semicolons to Join Independent Clauses** Proofread your writing to find places where two independent clauses are joined with only a comma. Some of these sentences may include a conjunctive adverb. Use a semicolon to join them correctly.

**Rule: Use a semicolon to join independent clauses that are not already joined by a conjunction.** *Smart phones will get smarter; increased speed and bandwidth will increase their functions.*

**Rule: Use a semicolon to join independent clauses separated either by a conjunction, adverb, or a transitional expression.** *Smart phones existed in the early 90s; however, cell phones were not as widely used then as they are today. The idea of getting e-mail and texts on a phone was once revolutionary; in fact, some people did not think a keyboard would ever be popular on a handset.*

Name _____ Date _____ Selection _____

# Publishing and Presenting

Consider one of the following ways to present your writing:

**Share a multimedia presentation.** Use your research report as the basis for a multimedia presentation, and include graphics, music or sound effects, props, and other elements to engage your audience. If possible, rehearse your presentation with a live audience to coordinate the smooth integration of elements, and incorporate audience feedback to improve your presentation.

**Publish on the Internet.** Post your research report on a Web site that publishes student writing, or send it to a Web site editor for possible inclusion on a juried Web site.

## Rubric for Self-Assessment

Find evidence in your writing to address each category. Then, use the rating scale to grade your work. Circle the score that best applies for each category.

| Evaluating Your Research Report | not very | | | | | very |
|---|---|---|---|---|---|---|
| **Focus:** How well have you written about a topic that is appropriate to the length of your paper, stated a clear thesis on that topic, and maintained a focus on that thesis throughout your report? | 1 | 2 | 3 | 4 | 5 | 6 |
| **Organization:** How logical is your method of organization? How clearly have you linked all your ideas to your thesis and to each other? | 1 | 2 | 3 | 4 | 5 | 6 |
| **Support/Elaboration:** How well have you supplied sufficient and relevant support for your thesis from credible and authoritative sources? How well have you incorporated well-chosen quotations? | 1 | 2 | 3 | 4 | 5 | 6 |
| **Style:** How effectively have you created a formal style and objective tone that are appropriate to your task, your purpose, and your audience? | 1 | 2 | 3 | 4 | 5 | 6 |
| **Conventions:** How free is your research report from errors in grammar, spelling, and punctuation? | 1 | 2 | 3 | 4 | 5 | 6 |

# Writing 9a

> **9a. Draw evidence from literary or informational texts to support analysis, reflection, and research.**
> - **Apply *grades 9–10 Reading standards* to literature (e.g., "Analyze how an author draws on and transforms source material in a specific work [e.g., how Shakespeare treats a theme or topic from Ovid or the Bible or how a later author draws on a play by Shakespeare]").**

## Explanation

When you analyze literature, you may be asked to show how an author used another source to develop his or her own work. To do this, you must draw evidence from several sources to explain how the author used and transformed the original material. For example, if you were asked to analyze how Shakespeare used Plutarch's *Lives*—especially those of Brutus, Antony, and Caesar— to write *Julius Caesar*, you might do the following:

1. Use the **primary source.** Read Plutarch and identify characters, events, conflicts, themes, or language that are similar to those in Shakespeare's *Julius Caesar.* Take notes and record bibliographical information from the source.

2. Check **secondary sources**. Find what others have to say about how Shakespeare used source material to write *Julius Caesar*. These authors will share their own research, opinions, and ideas on the topic. Take careful notes and record bibliographical information.

3. Use a combination of information from primary and secondary sources to support your analysis.

Then develop a thesis that tells specifically how Shakespeare used or transformed the primary source. Support your thesis with quoted, summarized, and paraphrased evidence that you cite in both a bibliography and footnotes or endnotes.

## Academic Vocabulary

**primary source**  an original literary work, or the source of a subsequent literary work

**secondary source**  a document that relates information about, interprets, or analyzes an event or literary work(s)

## Apply the Standard

Use the worksheet that follows to help you apply the standard as you write. Several copies have been provided for you to use with different assignments.

- Analyzing Literature

Name _____  Date _____  Assignment _____

# Analyzing Literature

Use the organizer below to record information from your sources and develop your thesis.

---

**Primary Source**

**Bibliographic Information:**

**Evidence (with page numbers):**

---

**Secondary Sources**

**Source 1, Bibliographic Information:**

**Evidence (with page numbers):**

**Source 2, Bibliographic Information:**

**Evidence (with page numbers):**

---

**Thesis**

---

Name _____ Date _____ Assignment _____

# Analyzing Literature

Use the organizer below to record information from your sources and develop your thesis.

| Primary Source |
| --- |
| **Bibliographic Information:**<br><br><br>**Evidence (with page numbers):** |
| **Secondary Sources** |
| **Source 1, Bibliographic Information:**<br><br>**Evidence (with page numbers):**<br><br><br><br>**Source 2, Bibliographic Information:**<br><br>**Evidence (with page numbers):** |
| **Thesis** |
| |

Name _____ Date _____ Assignment _____

# Analyzing Literature

Use the organizer below to record information from your sources and develop your thesis.

| **Primary Source** |
| --- |
| **Bibliographic Information:**<br><br>**Evidence (with page numbers):** |
| **Secondary Sources**<br><br>**Source 1, Bibliographic Information:**<br><br>**Evidence (with page numbers):**<br><br><br>**Source 2, Bibliographic Information:**<br><br>**Evidence (with page numbers):** |
| **Thesis** |
| |

# Writing 9b

> 9. **Draw evidence from literary or informational texts to support analysis, reflection, and research.**
> - Apply grades 9–10 *Reading standards* to literary nonfiction (e.g., "Delineate and evaluate the argument and specific claims in a text, assessing whether the reasoning is valid and the evidence is relevant and sufficient; identify false statements and fallacious reasoning").

## Explanation

In an argument, a writer states a position on an issue. This position is called the **claim.** When you write an evaluation of an argument, you must decide whether the claim is reasonable and the support is both logical and adequate. The claim must be reasonable; if not, you should discredit the argument. The support must be logical, rather than strictly emotional.

Choose a text that contains an argument to evaluate, such as an editorial or a speech. Then take notes for your essay. Here are some points to keep in mind as you take notes:

- A sound argument contains a clearly stated opinion.
- The writer's claim is supported by valid reasons and relevant evidence, such as facts, examples, statistics, and expert testimony.
- Reasons are logical and presented in an order that makes sense.
- The writer gives evidence against opposing points of view.

In your evaluation, be sure to identify any false statements or **fallacious** reasoning that the writer uses to support his or her argument. Here are some common logical fallacies:

**bandwagon**—a call to do something because everyone else is doing it

**overgeneralization**—an inference based on too little evidence

**either/or argument**—a false assumption that only two choices are possible

**false analogy**—a suggestion that because two things are alike in one way, they are alike in other ways

***non sequitur***—a conclusion that does not follow, or arise logically, from the facts

## Academic Vocabulary

**claim** a brief statement of position on an issue that offers the writer's perspective

**fallacious** containing or involving a mistaken belief or idea; untrue; faulty

## Apply the Standard

Use the worksheet that follows to help you apply the standard as you complete your writing assignments. Several copies of the worksheet have been provided for you.

- Evaluating an Argument

Name _____ Date _____ Selection _____

# Evaluating an Argument

Use the organizer below to take notes for an essay in which you evaluate a writer's argument. Use specific details from the text to explain your responses.

| Title: | Form (e.g., essay, speech): |
|--------|------------------------------|

**Writer's claim:**

| Evaluation Questions | Response | Evidence from Text |
|----------------------|----------|---------------------|
| Is an opinion clearly stated? | ❑ Yes  ❑ No | |
| Is the claim supported by reasons and evidence? | ❑ Yes  ❑ No | |
| Do the reasons make sense? Is the evidence factual? | ❑ Yes  ❑ No | |
| Are reasons and evidence presented in an order that makes sense? | ❑ Yes  ❑ No | |
| Does the writer acknowledge and give evidence against an opposing point of view? | ❑ Yes  ❑ No | |

Has the writer included any logical fallacies or false statements? Give examples.

❑ **Bandwagon:** ...........................................................................................

❑ **Overgeneralization:** ...............................................................................

❑ **Either/or argument:** ...............................................................................

❑ **False analogy:** ........................................................................................

❑ **Non sequitur:** .........................................................................................

❑ **Other:** ....................................................................................................

For use with Writing 9b

Name _____ Date _____ Selection _____

# Evaluating an Argument

Use the organizer below to take notes for an essay in which you evaluate a writer's argument. Use specific details from the text to explain your responses.

| Title: | Form (e.g. essay, speech): |
|---|---|

**Writer's claim:**

| Evaluation Questions | Response | Evidence from Text |
|---|---|---|
| Is an opinion clearly stated? | ❑ Yes<br>❑ No | |
| Is the claim supported by reasons and evidence? | ❑ Yes<br>❑ No | |
| Do the reasons make sense? Is the evidence factual? | ❑ Yes<br>❑ No | |
| Are reasons and evidence presented in an order that makes sense? | ❑ Yes<br>❑ No | |
| Does the writer acknowledge and give evidence against an opposing point of view? | ❑ Yes<br>❑ No | |

Has the writer included any logical fallacies or false statements? Give examples.

❑ **Bandwagon:** ....................................................................................................................

❑ **Overgeneralization:** .........................................................................................................

❑ **Either/or argument:** .........................................................................................................

❑ **False analogy:** ..................................................................................................................

❑ **Non sequiter:** ...................................................................................................................

❑ **Other:** ..............................................................................................................................

Name _____ Date _____ Selection _____

# Evaluating an Argument

Use the organizer below to take notes for an essay in which you evaluate a writer's argument. Use specific details from the text to explain your responses.

| Title: | Form (e.g. essay, speech): | |
|---|---|---|
| **Writer's claim:** | | |

| Evaluation Questions | Response | Evidence from Text |
|---|---|---|
| Is an opinion clearly stated? | ❏ Yes <br> ❏ No | |
| Is the claim supported by reasons and evidence? | ❏ Yes <br> ❏ No | |
| Do the reasons make sense? Is the evidence factual? | ❏ Yes <br> ❏ No | |
| Are reasons and evidence presented in an order that makes sense? | ❏ Yes <br> ❏ No | |
| Does the writer acknowledge and give evidence against an opposing point of view? | ❏ Yes <br> ❏ No | |

Has the writer included any logical fallacies or false statements? Give examples.

❏ **Bandwagon:** ...............................................................................................

❏ **Overgeneralization:** ...................................................................................

❏ **Either/or argument:** ...................................................................................

❏ **False analogy:** ...........................................................................................

❏ *Non sequiter:* ..............................................................................................

❏ **Other:** .......................................................................................................

C

# Writing 10

> 10. Write routinely over extended time frames (time for research, reflection, and revision) and shorter time frames (a single sitting or a day or two) for a range of tasks, purposes, and audiences.

## Explanation

Some writing assignments extend over a long period to allow time for the student to reflect on a topic, gather research, write, and revise. Others, such as a business letter, are shorter and require only a single class period or a day or two to complete. A business letter can serve a variety of purposes—to request information, request an interview, lodge a complaint, or offer a proposal. Effective business letters are clear, direct, courteous, and formatted according to established conventions. Follow these steps:

### Prewriting:

- Identify your audience and write a clear statement of purpose.
- Gather information that helps explain why you are writing and what you want.
- List and arrange key points that will make your message clear.

### Drafting:

- Create your format: two choices are **block format** or **modified block format.** Include a heading, inside address, greeting, body, closing, and signature.
- State your purpose clearly in the first sentence. Include only necessary information in the body text—and nothing more.
- Consider how you will use style and tone to create your **voice.** Be confident, but not arrogant or pushy. Avoid informal language, slang, and exclamation points.

### Revising and Editing:

- Check your format: Have you consistently and correctly formatted your letter?
- Refine your voice: Are your style and tone formal, direct, and businesslike?

## Academic Vocabulary

**block format**  each part of the letter begins at the left margin, and a double space is used between paragraphs

**modified block format**  some parts of the letter are indented to the center of the page

**voice**  the writer's distinctive "sound" or way of "speaking" on the page

## Apply the Standard

Use the worksheet that follows to help you apply the standard as you complete your writing assignments.

- Writing a Business Letter

Name _____  Date _____  Selection _____

# Writing a Business Letter

Use the organizer to plan your business letter and the checklist to check your formatting.

| Purpose: |
| --- |
| Audience: |

| Important Background Information: | Key Points: |
| --- | --- |
| | |

## Checklist

- ☐ I have used the block or modified block format.
- ☐ The inside address tells where the letter will be sent.
- ☐ The greeting is punctuated with a colon.
- ☐ The body paragraphs are not indented and I have double-spaced between them.
- ☐ I have included a closing (e.g. *Sincerely, Respectfully yours, Yours truly*), my signature, and my typed name.

A

For use with Writing 10a

# Writing 10

> **10. Write routinely over extended time frames (time for research, reflection, and revision) and shorter time frames (a single sitting or a day or two) for a range of tasks, purposes, and audiences.**

## Explanation

An editorial is an example of writing that may be completed over an extended time frame. An editorial is a brief persuasive essay that presents and defends an opinion. You might write an editorial to present your position on a controversial development in sports. Effective editorials focus on presenting an argument and developing it with strong evidence. They are written in a formal style and maintain an objective tone.

### Prewriting:

- Write a thesis statement that clearly and firmly states your position on an issue.

- Gather evidence from sources to support your argument.

- List counterarguments and gather evidence to use against them.

- List any **biases,** expectations, and potential misunderstandings that your audience might have. Make notes about how you will address and counter them.

### Drafting:

- Present the points you use to support your thesis in order, from least important to most important. Then acknowledge and respond to at least one counterargument.

- Provide ample evidence, including statistics, expert opinions, personal observations, and testimonials, to explain and support each main point you make.

- Close with a restatement of your thesis and a final, memorable thought.

### Revising and Editing:

- Replace weak words with words that will add power to your argument.

- Check your evidence: As needed, add information, explanation, and evidence that shows you understand your readers' biases and counterarguments.

## Academic Vocabulary

**bias**  a tendency toward a particular opinion; a predetermined way of thinking

## Apply the Standard

Use the worksheet that follows to help you apply the standard as you complete your writing assignments. Several copies of the worksheet have been provided for you.

- Writing an Editorial

Name _____ Date _____ Selection _____

# Writing an Editorial

Use the organizer to plan an editorial.

| Thesis: |
| --- |
| |
| **Main Points:** |
| 1. |
| 2. |
| 3. |

| My Audience's Opposition | Responses and Evidence to Counter My Audience's Opposition |
| --- | --- |
| • **Counterargument(s):** | |
| • **Bias(es):** | |
| • **Expectation(s):** | |
| • **Potential Misunderstanding(s):** | |

| Final Memorable Thought: |
| --- |
| |

A

For use with Writing 10b

Name _____ Date _____ Selection _____

# Writing an Editorial

Use the organizer to plan an editorial.

| Thesis: |
| --- |
| |

| Main Points: |
| --- |
| 1. |
| 2. |
| 3. |

| My Audience's Opposition | Responses and Evidence to Counter My Audience's Opposition |
| --- | --- |
| • Counterargument(s):<br><br>• Bias(es):<br><br>• Expectation(s):<br><br>• Potential Misunderstanding(s): | |

| Final Memorable Thought: |
| --- |
| |

B

Name _____ Date _____ Selection _____

# Writing an Editorial

Use the organizer to plan an editorial.

| Thesis: |
| --- |
| Main Points:<br><br>1.<br><br>2.<br><br>3. |

| My Audience's Opposition | Responses and Evidence to Counter My Audience's Opposition |
| --- | --- |
| • Counterargument(s):<br><br>• Bias(es):<br><br>• Expectation(s):<br><br>• Potential Misunderstanding(s): |  |

| Final Memorable Thought: |
| --- |

C

# Writing 10

> **10. Write routinely over extended time frames (time for research, reflection, and revision) and shorter time frames (a single sitting or a day or two) for a range of tasks, purposes, and audiences.**

## Explanation

A reflective essay is an example of writing that can be completed in one or two class periods or over a day or two. A reflective essay describes a personal experience, memory, object, or idea and explains its significance. For example, you might write a reflective essay about a conversation that changed you. Effective reflective essays are written in the first person and use clear, concrete language, vivid imagery, and a personal style.

**Prewriting:**

- Choose a topic that you can describe dramatically and vividly, as well as a topic that has a personal meaning or significance that you can share with an audience.

- Brainstorm sensory images that you associate with your topic.

**Drafting:**

- Use an effective organizational pattern, such as chronological order for a series of events or order of importance for a reflection on an object.

- Consider including **figurative language** to enliven your writing.

- End by emphasizing the significance of the event, memory, object, or idea.

**Revising and Editing:**

- Check for **unity:** Does every word or phrase in the essay contribute to describing the experience, memory, object, or idea?

- Check for word choice: Are the words precise, vivid, and interesting?

## Academic Vocabulary

**figurative language**  words and phrases that describe a thing in terms of something else

**unity**  a quality that exists when everything in a piece of writing works together to support a single idea or to create one dominant impression

## Apply the Standard

Use the worksheet that follows to help you apply the standard as you complete your writing assignments.

- Writing a Reflective Essay

Name _____ Date _____ Selection _____

# Writing a Reflective Essay

Use the organizer to plan a reflective essay.

| Reflection on: |
| --- |

| Details of the Setting: |
| --- |

| Events or Main Ideas (after listing, use circles and arrows to create the most effective order):<br><br>1.<br><br>2.<br><br>3. | Images (sights, sounds, smells, etc.): |
| --- | --- |

| Significance: |
| --- |

# Writing 10

> 10. Write routinely over extended time frames (time for research, reflection, and revision) and shorter time frames (a single sitting or a day or two) for a range of tasks, purposes, and audiences.

## Explanation

A how-to essay is an example of writing that can be completed in one class period or over a day or two. A how-to essay provides step-by-step instructions for completing a specific task. For example, you might write a how-to essay to give your audience instructions for building a model airplane or rocket or for preparing for achievement tests. Effective how-to essays are well organized and written in a very clear, direct style.

**Prewriting:**

- List materials needed, as well as safety rules or other requirements.

- Brainstorm one or more examples to demonstrate the activity.

- Jot down each step required to complete the activity.

**Drafting:**

- State your purpose and list any materials your audience will need, as well as any other rules or requirements.

- List the steps in **sequential order.** Consider using bullets or numbering to clarify the sequence, or add drawings or other graphics for clarity.

- Identify common problems the audience may encounter and provide solutions.

- Close by presenting final thoughts about the activity or process.

**Revising and Editing:**

- Check that your reader can actually perform each step based on your instructions.

- Check your transitions: Do numbers, bullets, and words and phrases such as *first, next,* and *then* help readers follow the sequence?

## Academic Vocabulary

**sequential order**   the organization of steps or events in order, from first to last

## Apply the Standard

Use the worksheet that follows to help you apply the standard as you complete your writing assignments.

- Writing a How-to Essay

Name _____ Date _____ Selection _____

# Writing a How-to Essay

Use the organizer to plan and prewrite a how-to essay.

| Purpose: | |
|---|---|
| **Materials and Other Requirements:** | |

| Steps in Order: | Example that Demonstrates the Activity or Process: |
|---|---|
| 1. | |
| 2. | |
| 3. | |
| 4. | |
| 5. | |

| Common Problems: | Solutions: |
|---|---|

| Final Thoughts: |
|---|

For use with Writing 10d

# Speaking and Listening Standards

# Speaking and Listening 1

> **1. Initiate and participate effectively in a range of collaborative discussions (one-on-one, in groups, and teacher-led) with diverse partners on grades 9–10 topics, texts, and issues, building on others' ideas and expressing their own clearly and persuasively.***

## Workshop: Present a Multimedia Presentation

**Multimedia presentations** combine a variety of media, such as graphics, images, and music, to convey information to an audience. You encounter multimedia presentations daily on television and the Internet, as well as in school or the workplace. They can be used for selling goods and services, communicating goals and agendas, and informing audiences. Examples of multimedia presentations include slide shows, Web pages, advertisements, and documentaries.

## Assignment

Write, produce, and deliver a multimedia presentation to your class on a topic that interests you. In your presentation, include these elements:

✓ integrated text, graphics, images, and sound components
✓ the use of a wide range of media, such as newspaper clippings, photos, audio recordings, and video clips
✓ a main idea that is supported by detailed evidence
✓ a scripted and logical organization to present a focused message to a specific audience
✓ appropriate eye contact, adequate volume, and clear pronunciation
✓ language that is appropriate and that follows the rules of Standard English

## *Additional Standards

**Speaking and Listening**

**1.** Initiate and participate effectively in a range of collaborative discussions (one-on-one, in groups, and teacher-led) with diverse partners on grades 9–10 topics, texts, and issues, building on others' ideas and expressing their own clearly and persuasively.

**1.a.** Come to discussions prepared, having read and researched material under study; explicitly draw on that preparation by referring to evidence from texts and other research on the topic or issue to stimulate a thoughtful, well-reasoned exchange of ideas.

**1.b.** Work with peers to set rules for collegial discussions and decision-making

(e.g., informal consensus, taking votes on key issues, presentation of alternate views), clear goals and deadlines, and individual roles as needed.

**1.c.** Propel conversations by posing and responding to questions that relate the current discussion to broader themes or larger ideas; actively incorporate others into the discussion; and clarify, verify, or challenge ideas and conclusions.

**1.d.** Respond thoughtfully to diverse perspectives, summarize points of agreement and disagreement, and, when warranted, qualify or justify their own views and understanding and make new connections in light of

the evidence and reasoning presented.

**2.** Integrate multiple sources of information presented in diverse media or formats (e.g., visually, quantitatively, orally) evaluating the credibility and accuracy of each source.

**4.** Present information, findings, and supporting evidence clearly, concisely, and logically such that listeners can follow the line of reasoning and the organization, development, substance, and style are appropriate to purpose, audience, and task.

**5.** Make strategic use of digital media (e.g., textual, graphical, audio, visual, and interactive elements)

in presentations to enhance understanding of findings, reasoning, and evidence and to add interest.

**6.** Adapt speech to a variety of contexts and tasks, demonstrating command of formal English when indicated or appropriate.

**Language**

**6.** Acquire and use accurately general academic and domain-specific words and phrases, sufficient for reading, writing, speaking, and listening at the college and career readiness level; demonstrate independence in gathering vocabulary knowledge when considering a word or phrase important to comprehension or expression.

Name _____ Date _____ Assignment _____

# Choose and Narrow Your Topic

A multimedia presentation can be challenging. You must choose a topic that is rich enough that you will be able to find a variety of media materials to use in your presentation. Yet, the topic cannot be so broad that it loses focus.

**Choose your topic.** To choose a subject for your multimedia presentation, consider things you enjoy or that interest you. Then find a single example within a broad subject. The general topics you initially think of will probably be too broad to be manageable. For example, the Olympics is too broad a topic to address effectively. However, the history of a single sport or the development of one athlete's career is manageable.

To help you choose potential topics, use the media checklist below as you do some initial research. Choose two general topics that interest you and do a quick search for materials you can use in your presentation. List the various types of media that you can find that provide good information on those subjects. Then review your chart, and choose the topic that offers the richest possibilities.

| Topic 1: .................................................................................................................... | |
|---|---|
| ❏ Music<br>❏ Videos<br>❏ Art<br>❏ Photographs<br>❏ Web Pages<br>❏ Interviews | Example: ................................................................<br>Example: ................................................................<br>Example: ................................................................<br>Example: ................................................................<br>Example: ................................................................<br>Example: ................................................................ |
| Topic 2: .................................................................................................................... | |
| ❏ Music<br>❏ Videos<br>❏ Art<br>❏ Photographs<br>❏ Web Pages<br>❏ Interviews | Example: ................................................................<br>Example: ................................................................<br>Example: ................................................................<br>Example: ................................................................<br>Example: ................................................................<br>Example: ................................................................ |

**Collaborate and decide.** Next, consult with a group of classmates to solidify your choice. In a collaborative discussion, ask students in your group for feedback about your ideas, including whether the topic is too narrow or too broad. Listen for suggestions about your ideas, and respond to and ask questions of the group to help clarify your main idea.

**For use with Speaking and Listening 1**

Name _____ Date _____ Assignment _____

# Plan and Research Your Presentation

**Research your topic.** Now you must dig deeper into your topic. As you gather materials, look for varying points of view on your topic. Consult your library for audio or video clips, documentaries, music, and art resources. Search the Internet for photographs, recordings, cartoons, and archives of periodicals. Keep careful notes about your sources so that you can accurately cite them.

Take notes to capture or identify the most useful information you find in each source. Conduct further research to settle any discrepancies you find among your sources. Be sure to consider the reliability of sources as you plan. Evaluating sources is especially important on the Internet. Some Web pages may include information that is unreliable, invalid, or inaccurate. The most reliable Web sites tend to have URLs ending in **.edu** and **.gov**.

Use the graphic organizer to help you research and take notes.

| Source | Useful Information | Reliability |
|---|---|---|
| (Name, type, author, date) | | Is this source<br>❑ useful?<br>❑ current?<br>❑ accurate?<br>❑ free from bias? |
| (Name, type, author, date) | | Is this source<br>❑ useful?<br>❑ current?<br>❑ accurate?<br>❑ free from bias? |
| (Name, type, author, date) | | Is this source<br>❑ useful?<br>❑ current?<br>❑ accurate?<br>❑ free from bias? |

Name _____  Date _____  Assignment _____

# Organize Your Multimedia Presentation

**Write a thesis.** Review your notes and researched materials. Write a thesis—one clear statement that will express the focus of your presentation. All aspects of your presentation, from script to visuals, graphics, audio, and charts, should support this main idea.

**Thesis Statement:** ...............................................................................................................

..........................................................................................................................................

**Choose a structure.** Use your thesis statement and knowledge of your audience to choose an organizational structure. Consider these options.

- **Chronological order:** present events in the order in which they occur. This structure works well for reporting on a historical event or a person's life.

  I. Introduction

  II. Significant Event #1

  III. Significant Event #2

  IV. Significant Event #3

  V. Conclusion

- **Order of importance:** present details in order of increasing or decreasing significance. This is ideal for building an argument.

  I. Introduction

  II. Less important point

  III. More important point

  IV. Most important point

  V. Conclusion

- **Comparison-and-contrast:** present similarities and differences. This is ideal for reporting on two related subjects.

  I. Introduction

  II. Discussion of first subject

  III. Discussion of second subject

  IV. How two subjects are alike and different

  V. Conclusion

Name _____ Date _____ Assignment _____

# Draft Your Script

**Write a draft.** Consider drafting your script as a two-column chart. Use it to note what will occur at any given moment. Careful planning will lead to great delivery. Make sure the wording of your presentation is clear and specific. Avoid repeating in words what other media are already communicating to the viewer in sounds or visuals.

**Thesis statement:** ....................................................................................................................................

| Narration | Multimedia Elements |
|---|---|
| **I. Introduction** | ❑ Video:<br>❑ Audio:<br>❑ Graphic:<br>❑ Text:<br>❑ Other: |
| **II.** | ❑ Video:<br>❑ Audio:<br>❑ Graphic:<br>❑ Text:<br>❑ Other: |
| **III.** | ❑ Video:<br>❑ Audio:<br>❑ Graphic:<br>❑ Text:<br>❑ Other: |
| **IV.** | ❑ Video:<br>❑ Audio:<br>❑ Graphic:<br>❑ Text:<br>❑ Other: |
| **V. Conclusion:** | ❑ Video:<br>❑ Audio:<br>❑ Graphic:<br>❑ Text:<br>❑ Other: |

Name _____ Date _____ Assignment _____

# Rehearse Your Presentation

**Use presentation techniques.** Use these tips to help you practice your delivery:

- **Eye contact:** Use eye contact to connect with your audience.

- **Speaking rate:** Pause to emphasize important ideas or for effect where useful. Slow down as you move from one multimedia component to the next.

- **Volume:** Project your voice so everyone in your audience can hear you—especially if you have incorporated music or other sound effects.

- **Language:** Use academic and domain-specific words and phrases correctly.

- **Integration of Multimedia:** Edit and weave multimedia elements throughout your presentation. Choose a few strong elements that are clearly relevant to the presentation.

**Practice and revise.** Hold a test-run for a small group of classmates, incorporating all multimedia elements. As you rehearse, you may find that certain planned music, sound effects, or graphics are not working. Now is the time to fix any problems.

Ask for feedback and comments on sections that lack clarity or seem unpolished. Consider eliminating elements that are distracting or overly complicated. Review your script for overuse of one form of media. If you decide that your presentation lacks variation, replace repetitive elements with different media formats.

| Presentation Technique | Listening Rubric |
| --- | --- |
| Eye contact | ❑ Did the speaker maintain eye contact?<br>❑ Did you feel the speaker was speaking directly to you? |
| Speaking rate | ❑ Was the speaker's delivery evenly-paced and clear?<br>❑ Did you feel the speaker used pauses effectively?<br>❑ Did the speaker's words match up with the components on screen? |
| Volume | ❑ Was the speaker loud enough for everyone to hear?<br>❑ Did the speaker vary his or her tone for dramatic effect? |
| Language | ❑ Did the speaker use academic and domain-specific language correctly? |
| Integration of Multimedia | ❑ Did the speaker integrate multimedia effectively?<br>❑ Were multimedia elements relevant and informative? |

Name _____  Date _____  Assignment _____

# Discuss and Evaluate

After you complete your presentation, participate with classmates in a discussion of the the content and delivery of your speech.

**Discuss and evaluate the technical presentation.** Try to reach an agreement on what worked well in your presentation and what did not. If a consensus cannot be reached, then summarize the points of agreement and disagreement among group members. Refer to the Guidelines below to ensure that your discussion is productive.

# Guidelines for Discussion

Prepare for the discussion by reviewing the guidelines below for holding a productive discussion.

- Help the group set goals for the discussion and assign roles, such as leader and note-taker.

- Ask and answer questions in a way that maintains focus as well as meets the goals of the group.

- Be open to new ideas suggested by others and change your perspective to take such ideas into account when appropriate.

- Make sure all group members have a chance to express his or her views within the discussion.

| Discussion Rubric | Notes |
|---|---|
| ❏ Did each member of the group participate in the discussion? <br> ❏ Was each member of the group able to freely express his or her opinion? | |
| ❏ Did a leader guide the discussion? <br> ❏ Was someone taking notes to share with the group at the end of the discussion? | |
| ❏ Did group participants ask questions and answer those posed by others? <br> ❏ Were group participants' questions and answers focused on the topic? | |
| ❏ Did group members accept comments from others? <br> ❏ Were group members open to new ideas and perspectives? | |

**For use with Speaking and Listening 1**

Name _____ Date _____ Assignment _____

# Self-Assessment

After you've completed your presentation, you should reflect on your speech. Ask yourself how well you thought it went. Consider the logic and organization of your speech. Think about whether or not your delivery effectively met the needs of your audience and how well you integrated multimedia elements into your presentation. Also consider how your classmates reacted to your presentation and whether or not the group discussion helped you to realize anything about your speech.

**Use a rubric for self-assessment.** Combine your self-evaluation with what you learned from your classmates' response to your presentation. Then, apply those insights as you fill in the rubric below. Use the rating scale to grade your work, and circle the score that best applies to each category.

## Self-Assessment Rubric

| Criteria | Rating Scale | | | | | |
|---|---|---|---|---|---|---|
| | not very | | | | | very |
| **Focus:** How effectively did I focus my presentation to meet the needs of my specific audience? | 1 | 2 | 3 | 4 | 5 | 6 |
| **Organization:** How logically did I organize my presentation so that listeners could easily follow it? | 1 | 2 | 3 | 4 | 5 | 6 |
| **Support/Elaboration:** How effectively did I integrate my images, graphics, sounds, and script while supporting main points with examples and detailed evidence? | 1 | 2 | 3 | 4 | 5 | 6 |
| **Delivery:** How well did I create an appropriate tone, while making eye contact with listeners, maintaining an adequate volume, and speaking clearly? | 1 | 2 | 3 | 4 | 5 | 6 |
| **Conventions:** How free was my presentation from errors in grammar, spelling, and punctuation? | 1 | 2 | 3 | 4 | 5 | 6 |

For use with Speaking and Listening 1

# Speaking and Listening 2

> **2. Integrate multiple sources of information presented in diverse media or formats (e.g., visually, quantitatively, orally) evaluating the credibility and accuracy of each source.**

## Explanation

When you create a multimedia presentation, you must **integrate**, or bring together, information from both print and nonprint media. Sources could include newspapers, magazines, books, or other texts, as well as such nonprint sources as video clips, television ads, videos, and music CDs. This information might be presented visually, quantitatively, and orally. To effectively integrate diverse media sources, you should consider and select the most appropriate media for communicating your topic and organize them into a clear and effective presentation.

When gathering information for a presentation, it is important to **evaluate** the **credibility** of each source you use. Many factors can affect the credibility and accuracy of a source. These factors include an author's or a sponsor's personal interest and feelings, the method in which the original information was gathered, and the age of the source. Also consider the intended audience and purpose of the coverage. Examine the authority and objectivity of your sources, and eliminate any that are biased. Determine the accuracy of each by checking it against other sources.

## Examples

- Learn about your topic by gathering different media sources. Then, carefully read through or view each source and take notes. Look for similarities and differences in the way information is presented.
- Look for any discrepancies between sources to evaluate their accuracy. Ask yourself if the source is presented in a way that is useful, authoritative, and free from bias. If you are not sure whether a source is reliable, compare it to other sources. If other sources give much of the same information and facts, you can be more confident that the source is reliable.
- Evaluating sources is especially important on the Internet. Many Web pages are written by people who are not authorities on a topic. These sources may include information that is unreliable, invalid, or inaccurate. Web sites that end with the URLs *.edu* and *.gov* are often the most reliable.
- Choose audio and visual materials carefully, integrating them into your presentation to illustrate information for maximum clarity and to provoke a specific emotional response from your audience.

## Academic Vocabulary

**integrate**  to bring parts together to create a cohesive whole

**evaluate**  to analyze or judge the value of something

**credibility**  the capacity to inspire belief; authoritative and trustworthy

## Apply the Standard

Use the worksheet that follows to help you apply the standard. Several copies of the worksheet have been provided for you to use with different assignments.

- Integrating Multiple Sources of Information

Name _____ Date _____ Selection _____

# Integrating Multiple Sources of Information

Use this graphic organizer to analyze your sources. Record information about each source in the left-hand column, and note which point you think the information most effectively supports in your presentation. Then evaluate each source, and check the appropriate boxes in the right-hand column.

| Source | Evaluation |
|---|---|
| **1)** Source Name:<br><br>Format:<br><br>Audience and Purpose:<br><br>Content:<br><br>Point it supports: | Is this source<br>❏ useful?<br>❏ current?<br>❏ accurate?<br>❏ unbiased? |
| **2)** Source Name:<br><br>Format:<br><br>Audience and Purpose:<br><br>Content:<br><br>Point it supports: | Is this source<br>❏ useful?<br>❏ current?<br>❏ accurate?<br>❏ unbiased? |
| **3)** Source Name:<br><br>Format:<br><br>Audience and Purpose:<br><br>Content:<br><br>Point it supports: | Is this source<br>❏ useful?<br>❏ current?<br>❏ accurate?<br>❏ unbiased? |

A          **For use with Speaking and Listening 2**

Name _____ Date _____ Selection _____

# Integrating Multiple Sources of Information

Use this graphic organizer to analyze your sources. Record information about each source in the left-hand column, and note which point you think the information most effectively supports in your presentation. Then evaluate each source, and check the appropriate boxes in the right-hand column.

| Source | Evaluation |
|---|---|
| **1)** Source Name:<br><br>Format:<br><br>Audience and Purpose:<br><br>Content:<br><br>Point it supports: | Is this source<br>❑ useful?<br>❑ current?<br>❑ accurate?<br>❑ unbiased? |
| **2)** Source Name:<br><br>Format:<br><br>Audience and Purpose:<br><br>Content:<br><br>Point it supports: | Is this source<br>❑ useful?<br>❑ current?<br>❑ accurate?<br>❑ unbiased? |
| **3)** Source Name:<br><br>Format:<br><br>Audience and Purpose:<br><br>Content:<br><br>Point it supports: | Is this source<br>❑ useful?<br>❑ current?<br>❑ accurate?<br>❑ unbiased? |

Name _____ Date _____ Selection _____

# Integrating Multiple Sources of Information

Use this graphic organizer to analyze your sources. Record information about each source in the left-hand column, and note which point you think the information most effectively supports in your presentation. Then evaluate each source, and check the appropriate boxes in the right-hand column.

| Source | Evaluation |
|---|---|
| **1)** Source Name:<br><br>Format:<br><br>Audience and Purpose:<br><br>Content:<br><br>Point it supports: | Is this source<br>❏ useful?<br>❏ current?<br>❏ accurate?<br>❏ unbiased? |
| **2)** Source Name:<br><br>Format:<br><br>Audience and Purpose:<br><br>Content:<br><br>Point it supports: | Is this source<br>❏ useful?<br>❏ current?<br>❏ accurate?<br>❏ unbiased? |
| **3)** Source Name:<br><br>Format:<br><br>Audience and Purpose:<br><br>Content:<br><br>Point it supports: | Is this source<br>❏ useful?<br>❏ current?<br>❏ accurate?<br>❏ unbiased? |

C   **For use with Speaking and Listening 2**

# Speaking and Listening 3

> **3. Evaluate a speaker's point of view, reasoning, and use of evidence and rhetoric, identifying any fallacious reasoning or exaggerated or distorted evidence.**

## Explanation

Good listeners evaluate how well a speaker communicates his or her point of view. Speakers must use effective **reasoning** and relevant **evidence** to support and defend their ideas. Reasoning can include appeals to logic or emotion. Relevant evidence includes statistics, expert opinions, and testimonials. Speakers also use **rhetorical devices,** which are techniques intended to persuade listeners. They include:

- parallelism: similar grammatical structures expressing related ideas
- repetition: reusing a key word or idea for emphasis
- analogy: drawing a comparison between two unlike things

It is important to identify distorted evidence and fallacious, or flawed, reasoning when evaluating a speech. Some common logical fallacies are:

- red herring: introducing an irrelevant point as a distraction
- overgeneralization: a conclusion drawn from insufficient evidence

## Examples

- Reasoning includes emotional appeals. For example, a speaker who would like to expand theater programs in a community might appeal to emotion by saying that doing so would keep local children out of trouble.
- A good speech is supported by relevant evidence. For example, a speaker arguing for making air bags mandatory might include testimonials from people who were injured in cars that did not have air bags.
- Rhetorical devices add emphasis and help persuade. For example, a class president trying to persuade the school board to increase funding for school programs might use parallelism for emphasis: "We want to learn. We want to grow. We want to succeed."
- Fallacious reasoning is unsupported and weak. For example, a political candidate might use an overgeneralization when she promises to cut spending, but does not offer details about which cuts she intends to make.

## Academic Vocabulary

**evidence**  something that provides proof of a claim

**reasoning**  using reason, or logical thinking, to make judgments or form conclusions

**rhetorical device**  a verbal technique used to add emphasis and persuade

## Apply the Standard

Use the worksheets that follow to help you apply the standard. Several copies of each worksheet have been provided for you to use with different assignments.

- Evaluating Point of View and Reasoning
- Evaluating Evidence

Name _____ Date _____ Assignment _____

# Evaluating Point of View and Reasoning

Use this chart to evaluate a speaker's point of view and reasoning. Then identify any rhetorical devices and describe their effects.

| Topic: | |
|---|---|
| **Speaker's point of view:** | **Is it**<br>❏ clearly stated?<br>❏ convincing? |
| **Type of reasoning:** | **Does the speaker include any common logical fallacies?**<br>❏ Red herring<br>❏ Overgeneralization<br><br>Examples: |
| **Rhetorical devices:** | **Does the speaker use any rhetorical devices?**<br>❏ Parallelism<br>❏ Analogy<br>❏ Repetition<br><br>Examples: |
| **What effect does the speaker's use of rehetorical devices have on his or her audience?** | |

Name _____ Date _____ Assignment _____

# Evaluating Point of View and Reasoning

Use this chart to evaluate a speaker's point of view and reasoning. Then identify any rhetorical devices and describe their effects.

| Topic: | |
|---|---|
| **Speaker's point of view:** | **Is it**<br>❑ clearly stated?<br>❑ convincing? |
| **Type of reasoning:** | **Does the speaker include any common logical fallacies?**<br>❑ Red herring<br>❑ Overgeneralization<br><br>Examples: |
| **Rhetorical devices:** | **Does the speaker use any rhetorical devices?**<br>❑ Parallelism<br>❑ Analogy<br>❑ Repetition<br><br>Examples: |
| **What effect does the speaker's use of rehetorical devices have on his or her audience?** | |

Name _____ Date _____ Assignment _____

# Evaluating Point of View and Reasoning

Use this chart to evaluate a speaker's point of view and reasoning. Then identify any rhetorical devices and describe their effects.

| Topic: | |
|---|---|
| **Speaker's point of view:** | **Is it**<br>❑ clearly stated?<br>❑ convincing? |
| **Type of reasoning:** | **Does the speaker include any common logical fallacies?**<br>❑ Red herring<br>❑ Overgeneralization<br><br>Examples: |
| **Rhetorical devices:** | **Does the speaker use any rhetorical devices?**<br>❑ Parallelism<br>❑ Analogy<br>❑ Repetition<br><br>Examples: |
| **What effect does the speaker's use of rehetorical devices have on his or her audience?** | |

Name _____ Date _____ Assignment _____

# Evaluating Evidence

Use this chart to analyze the relevance, quality, and credibility of the evidence that a speaker provides to support or oppose a point of view.

| |
|---|
| **Topic:** |
| **Speaker's Point of View:** |
| **Audience:** |
| **Supporting Evidence:**<br><br>**The evidence is**<br>❏ relevant.<br>❏ of good quality.<br>❏ credible.<br>❏ exaggerated or distorted. |
| **Evaluate how well the evidence supports the speaker's point of view.** |

A

Name _____ Date _____ Assignment _____

# Evaluating Evidence

Use this chart to analyze the relevance, quality, and credibility of the evidence that a speaker provides to support or oppose a point of view.

| Topic: |
| --- |

| Speaker's Point of View: |
| --- |

| Audience: |
| --- |

**Supporting Evidence:**

**The evidence is**
- ❏ relevant.
- ❏ of good quality.
- ❏ credible.
- ❏ exaggerated or distorted.

| Evaluate how well the evidence supports the speaker's point of view. |
| --- |

Name _____ Date _____ Assignment _____

# Evaluating Evidence

Use this chart to analyze the relevance, quality, and credibility of the evidence that a speaker provides to support or oppose a point of view.

| |
|---|
| **Topic:** |
| **Speaker's Point of View:** |
| **Audience:** |
| **Supporting Evidence:**<br><br>**The evidence is**<br>❑ relevant.<br>❑ of good quality.<br>❑ credible.<br>❑ exaggerated or distorted. |
| **Evaluate how well the evidence supports the speaker's point of view.** |

# Speaking and Listening 4

> **4. Present information, findings, and supporting evidence clearly, concisely, and logically such that listeners can follow the line of reasoning and the organization, development, substance, and style are appropriate to purpose, audience, and task.**

## Explanation

When preparing a speech or presentation, you must first identify your audience, purpose, and task. Ask yourself who will be listening to your speech and what you want them to know, believe, or do. Also, anticipate what will interest your audience and what may bore or confuse them. Then, choose information and **evidence** that will satisfy their curiosity, be persuasive, and answer their questions. Since listeners typically cannot ask a speaker to slow down or repeat information, you should organize supporting ideas **logically** and connect them clearly to the main idea. Doing so will help listeners follow your argument.

Here are three possible ways of organizing your speech:

- *Problem-and-Solution* Identify a problem and then offer reasonable solutions.
- *Cause-and-Effect* Show the causes and effects leading to an event or problem.
- *Order of Importance* Present information from least important to most important or vice versa.

## Examples

- Suppose you are concerned that there are not enough parking spaces for students at your school. You could give a speech about this topic using the problem-and-solution organizational structure. Highlight the nature of the problem first. Then, appealing to your audience's concerns, propose and explain a possible solution.
- If you are concerned about the harmful effects of a huge new parking garage in the center of your town, you might organize a presentation using a cause-and-effect approach. Begin by describing the new garage (the cause), and then explain its harmful effects on traffic and pedestrians.
- Imagine you want to describe the benefits a new teen center would provide to your community. You might begin with the least important benefit (improving the appearance of a particular building) and move to the most important (providing teens with a safe and stimulating place to go after school).

## Academic Vocabulary

**evidence**  factual proof or support

**logically**  in a manner based on proof or evidence; reasonably

## Apply the Standard

Use the worksheets that follow to help you apply the standard. Several copies of each worksheet have been provided for you to use with different assignments.

- Presenting a Speech Effectively
- Organizing Information

Name _____ Date _____ Assignment _____

# Presenting a Speech Effectively

Use the top portion of the organizer to plan your speech. Use the lower portion as a checklist when drafting your speech.

**PLAN**

**Topic**



**Audience**



**Purpose**



**Occasion or Task**



**Types of Organization**

❏ Problem-and-Solution
❏ Cause-and-Effect
❏ Order of Importance
❏ Other (Explain) ...................................................................................

**SPEECH CHECKLIST**

Analyze the effectiveness of your speech:

❏ Do you present information, findings, and evidence clearly?
❏ Do you use valid evidence from reliable sources?
❏ Do you organize details logically so listeners can follow your reasoning?
❏ Does your style support your point of view and the speech's purpose?
❏ Does your structure support your point of view and the speech's purpose?

A

For use with Speaking and Listening 4

Name _____ Date _____ Assignment _____

# Presenting a Speech Effectively

Use the top portion of the organizer to plan your speech. Use the lower portion as a checklist when drafting your speech.

**PLAN**

**Topic**

**Audience**

**Purpose**

**Occasion or Task**

**Types of Organization**

❑ Problem-and-Solution
❑ Cause-and-Effect
❑ Order of Importance
❑ Other (Explain) ...............................................................................

**SPEECH CHECKLIST**

**Analyze the effectiveness of your speech:**

❑ Do you present information, findings, and evidence clearly?
❑ Do you use valid evidence from reliable sources?
❑ Do you organize details logically so listeners can follow your reasoning?
❑ Does your style support your point of view and the speech's purpose?
❑ Does your structure support your point of view and the speech's purpose?

Name _____ Date _____ Assignment _____

# Presenting a Speech Effectively

Use the top portion of the organizer to plan your speech. Use the lower portion as a checklist when drafting your speech.

**PLAN**

Topic

Audience

Purpose

Occasion or Task

**Types of Organization**

❏ Problem-and-Solution
❏ Cause-and-Effect
❏ Order of Importance
❏ Other (Explain) ........................................................................................

**SPEECH CHECKLIST**

Analyze the effectiveness of your speech:

❏ Do you present information, findings, and evidence clearly?
❏ Do you use valid evidence from reliable sources?
❏ Do you organize details logically so listeners can follow your reasoning?
❏ Does your style support your point of view and the speech's purpose?
❏ Does your structure support your point of view and the speech's purpose?

C

**For use with Speaking and Listening 4**

Name _____ Date _____ Assignment _____

# Organizing Information

Use the graphic organizer below to help you decide which type of organization works best for your speech. Try filling out each section. Then, explain which structure works best for your topic.

| Topic |
|---|
| **Problem-and-Solution** |
| Thesis/Problem: ............................................................................................................... |
| Who is affected? ............................................................................................................... |
| What are the possible solutions? |
| 1) ............................................................................................................... |
| 2) ............................................................................................................... |
| 3) ............................................................................................................... |
| **Cause-and-Effect** |
| Cause of event or problem: ............................................................................................. |
| Effect ............................................................................................................... |
| Effect ............................................................................................................... |
| Effect ............................................................................................................... |
| **Order of Importance** |
| Most to Least |
| 1) ............................................................................................................... |
| 2) ............................................................................................................... |
| 3) ............................................................................................................... |
| Least to Most |
| 1) ............................................................................................................... |
| 2) ............................................................................................................... |
| 3) ............................................................................................................... |
| **Which type of organization works best and why?** |
| |

Name _____ Date _____ Assignment _____

# Organizing Information

Use the graphic organizer below to help you decide which type of organization works best for your speech. Try filling out each section. Then, explain which structure works best for your topic.

| Topic |
|---|
| **Problem-and-Solution** |
| Thesis/Problem: ............................................................................................................................ |
| Who is affected? ............................................................................................................................ |
| What are the possible solutions? |
| 1) ................................................................................................................................................ |
| 2) ................................................................................................................................................ |
| 3) ................................................................................................................................................ |
| **Cause-and-Effect** |
| Cause of event or problem: .......................................................................................................... |
| Effect ........................................................................................................................................... |
| Effect ........................................................................................................................................... |
| Effect ........................................................................................................................................... |
| **Order of Importance** |
| Most to Least |
| 1) ................................................................................................................................................ |
| 2) ................................................................................................................................................ |
| 3) ................................................................................................................................................ |
| Least to Most |
| 1) ................................................................................................................................................ |
| 2) ................................................................................................................................................ |
| 3) ................................................................................................................................................ |
| **Which type of organization works best and why?** |
| |

B

**For use with Speaking and Listening 4**

Name _____ Date _____ Assignment _____

# Organizing Information

Use the graphic organizer below to help you decide which type of organization works best for your speech. Try filling out each section. Then, explain which structure works best for your topic.

| **Topic** |
| --- |
| **Problem-and-Solution** |
| Thesis/Problem: ................................................................................................................................... |
| Who is affected? ................................................................................................................................. |
| What are the possible solutions? |
| 1) ....................................................................................................................................................... |
| 2) ....................................................................................................................................................... |
| 3) ....................................................................................................................................................... |
| **Cause-and-Effect** |
| Cause of event or problem: ................................................................................................................ |
| Effect ................................................................................................................................................. |
| Effect ................................................................................................................................................. |
| Effect ................................................................................................................................................. |
| **Order of Importance** |
| Most to Least |
| 1) ....................................................................................................................................................... |
| 2) ....................................................................................................................................................... |
| 3) ....................................................................................................................................................... |
| Least to Most |
| 1) ....................................................................................................................................................... |
| 2) ....................................................................................................................................................... |
| 3) ....................................................................................................................................................... |
| **Which type of organization works best and why?** |
| |

# Speaking and Listening 5

> **5. Make strategic use of digital media (e.g., textual, graphical, audio, visual, and interactive elements) in presentations to enhance understanding of findings, reasoning, and evidence and to add interest.**

## Explanation

To give an effective multimedia presentation, make **strategic** use of digital media. Digital media can include a variety of formats.

- **textual elements,** such as titles and captions

- **graphical elements,** such as charts, maps, and diagrams

- **audio elements,** such as background music, sound clips, and interviews

- **visual elements,** such as still photographs and video clips

- **interactive elements,** such as instant messaging or games

A few strong elements with clear meaning and relevance are better than many elements that are not clearly connected to your topic or argument. As you consider which elements to use, think about their intended impact. Ask yourself: How do these elements communicate information? How might different elements change my presentation? How do they support the main points I want to make?

## Examples

- Using media throughout the presentation, rather than clustered at one point, improves pacing. For example, in a presentation on migration of peoples, use maps at various points throughout rather than showing several maps at once.

- Visuals and any captions or other text should be large and clear enough to be seen at a distance. Sound components should not drown out the presentation.

- Formats communicate information differently. For example, photographs provide information and prompt an emotional response, while charts and graphs present complex information quickly and easily. For migration, a graph or map might be the best choice for sharing statistics or showing routes; but a photograph of a family walking with all their belongings could prompt a strong emotional response.

## Academic Vocabulary

**strategic**  integral or essential to a carefully made plan

## Apply the Standard

Use the worksheet that follows to help you apply the standard.

- Using Digital Media

Name _____ Date _____ _____

# Using Digital Media

In the chart, describe the digital media elements you will include in your presentation and plan how you will use each element.

**Topic:** ...........................................................................................................................................

| Digital Media Elements |
| --- |
| **Ideas and Information:** |
| How it enhances understanding:<br><br>Where to include it: |
| **Graphical Element:** |
| How it enhances understanding:<br><br>Where to include it: |
| **Audio Element:** |
| How it enhances understanding:<br><br>Where to include it: |
| **Visual Element:** |
| How it enhances understanding:<br><br>Where to include it: |
| **Interactive Element:** |
| How it enhances understanding:<br><br>Where to include it: |

A

# Speaking and Listening 6

> **6. Adapt speech to a variety of contexts and tasks, demonstrating command of formal English when indicated or appropriate.**

## Explanation

When you speak in different situations and for different reasons, you need to **adapt,** or adjust your speech. Think about your task, or the reason you are speaking. Think also about the **context** in which you will speak. Ask yourself these questions: Who is in the audience, and what do they know about your subject? Are you delivering a formal presentation? Is your purpose to persuade, to inform, to describe, or to entertain?

Keep the context and task in mind as you adapt your presentation. Knowing how much depth to go into and what method of delivery to use depends on these factors. Remember to speak at an appropriate volume and rate. Make eye contact, vary your facial expressions, and use effective gestures.

As you adapt your speech, make sure that your audience can understand you. When you deliver a presentation, use **formal English** to communicate your ideas. Formal English shows that you respect both your subject and your audience. Avoid using casual, everyday language and slang when speaking.

## Examples

- To identify ways to adapt your speech, be mindful of the context. For example, a classroom presentation requires formal speech while a group discussion is more informal. When working with a partner, use casual but polite speech.

- Keep your task in mind as you determine ways to adapt your presentation. For example, when attempting to entertain, speak expressively and use pauses, gestures, and facial expressions. To persuade, vary volume dramatically and maintain eye contact. To inform, speak with authority and provide solid reasons and support.

- Avoid slang terms and informal expressions, such as *like, you know,* and *I mean.*

## Academic Vocabulary

**adapt** to change for a situation or purpose

**context** the circumstances or situation

## Apply the Standard

Use the worksheets that follow to help you apply the standard. Several copies of each worksheet have been provided for you.

- Adapting a Speech
- Using Appropriate Language

Name _____ Date _____ Selection _____

# Adapting a Speech

Use this chart to help you adapt your speech to the appropriate context, audience, and task.

**Topic:** .....................................................................................................................................

| |
|---|
| **Context:**<br>❑ formal classroom presentation<br>❑ impromptu speech<br>❑ group discussion<br>❑ partner talk |
| **Audience:**<br>❑ class and teacher<br>❑ small group<br>❑ partner |
| **Task:**<br>❑ to persuade<br>❑ to entertain<br>❑ to describe<br>❑ to inform |
| **How I will adapt my delivery:** |

Name _____ Date _____ Selection _____

# Adapting a Speech

Use this chart to help you adapt your speech to the appropriate context, audience, and task.

**Topic:** .................................................................................................................

| Context: |
| --- |
| ❑ formal classroom presentation |
| ❑ imprompt speech |
| ❑ group discussion |
| ❑ partner talk |

| Audience: |
| --- |
| ❑ class and teacher |
| ❑ small group |
| ❑ partner |

| Task: |
| --- |
| ❑ to persuade |
| ❑ to entertain |
| ❑ to describe |
| ❑ to inform |

| How I will adapt my delivery: |
| --- |
| |

B

For use with Speaking and Listening 6

Name _____ Date _____ Selection _____

# Adapting a Speech

Use this chart to help you adapt your speech to the appropriate context, audience, and task.

**Topic:** ....................................................................................................................................

---

**Context:**

❏ formal classroom presentation

❏ imprompt speech

❏ group discussion

❏ partner talk

---

**Audience:**

❏ class and teacher

❏ small group

❏ partner

---

**Task:**

❏ to persuade

❏ to entertain

❏ to describe

❏ to inform

---

**How I will adapt my delivery:**

---

Name _____ Date _____ Selection _____

# Using Appropriate Language

Complete the following chart to check that you are using appropriate language for your presentation.

**Topic:** .................................................................................................................

| Context: |
| --- |
| Task: |

<table>
<tr><td>Do you<br>❏ use formal English?<br><br>Explain:...................................<br><br>❏ use informal English?<br><br>Explain:...................................</td><td>Do you<br>❏ avoid temporizing words?<br>❏ avoid common usage problems?<br>❏ avoid incomplete sentences?</td></tr>
<tr><td colspan="2">How might you improve or adjust the language you use? Explain:</td></tr>
</table>

Name _____ Date _____ Selection _____

# Using Appropriate Language

Complete the following chart to check that you are using appropriate language for your presentation.

**Topic:** .......................................................................................................

| Context: |
|---|

| Task: |
|---|

**Do you**
❏ use formal English?

Explain:................................................

❏ use informal English?

Explain:................................................

**Do you**
❏ avoid temporizing words?
❏ avoid common usage problems?
❏ avoid incomplete sentences?

**How might you improve or adjust the language you use? Explain:**

COMMON CORE COMPANION • COMMON CORE COMPANION • COMMON CORE COMPANION

Name _____ Date _____ Selection _____

# Using Appropriate Language

Complete the following chart to check that you are using appropriate language for your presentation.

**Topic:**..................................................................................................................................

| Context: |
|---|

| Task: |
|---|

| Do you | Do you |
|---|---|
| ❏ use formal English? | ❏ avoid temporizing words? |
| | ❏ avoid common usage problems? |
| Explain:................................................ | ❏ avoid incomplete sentences? |
| | |
| ❏ use informal English? | |
| | |
| Explain:................................................ | |

| How might you improve or adjust the language you use? Explain: |
|---|

For use with Speaking and Listening 6

# Language Standards

# Language 1a

---

**1a. Demonstrate command of the conventions of standard English grammar and usage when writing or speaking.**

  **• Use parallel structure.**

---

## Explanation

**Parallelism** is the use of similar grammatical forms or patterns to express similar ideas. Writers and speakers use parallelism to connect ideas and to make them memorable.

## Examples

Parallel constructions place equal ideas in words, phrases, or clauses of similar types. Ideas are not parallel if the grammatical structure shifts.

- **Similar types of words**
  **Nonparallel:** *We went **fishing, swimming,** and **on a hike**.*
  (The phrase *on a hike* is a shift in the grammatical structure.)
  **Parallel:** *We went **fishing, swimming,** and **hiking**.*

- **Similar types of phrases**
  **Nonparallel:** *Helen enjoys singing **in the chorus** and **to sing in the town choir**.*
  (A prepositional phrase is followed by an infinitive phrase.)
  **Parallel:** *Helen enjoys singing **in the chorus** and **in the town choir**.*

  **Nonparallel:** *They want **to practice, be making progress,** and **playing a great concert**.*
  (The second and third phrases create a confusing shift in grammatical structure.)
  **Parallel:** *They want **to practice, to make progress,** and **to play a great concert**.*
  (Three infinitive phrases create parallelism and show equal ideas.)

- **Similar types of clauses**
  **Nonparallel:** *Interesting hobbies include those **that require imagination** or **building skills**.*
  (An adjectival clause is followed by a participial phrase.)
  **Parallel:** *Interesting hobbies include those **that require imagination** or **that build skills**.*
  (The two adjectival clauses create a parallel structure.)

Name _____ Date _____ Assignment _____

# Apply the Standard

Rewrite each sentence so that it contains parallel structures.

1. Angelica loves skateboarding and to ski. ........................................

2. She has strong muscles, good balance, and is fearless. ........................................

3. She began skateboarding when she was five and skied since she was eight.
........................................

4. This year, she started teaching other kids and works in the ski shop. ........................................

5. She says that when people ski, they must use their legs, their arms, and think, too.
........................................

6. Last year, Angelica was happy when one of her students entered a race and in a downhill competition. ........................................

7. It was the student who was a very timid skier at first and having a hard time with his balance.
........................................

8. Angelica urged him to keep practicing, work hard, and overcoming his fears.
........................................

9. Imagine how proud she was when he won the race and thanking her for her support.
........................................

10. After that, Angelica suggested that he become a skiing teacher and to help younger skiers advance.
........................................

11. Today, he works at the ski school and being a great slalom skier. ........................................

12. It is hard for Angelica to remember him as the student who was afraid of losing his balance and to fall. ........................................

# Language 1b

> **1b. Demonstrate command of the conventions of standard English grammar and usage when writing or speaking.**
>
> • **Use various types of phrases (noun, verb, adjectival, adverbial, participial, prepositional, absolute) and clauses (independent, dependent, noun, relative, adverbial) to convey specific meanings and add variety and interest to writing or presentations.**

## Explanation

A **phrase** is a group of words functioning together that does not have a subject and a verb. Types of phrases include prepositional phrases, noun phrases, verb phrases, participial phrases, and absolute phrases. A **clause** is a group of words functioning together that *does* contain a subject and a verb. There are two types of clauses: independent ("main") clauses and dependent ("subordinate") clauses. Within the category of dependent clauses are three kinds: noun clauses, relative ("adjectival") clauses, and adverbial clauses.

## Examples
### PHRASES

A **prepositional phrase** includes a preposition (*at, in, for*) and a noun or pronoun that is the object of the preposition. Two types of prepositional phrases are an adjectival phrase and an adverbial phrase.

> An **adjectival phrase** modifies a noun or pronoun.
> > *The man <u>in the white car</u> is my uncle.* (Which man?)

> An **adverbial phrase** modifies a verb, an adjective, or an adverb.
> > *We'll read this poem <u>in the morning.</u>* (When?)

There are also several other kinds of phrases. A **noun phrase** is a noun or pronoun and its modifiers.

> > *<u>My favorite poet</u> is William Butler Yeats.*

A **verb phrase** is a main verb with its auxiliary, or helping, verbs. The entire phrase serves as the verb.

> > *Tomorrow, I <u>will be visiting</u> my aunt in Tucson.*

A **participial phrase** contains a present or past participle (*walking, walked*) and its modifiers or complements. In a sentence, a participial phrase acts as an adjective.

> > *<u>Walking out the door</u>, I dropped my books.* (present participle)
> > *<u>Covered with mud</u>, the dog jumped into my lap.* (past participle)

### CLAUSES

An **independent or main clause** expresses a complete thought and can stand alone as a complete sentence. A **dependent or subordinate clause** does *not* express a complete thought. Therefore, it cannot stand alone as a complete sentence. A subordinate **relative or adjectival clause** modifies a noun, and a subordinate **adverbial clause** modifies a verb. A subordinate **noun clause** acts as a noun.

> **Relative or adjectival clause:** *Holly Tyson, <u>who is my neighbor</u>, is a famous author.*
> **Adverbial clause:** *<u>When Ms. Tyson came to our class</u>, she gave us some writing tips.*
> **Noun clause:** *<u>Whoever wants to be a writer</u> should write in a journal every day.*

Name _____ Date _____ Assignment _____

# Apply the Standard

**A.** Underline the answer that correctly identifies each phrase or clause. Then use each one in a sentence.

**1.** after the game (adjectival phrase, adverbial phrase)

.............................................................................................................

**2.** a talented musician (prepositional phrase, noun phrase)

.............................................................................................................

**3.** running to the bus (participial phrase, adjectival phrase)

.............................................................................................................

**4.** who enjoys baseball games (independent clause, adjectival or relative clause)

.............................................................................................................

**5.** baked and frosted (participial phrase, prepositional phrase)

.............................................................................................................

**6.** whatever you want (noun clause, noun phrase)

.............................................................................................................

**7.** over tragedies (prepositional phrase, verb phrase)

.............................................................................................................

**8.** before you answer that question (adverbial clause, adverbial phrase)

.............................................................................................................

**B.** Complete each sentence by adding the type of phrase or clause shown in parentheses.
   **Example:** Martin Anderson, (adjectival or relative clause), is a science teacher at our school.
   **Sample answer:** *Martin Anderson, who wrote a biology textbook, is a science teacher at our school.*

**1.** (Noun clause) is a good answer to the question.

.............................................................................................................

**2.** We will continue this discussion (adverbial phrase).

.............................................................................................................

**3.** Tomorrow we (verb phrase).

.............................................................................................................

**4.** I introduced my parents to Jim, (adjectival or relative clause).

.............................................................................................................

# Language 2a

> **2a. Demonstrate command of the conventions of standard English capitalization, punctuation, and spelling when writing.**
>
> - **Use a semicolon (and perhaps a conjunctive adverb) to link two or more closely related independent clauses.**

## Explanation

A comma and a conjunction (*and, but, or*) are used to join two or more independent clauses to form a compound sentence.

Use a **semicolon** to join independent clauses that are *not* joined by a conjunction. Additionally, use a semicolon and a **conjunctive adverb** (*however, for example, nevertheless*) followed by a comma to join two independent clauses.

Finally, use semicolons to separate items in a series when one or more of the items includes a comma.

## Examples

**1. Use a comma and a conjunction:**

*Jim will cook the pasta, **and** I will prepare the sauce.*

*Please hurry, **or** we will be late.*

**2. Use a semicolon when the clauses are *not* joined by a conjunction:**

*Helen is not feeling **well; please** call the nurse.*

*The decorations are **finished; let** the party begin!*

**3. Use a semicolon and a conjunctive adverb, followed by a comma:**

*John was absent **yesterday; therefore**, he missed the quiz.*

*As a child, I was afraid of large **dogs; however,** your dog has cured me of that.*

Here are commonly used conjunctive adverbs. Note their different meanings and uses.

| To show similarity | *similarly, likewise* |
| --- | --- |
| To show contrast | *however, nevertheless* |
| To show an effect or conclusion | *therefore, thus, consequently, accordingly* |
| To show an alternative | *instead, otherwise* |
| To show additional or stronger information | *additionally, furthermore, moreover* |
| To provide an example | *for example, for instance* |

**4. Use semicolons to separate items in a series when one or more items contains a comma:**

*Winners in the essay contest were **James Ali, first place; Ana Chin, second place;** and Myron Dobbs, third place.*

Name _____ Date _____ Assignment _____

# Apply the Standard

**A.** Each sentence is missing one or more semicolons. Add semicolons where they are needed.

**1.** I live in Texas, where ponds do not freeze in the winter consequently, I had never skated on a pond.

**2.** I didn't have any warm winter clothes additionally, I didn't think to bring my skates.

**3.** Luckily, my cousin Petros had enough warm clothes to share otherwise, I would have frozen!

**4.** He loaned me a thick parka, which fit perfectly I brought one that was too small.

**5.** He didn't have an extra pair of skates accordingly, I rented a pair at the local sporting goods store.

**B.** Rewrite each pair of sentences as a single sentence. Follow the directions in parentheses. Remember to place a comma after a conjunctive adverb.

**1.** My great grandfather grew up in France. He moved here in 1946. (Use a semicolon and *however*.)

.......................................................................................

**2.** French men were called to duty during the war. He became a submariner. (Use a semicolon and *thus*.)

.......................................................................................

**3.** World War II submarines did not have modern technology. They lacked sonar. (Use a semicolon and *for example*.)

.......................................................................................

**4.** Without sonar, they could not detect other submarines. There were many collisions and close calls. (Use a semicolon and *therefore*.)

.......................................................................................

**5.** Great Grandpa's submarine and its crew remained safe. They were very lucky. (Use a semicolon.)

.......................................................................................

**C.** Write a sentence using the elements shown. Remember to use a comma after a conjunctive adverb.

**1.** a semicolon .................................................................................

**2.** a semicolon and *similarly* ..............................................................

**3.** a semicolon and *for instance* .........................................................

**4.** a semicolon and *furthermore* ..........................................................

**5.** semicolons to separate items in a series ...........................................

.......................................................................................

# Language 2b

> **2b. Demonstrate command of the conventions of standard English capitalization, punctuation, and spelling when writing.**
>
> • **Use a colon to introduce a list or quotation.**

## Explanation

The **colon** is a punctuation mark that has three main functions.

• **To introduce a list**

Use a colon to introduce a list of items that follows an independent clause.

• **To introduce a direct quotation**

Use a colon to introduce a direct quotation from a person or another work of literature.

• **To end the salutation of a business letter**

When you write an informal personal letter, end the salutation with a comma. However, when you write a formal business letter, end the salutation with a colon.

## Examples

• **To introduce a list that follows an independent clause**

*The gym offers several activities: yoga, weight training, swimming, and cycling.*

**Do *not* use a colon if the list is the direct object of the verb.**

*The gym offers yoga, weight training, swimming, and cycling.*

• **To introduce a direct quotation from another work of literature**

*This sentence appears in Jack London's short story, "The King of Mazy May": "Walt was born a thousand miles or so down the Yukon, in a trading post below the Ramparts."*

• **To end the salutation of a business letter**

*Dear Mr. Tsao:*

*Dear Ms. Lipkin:*

Name _____ Date _____ Assignment _____

# Apply the Standard

**A.** Some of these sentences are missing a colon. Add colons where they are needed. If a sentence is correctly punctuated and does not require the addition of a colon, write *No colon* on the line.

1. This is one of my favorite Mark Twain stories "Stage Fright." ................................

2. Maya Angelou speaks of childhood fears "Panthers in the park, strangers in the dark." ...............

3. I think these are the best American writers Ernest Hemingway and F. Scott Fitzgerald. ...............

4. For a report on Edgar Allan Poe, I read "The Tell-Tale Heart" and "The Black Cat." ...............

5. Lensey Namioka begins her story "The All-American Slurp" with this sentence "The first time our family was invited out to dinner in America, we disgraced ourselves while eating celery."

................................................................

**B.** Rewrite each item, adding a colon where one is needed. If the item or the sentence does not need a colon, write *No colon* on the line.

1. Dear Mayor O'Hanihan ................................................

2. There are four herbs in our classroom garden rosemary, thyme, parsley, and oregano.

................................................................

3. Dear Aunt Louise ................................................

4. In *Casablanca,* Humphrey Bogart speaks this romantic line "We'll always have Paris."

................................................................

5. Supplies that I need to buy at the pharmacy include toothpaste, mouthwash, and iodine.

................................................................

**C.** Follow each direction.

1. Write an original sentence in which a colon introduces a direct quotation.

................................................................

2. Write a correctly punctuated salutation for an informal personal letter. ...............

3. Write a correctly punctuated salutation for a formal business letter. ...............

4. Write an original sentence in which a colon introduces a list.

................................................................

# Language 2c

> **2c. Demonstrate command of the conventions of standard English capitalization, punctuation, and spelling when writing.**
> - **Spell correctly.**

## Explanation

A carefully researched and written report will not be effective if it is filled with spelling errors. These guidelines will help you to prevent—or correct—spelling errors.

## Examples

**Words with suffixes** can present spelling problems. Some suffixes have similar sounds. Keep a list of words with such suffixes in your notebook. When using words with suffixes in your writing, you should always double check the spelling. Here are some examples.

| **Words ending in –*ize* or –*yze*** | | **Words ending in –*able* or –*ible*** | |
|---|---|---|---|
| *analyze* | *motorize* | *capable* | *sensible* |

| **Words ending in –*ance* or –*ence*** | | **Words ending in –*ant* or –*ent*** | |
|---|---|---|---|
| *resistance* | *suspense* | *servant* | *parent* |

**Words with double letters** can also cause spelling problems. Here are examples.

    *accommodate    accessible    dilemma    occurrence    embarrass*

**Words with silent vowels** are tricky, too. Often, errors occur with words in which two vowels together make only one vowel sound. Here are examples.

    *maintain    boulevard    familiar    biscuit    restaurant    breakfast*

**Homophones** are words that sound alike but have different meanings. Therefore, they are easily confused with one another. A spell checker will not help you to catch such errors. This chart lists some examples.

| | |
|---|---|
| **past**—"before the present"<br>*This past year, I lived in Cleveland.* | **passed**—"moved by"<br>*On our way home, we passed the park.* |
| **its**—a possessive pronoun<br>*The turtle went into its shell.* | **it's**—a contraction ("it is" or "it has")<br>*It's been a long time since I heard that song.* |
| **whose**—a possessive pronoun<br>*Whose coat is that?* | **who's**—a contraction ("who is" or "who has")<br>*Who's going to be our next president?* |
| **your**—a possessive pronoun<br>*Will your friends meet us at the movies?* | **you're**—a contraction ("you are")<br>*I know you're going to enjoy this book.* |
| **affect**—(verb) "to influence or change"<br>*A storm will affect our plans for a picnic.* | **effect**—(noun) "result or consequence"<br>*The poem had a great effect on the audience.* |
| **led**—(past tense of the verb *lead*)<br>*Our float led the parade.* | **lead**—(noun) "a heavy metal"<br>*The pipes were made of lead.* |
| **stationary**—"in a fixed position"<br>*The cabinet has been bolted to the wall; it is stationary.* | **stationery**—"writing paper"<br>*I used my best stationery to write that letter.* |

Name _____ Date _____ Assignment _____

# Apply the Standard

**A.** Each sentence contains one or more misspelled or misused words. Circle the errors. Then write each correct spelling on the line provided. If the sentence is correct as is, write *Correct*.

1. You're parants were kind to take us to that restarant for breakfast on Saturday.

   ...........................................................................................................................

2. I need to by some stationary to write them a thank-you note.

   ...........................................................................................................................

3. Meanwhile, please tell them how much I enjoyed the eggs and biscits.

   ...........................................................................................................................

4. Its always a grat treat to go out for brekfast.

   ...........................................................................................................................

5. Also, I've past that restaurant many times, but have never dined there in the passed.

   ...........................................................................................................................

6. Going there with your famly had a great affect on my entire day.

   ...........................................................................................................................

7. When a day is lead off by such a wonderful meal, its often a sign that the whole day will be grand!

   ...........................................................................................................................

8. You're a great frend for including me in your weekend plans.

   ...........................................................................................................................

**B.** Use each pair of words in a sentence or two. Make the meanings of the two words clear.

1. *who's, whose*....................................................................................................

   ...........................................................................................................................

2. *stationary, stationery*.....................................................................................

   ...........................................................................................................................

3. *its, it's*................................................................................................................

   ...........................................................................................................................

4. *affect, effect*....................................................................................................

   ...........................................................................................................................

5. *past, passed*.....................................................................................................

   ...........................................................................................................................

# Language 3

> 3. Apply knowledge of language to understand how language functions in different contexts, to make effective choices for meaning or style, and to comprehend more fully when reading or listening.
>
> • Write and edit work so that it conforms to the guidelines in a style manual (e.g., *MLA Handbook,* Turabian's *Manual for Writers*) appropriate for the discipline and writing type.

## Explanation

Following the guidelines of an established style manual will help you to revise and present your written work effectively. The Modern Language Association (MLA), for example, has created a style guide that instructs writers on the correct rules to follow regarding grammar, punctuation, and capitalization, as well as the appropriate formats to use when citing reference sources, both in parenthetical citations within the body of the report and in the works-cited list (or bibliography) at the end of the report.

## Examples

• **Underlines or Italics in Titles:** Underline or italicize the titles of books, periodicals, plays, movies, CDs, and DVDs. Underline or italicize the word *the* only if it is part of the title. Do not underline or italicize *the* before the name of a magazine or newspaper.

  *For Whom the Bell Tolls* (book)        the *Houston Chronicle* (newspaper)

• **Quotation Marks in Titles:** Use quotation marks to punctuate the titles of stories, articles, poems, Internet Web pages, radio or television transcripts, and editorials.

  "The Legend of Sleepy Hollow" (story)        "The Hollow Men" (poem)

• **Capitalization in Titles:** Capitalize the first word and all important words in the titles of books, periodicals, plays, poems, stories, and articles. However, do not capitalize an article (*a, an, the*) unless it is the first word. Do not capitalize coordinating conjunctions (*and, or, but*) or prepositions of fewer than five letters (*with, in, on*).

  *Gone with the Wind* (novel)        *Twenty Thousand Leagues Under the Sea* (novel)

• **Format for Works-Cited List at End of Report:** Follow this order for each entry. List the entries in alphabetical order.

  **1.** Name of author, editor, translator, or group responsible for the work (last name first)

  **2.** Title of the work (title of article first, then title of book)

  **3.** Place of publication, publisher, and date of publication

  Salle, Blake. "New Trends in Software." *The Latest Technology.* New York: Dial, 2010.

  Saperstein, Morris. *Software for Your PC.* Chicago: Mason, 2009.

• **Format for Parenthetical Citation Within Report:** This is an abbreviated form of the full citation that will appear in your works-cited list at the end of the report. Include only the last name of the author, editor, translator, or responsible group, followed by a page reference.

  (Salle, 284)        (Saperstein, 118–119)

Name _____ Date _____ Assignment _____

# Apply the Standard

**A.** Each of these titles needs punctuation and capitalization. On the line, rewrite each one correctly.

1. **a newspaper:** the seattle times ........................................................................................

2. **a magazine article:** fossils found under the sea .................................................................

3. **a novel:** tender is the night ...........................................................................................

4. **a poem:** love is in the air .............................................................................................

5. **a CD:** songs from my childhood .....................................................................................

6. **a short story:** over the river and through the woods ...........................................................

7. **an Internet Web page:** rulers of ancient rome .................................................................

8. **a play:** voices within history ........................................................................................

**B.** On the lines provided, write a works-cited entry for each of these items. Be sure to use underlines, quotation marks, capitalization, and the appropriate format for each entry.

1. **an article:** native animals of new zealand, authored by Bev Nesbitt. It appears in a book titled endangered animals, which was published in 2010 in New York by Winstead.

........................................................................................................................

........................................................................................................................

2. **a novel:** a forgotten moment in time, published by Dole in 2010 in Chicago, and authored by Ron Nash

........................................................................................................................

........................................................................................................................

3. **a poem:** wandering beneath a starry night, which appears in a book titled the best poems of 2009. The poem is by Martha Strohl, and the book was published by Anchor in 2010 in Boston.

........................................................................................................................

........................................................................................................................

# Language 4a

---

**4a.** Determine or clarify the meaning of unknown and multiple-meaning words and phrases based on *grades 9–10 reading and content,* choosing flexibly from a range of strategies.

- Use context (e.g., the overall meaning of a sentence, paragraph, or text; a word's position or function in a sentence) as a clue to the meaning of a word or phrase.

---

## Explanation

Many words in the English language have more than one meaning. For example, the word *present* might be a noun that means "gift," an adjective that means "here" or "not absent," or a verb that means "to give something to somebody." When you come to a word with multiple meanings in your reading, look for context clues that will help you to figure out which meaning the author intended. Words and phrases surrounding the word may help, as well as the word's position or function in the sentence. Finally, the overall meaning of the sentence, or the main idea of the paragraph, might also provide clues.

## Examples

**Clues in Nearby Words and Phrases** Examples of this type of context clue include:

- **Restatement or definition:** The meaning of the word may be restated in other ways. *Use a chain saw to cut the large **branch**, or limb.* (*Branch* might mean "a tree limb" or "a local office," such as a *branch bank.* Clues show that the author is using the first meaning here.)

- **Opposite or contrast:** An antonym or a contrasting phrase may provide clues. *I'd like to change out of these **plain** clothes into something fancy for the party.* (Clues show that *plain* means "ordinary" in this sentence. It does not mean "a flat area of land.")

- **Illustration or example:** The context may provide an illustration or example clues. *If you want to donate some **change** to the charity, here are some dimes and quarters.* (The clues show that, in this sentence, *change* means "coins." It is not being used as a verb that means "to become different.")

**Clues in the Word's Function in the Sentence** If the word modifies a noun, it is an adjective. If it follows an article or an adjective, it is probably a noun. If it expresses action, it is a verb. If it modifies a verb, it is an adverb. Use this information to help you to determine the word's intended meaning.

*The **digest** provided a shortened version of the original article.* (*Digest* follows an article. Therefore, it is acting, in this instance, as a noun. This information, as well as clues in the sentence, show that the word means "a summary." In this sentence, it is not being used as a verb meaning "to break down food into a form that can be used by the body.")

**Clues in the Overall Meaning of the Sentence or Passage** Think about the overall meaning of the sentence or the main idea of the paragraph. Often the overall meaning will provide context clues.

*After that strenuous exercise, she felt a soreness in her right **calf**.* (*Calf* might mean "a young cow" or "a part of the leg." The overall meaning of this sentence shows that it means "a part of the leg.")

**REMEMBER:** If you are still unsure of a word's meaning after studying context clues, consult a dictionary.

Name _____ Date _____ Assignment _____

# Apply the Standard

**A.** Use context clues to choose a multiple-meaning word from the list that makes sense in each sentence. Write the word on the line. You will use some words more than once.

*broke    lock    positive    horn    panel    spare*

1. Which __ does he play? Is it a trumpet or a trombone? .................................................

2. Careless spending made the man totally __. ..............................................................

3. Are you __ that you mailed my letter? I doubt that you remembered. ...........................

4. A __ of experts will discuss the pros and cons of adopting the amendment. ..................

5. The soothing music had a very __ effect on the weary travelers. .................................

6. Be sure to __ the front door at night. .......................................................................

7. Jan and I were content until Jack decided to __ in on our conversation. ........................

8. There was a __ of beautiful auburn hair in my grandmother's scrapbook. .....................

9. Could you possibly __ a dollar? I will pay you back tomorrow. .....................................

10. Who __ the news to Mary about the surprise party? I thought it was a secret. .............

**B.** Use context clues to determine the meaning of the underlined multiple-meaning word in each sentence. Write your definition on the line.

1. Dr. Kohli opened her medical <u>practice</u> in the new building. .....................................

2. Dad cooked the chicken on a <u>spit</u> over charcoal on the grill. .....................................

3. Please <u>voice</u> your opinions at the end of my presentation. ........................................

4. Do you have anything to add that is <u>relative</u> to our conversation? .............................

5. Is he a real, professional doctor or a foolish <u>quack</u>? ................................................

6. What's wrong with your computer? Is it a <u>hardware</u> problem? ...................................

7. The crowd buzzed with <u>electricity</u> when the singer appeared. ...................................

8. I was really <u>touched</u> by your thoughtful note. .........................................................

9. Her new style of dress was more <u>jazzy</u> than her plain, solid colors. ...........................

10. I'd like to <u>pose</u> a question to the manager of the store. ..........................................

# Language 4b

> **4b.** Determine or clarify the meaning of unknown and multiple-meaning words and phrases based on *grades 9–10 reading and content,* choosing flexibly from a range of strategies.
>
> • Identify and correctly use patterns of word changes that indicate different meanings of parts of speech (e.g., *analyze, analysis, analytical; advocate, advocacy*).

## Explanation

When you come to an unfamiliar word in your reading, try breaking the word into its parts. Look for **affixes,** word parts that are added to a root or base word in order to change its meaning. There are two kinds of affixes—**prefixes,** which are attached *before* the root or base word, and **suffixes,** which are attached *after* the root or base word. Knowing the meanings of suffixes is important because suffixes determine both the meaning and the part of speech of the root or base word.

## Examples

This chart shows the meanings and specific functions of some common suffixes.

| Suffix | Function | Meaning | Example |
|--------|----------|---------|---------|
| *-ance* | changes root or base word to noun | "act, fact, or condition" | *utterance, reluctance* |
| *-ful* | changes root or base word to adjective | "full of, marked by" | *masterful* |
| *-like* | changes root or base word to adjective | "like" | *dreamlike* |
| *-ery* | changes root or base word to noun | "skill," "action," or "collection" | *jewelry, archery* |
| *-ous* | changes root or base word to adjective | "marked by" or "given to" | *famous, grievous* |
| *-ic* | changes root or base word to noun or adjective | "caused by," "dealing with" | *volcanic* |
| *-ible* | changes root or base word to adjective | "able," "likely" | *flexible* |
| *-fy* | changes root or base word to verb | "make," "cause" | *fortify* |
| *-ize* | changes root or base word to verb | "make," "cause to be" | *sterilize* |
| *-ness* | changes root or base word to noun | "quality," "state" | *shortness* |
| *-ation* | changes root or base word to noun | "action," "state," or "result" | *occupation, sanitation* |

Name _____ Date _____ Assignment _____

# Apply the Standard

**A.** Write the part of speech and the meaning of each underlined word.

1. To show their <u>resistance</u> to the king's unfair command, the villagers refused to pay taxes.

   Part of Speech: ................................... Meaning: ...................................

2. The gentleman with perfect manners was quite <u>chivalrous</u>.

   Part of Speech: ................................... Meaning: ...................................

3. On Memorial Day, the mayor made a speech to <u>glorify</u> our city's war heroes.

   Part of Speech: ................................... Meaning: ...................................

4. Let's come up with a <u>sensible</u> plan for solving this problem.

   Part of Speech: ................................... Meaning: ...................................

5. The Battle of Antietam was one of the bloodiest and most <u>horrific</u> events of the Civil War.

   Part of Speech: ................................... Meaning: ...................................

6. The dancer was <u>furious</u> when she discovered that her costume was not ready for the performance.

   Part of Speech: ................................... Meaning: ...................................

7. The dinner plates were made out of heavy, colorful <u>crockery</u>.

   Part of Speech: ................................... Meaning: ...................................

8. Horses were used less and less after we learned how to <u>motorize</u> vehicles.

   Part of Speech: ................................... Meaning: ...................................

**B.** Follow the directions to change each word from one part of speech to another.

1. Add a suffix to the verb *starve* to make it a noun. ...................................

2. Add a suffix to the verb *resent* to make it an adjective. ...................................

3. Add a suffix to the noun *angel* to make it an adjective. ...................................

4. Add a suffix to the noun *adventure* to make it an adjective. ...................................

5. Add a suffix to the adjective *tranquil* to make it a verb. ...................................

6. Add a suffix to the adjective *happy* to make it a noun. ...................................

# Language 4c

4c. Determine or clarify the meaning of unknown and multiple-meaning words and phrases based on *grades 9–10 reading and content,* choosing flexibly from a range of strategies.

- Consult general and specialized reference materials (e.g., dictionaries, glossaries, thesauruses), both print and digital, to find the pronunciation of a word or determine or clarify its precise meaning, its part of speech, or its etymology.

## Explanation

A **dictionary** is an alphabetical listing of all words. Each dictionary entry usually includes the definition, pronunciation, part of speech, and etymology of a word. A **thesaurus** provides synonyms and often antonyms for many words. Use a thesaurus when writing to increase your vocabulary or to find alternative words to express your precise meaning. Your library or classroom has dictionaries and thesauruses, or you can access them online.

## Examples

Notice the information this dictionary entry includes for the word *valiant.*

**val • iant** (val'-yənt) *adj.* [L *valere,* to be strong] **1** full of or characterized by valor or courage; brave **2** resolute; determined [made a *valiant* effort]

- A space or black dot inserted in the entry word indicates where the **syllables** break.

- Letters and symbols in parentheses show the word's **pronunciation.** Note the stress mark that indicates which syllable is stressed (VAL iant).

- The abbreviation *adj.* tells the **part of speech.** *Valiant* is an adjective. Other abbreviations used include *n.* (noun), *v.* (verb), and *adv.* (adverb).

- The word's **etymology,** or origin, often will appear in brackets. *Valiant* comes from the Latin word *valere,* which means "to be strong."

- The word's **definition** follows. If there is more than one definition for the word, each is numbered. Sometimes an example phrase or sentence appears to show how the word is used.

Now notice what this thesaurus entry for the word *valiant* includes.

**valiant** *adj.* **1.** bold, brave, chivalrous, courageous, dauntless, fearless, gallant, game, gritty, gutsy, heroic, high-spirited, lion-hearted, noble, steadfast

> *Antonyms:* afraid, cowardly

> **2.** determined, decided, dogged, firm, fixed, immutable, intent upon, purposeful, resolute

> *Antonyms:* cautious, irresolute, undecided, wishy-washy

Name _____ Date _____ Assignment _____

## Apply the Standard

Use the information in these dictionary and thesaurus entries to answer the questions.

## Dictionary entry:

fi • nal (fīn'-əl) *adj.* [L *finis,* end] **1** of or coming at the end; last; concluding [the *final* verse] **2** leaving no opportunity for further discussion or changes [my *final* decision]

## Thesaurus entry:

**final *adj.***

**1.** closing, concluding, ending, finishing, last, terminal, terminating, ultimate

*Antonyms:* beginning, commencing, first, opening, starting

**2.** absolute, conclusive, definitive, incontrovertible, irrefutable, settled,

*Antonyms:* continuing, debatable, inconclusive, on the table, refutable, temporary

1. Which syllable in *final* is the stressed syllable? ........................................................

2. What part of speech is *final*? ............................................................

3. From what language did *final* come, and what did the original word mean? ........................................

4. Why are the two dictionary definitions followed by material in brackets? ........................................

5. Which dictionary definition (1 or 2) relates to the use of *final* in this sentence?

   *Gary was really proud to get an A on his* <u>final</u> *exam.* ........................................

6. Use the other definition of *final* in an original sentence that shows its meaning.

   ........................................................................................................

7. Why does the thesaurus entry for *final* contain two numbered sections? ........................................

8. Rewrite the sentence below, using an appropriate synonym for *final* found in the thesaurus.

   *No one can make changes to the final plan that we agreed to follow.*

   ........................................................................................................

9. Rewrite the sentence below, using an appropriate synonym for *final* found in the thesaurus.

   *Tonight I will read the final chapter of the novel.*

   ........................................................................................................

10. Select an antonym for *final* from the thesaurus entry above. Use that antonym in a sentence that clearly shows its meaning.

    ........................................................................................................

# Language 4d

> **4d. Determine or clarify the meaning of unknown and multiple-meaning words and phrases based on grades 9–10 reading and content, choosing flexibly from a range of strategies.**
>
> • **Verify the preliminary determination of the meaning of a word or phrase (e.g., by checking the inferred meaning in context or in a dictionary).**

## Explanation

When you come to an unfamiliar word in your reading, look for **context clues** to figure out its meaning. Some clues might appear in nearby words or phrases or in the surrounding sentences. Others might be found in the unknown word's function in the sentence or in the overall meaning of the sentence or passage. Finally, you might find clues in the meaning of a word's root, prefix, or suffix. If you require further assistance, consult a dictionary.

## Examples

**Clues in nearby words and phrases:** Examples of this type of context clue include:

**Opposite or contrast:** *Before he won, Ben was modest, but now he's really <u>pompous.</u>*

(The clues suggest that *pompous* means "self-important" or "pretentious.")

**Example:** *The forest was green year-round due to the <u>conifers,</u> including pine trees and hemlocks.*

(The clues suggest that a *conifer* is an evergreen tree that bears cones.)

**Clues in the word's function in the sentence:** If the word is modified by an adjective, it is a noun. If it modifies a verb, it is an adverb. If it provides details about a person, place, or thing, it is an adjective.

*A <u>sumptuous</u> spread of food covered the buffet table from one end to the other.*

(*Sumptuous* is an adjective modifying "spread of food." *Sumptuous* means "huge or splendid.")

**Clues in the overall meaning of the sentence or passage:** Reread the passage to clarify and then read ahead to seek further context clues.

*A witness can <u>corroborate</u> the man's claim that he was not present at the crime scene.*

(The overall meaning of the sentence suggests that *corroborate* means "confirm" or "support.")

**Clues in the word's root or affixes:** You know the meanings of many roots, prefixes, and suffixes. Use that knowledge to unlock the meaning of an unfamiliar word.

*The poet's public life was quiet, but his private life was <u>scandalous.</u>*

(The suffix *-ous* means "marked by," and the word *scandal* means "a public outrage." Those clues suggest that *scandalous* means "outrageous" or "shocking.")

Name _____ Date _____ Assignment _____

# Apply the Standard

**A.** Use context clues to find the meaning of the underlined word or phrase. Write its definition on the line.

1. Did he tell the truth, or did he <u>prevaricate</u>? ................................................

2. As a <u>mariner</u>, my grandfather worked on many seagoing vessels. .....................

3. The souvenir shop sold inexpensive figurines, postcards, pennants, and other <u>sundries</u>.

...........................................................................................................

4. I think that "Little Guy" is a funny <u>misnomer</u> for that huge dog! ........................

5. Our team has many tough rivals, but our real <u>nemesis</u> is the Oak High team.

...........................................................................................................

6. I wanted an elegant costume for the party; by contrast, this chicken suit is <u>ludicrous</u>.

...........................................................................................................

7. The magician Harry Houdini was able to <u>extricate</u> himself from locked safes.

...........................................................................................................

8. I shop at sales, use coupons at the supermarket, and use other <u>frugal</u> practices.

...........................................................................................................

9. The lazy man <u>feigned</u> a sore back so that he wouldn't have to work very hard.

...........................................................................................................

10. At 94, Mrs. Ames says that her <u>longevity</u> is the result of a healthy lifestyle. ...........

**B.** Use context clues and clues in the word's function in the sentence, as well as in any prefixes, suffixes, or roots, to define the underlined word. Write the definition on the line.

1. No job is <u>unattainable</u> if you work hard and are determined. ...............................

2. Its dry, scaly skin made the movie monster look quite <u>reptilian</u>. ...........................

3. The child's behavior was <u>inexcusable</u>, and the babysitter was forced to punish him.

...........................................................................................................

4. My lack of natural rhythm is a <u>hindrance</u> when I try to dance. ...............................

5. After coming up to the surface, the submarine <u>resubmerged</u>. ...............................

# Language 5a

> **5a. Demonstrate understanding of figurative language, word relationships, and nuances in word meanings.**
> - **Interpret figures of speech (euphemism, oxymoron) in context and analyze their role in the text.**

## Explanation

**Figurative language** is language that is not meant to be taken literally. It includes several different **figures of speech.** They are literary devices that make unexpected comparisons or change the usual meaning of words. These figures of speech include similes, metaphors, personification, paradox, symbols, euphemism, and oxymoron.

To interpret figurative language, consider the context in which it is set. What is the author trying to express? How does the figure of speech help you better understand what is being described? What additional feeling or meaning does it convey?

## Examples

- A **simile** compares two unlike things using *like* or *as*.
  *He swims **like a fish.** The cave was **as dark as night.***

- A **metaphor** compares two unlike things by stating that one thing *is* another.
  *Her **expression is a window** into her deepest feelings.*

- **Personification** gives human characteristics to an object, animal, or idea.
  *The **alarm clock kept nagging** me to get out of bed.*

- A **symbol** is an object, person, animal, place, or image that represents something other than itself.
  *To me, **the ocean represents energy and freedom.***

- A **paradox** is an expression of two contradictory ideas that reveals a truth.
  *Twyla Tharp said, **"Art is the only way to run away without leaving home."***

- An **oxymoron** is similar to a paradox, although it is usually very brief—often just two or three words that express contradictory ideas.
  *new tradition*     *jumbo shrimp*     *vegetarian meatball*

- **Euphemism** is a soft way of expressing difficult, embarrassing, unpleasant, or tragic ideas.
  *a **restroom** (instead of "toilet room") a **cul de sac** (instead of "a dead end street")*

# Apply the Standard

**A.** On the line preceding each sentence, identify the type of figurative language that the underlined phrase represents. Write *simile, metaphor, personification, symbol, paradox, oxymoron,* or *euphemism.*

.................................. **1.** I don't like this hat because it is <u>pretty ugly</u>.

.................................. **2.** Many people feel that their <u>home is their castle</u>.

.................................. **3.** My <u>dog promised me</u> that he would save some time for a long walk with me.

.................................. **4.** A coded message both <u>increases communication and decreases communication</u>.

.................................. **5.** My grandfather said that he and his friend Ed are <u>as old as the hills</u>.

.................................. **6.** The judge sentenced the man to four years in a <u>correctional facility</u>.

.................................. **7.** After the argument, Laurie extended <u>the olive branch</u> to Josh by apologizing.

**B.** Write *simile, metaphor, personification, symbol, paradox, oxymoron,* or *euphemism* to identify each figure of speech. Then interpret each figure of speech by using your own words to tell what it means.

    *Example:* Inviting me to lunch was <u>awfully nice</u> of you.

        **Type:** oxymoron      **Interpretation:** It was very nice.

1. General Josephs <u>passed away</u> last night at the age of 94.

**Type:** ......................................    **Interpretation:** ......................................

2. The field was <u>as flat as a pancake</u>.

**Type:** ......................................    **Interpretation:** ......................................

3. His angry <u>words were a thorn in my side</u>.

**Type:** ......................................    **Interpretation:** ......................................

4. She had a <u>numb feeling</u> in her foot.

**Type:** ......................................    **Interpretation:** ......................................

5. As we grow older, we understand that <u>change is the only constant</u> in our lives.

**Type:** ......................................    **Interpretation:** ......................................

# Language 5b

> **5b.** Demonstrate understanding of figurative language, word relationships, and nuances in word meanings.
>
> • **Analyze nuances in the meaning of words with similar denotations.**

## Explanation

A word's **denotation** is its dictionary meaning, independent of other associations that the word may have. By contrast, a word's **connotations** are the ideas, emotions, or feelings associated with that word. A word's connotations might be positive, negative, or neutral.

## Examples

This chart shows five words that share the same denotation but have different connotations.

| Word | Denotation | Connotation | Example Sentence |
|---|---|---|---|
| **1.** big | large | **1.** large (neutral) | **1.** *Harry is a big dog.* |
| **2.** generous | | **2.** more than enough (positive) | **2.** *We have a generous supply of refreshments for the party.* |
| **3.** monstrous | | **3.** over-sized or too much (negative) | **3.** *The roads were clogged by a monstrous amount of snow.* |
| **4.** great | | **4.** impressively large (positive) | **4.** *A great amount of applause followed her solo.* |
| **5.** sufficient | | **5.** enough (positive) | **5.** *They had a sufficient amount of staff members to complete the job effectively.* |
| **6.** ponderous | | **6.** too large or unwieldy, due to weight or volume (negative) | **6.** *The movie star hired a secretary to take care of the ponderous amount of fan mail she received.* |

Name _____  Date _____  Assignment _____

# Apply the Standard

**A.** Use context clues and what you know about the meanings of words to tell whether the underlined word has a neutral, positive, or negative connotation. Circle your answer.

**1.** *neutral positive negative*  Tonight we will <u>dine</u> at seven o'clock.

**2.** *neutral positive negative*  Alice had a <u>minor</u> role in the play.

**3.** *neutral positive negative*  I was <u>aware</u> of someone knocking on the door late at night.

**4.** *neutral positive negative*  I was <u>on guard</u> for someone knocking on the door late at night.

**5.** *neutral positive negative*  I was <u>wary</u> of someone knocking on the door late at night.

**6.** *neutral positive negative*  It was a <u>remarkable</u> type of party.

**B.** Each item lists words with the same denotation but different connotations. On the line, write *neutral, positive,* or *negative* to identify each word's connotation. Then use each word in a sentence that makes its connotation clear.

**1. Denotation:** asked

    **a.** demanded            **Connotation:** ...........................................

**Sentence:** ...........................................

    **b.** requested            **Connotation:** ...........................................

**Sentence:** ...........................................

    **c.** questioned          **Connotation:** ...........................................

**Sentence:** ...........................................

**2. Denotation:** smart

    **a.** intelligent           **Connotation:** ...........................................

**Sentence:** ...........................................

    **b.** sly                    **Connotation:** ...........................................

**Sentence:** ...........................................

    **c.** wise                  **Connotation:** ...........................................

**Sentence:** ...........................................

# Language 6

> Acquire and use accurately general academic vocabulary and domain-specific words and phrases, sufficient for reading, writing, speaking, and listening at the college and career readiness level; demonstrate independence in gathering vocabulary knowledge when considering a word or phrase important to comprehension or expression.

## Explanation

In each of your classes, you frequently use many academic and domain-specific vocabulary words and phrases.

- **Academic words** are those that you use every day to distinguish between facts and opinions, analyze a table or graph, solve a math problem, and so on. Examples include *infer*, *differentiate*, *summarize*, and *evaluate*.

- **Domain-specific words** are words that are specific to a particular course of study. In a social studies course, examples include *equatorial*, *cultural*, and *longitude*. In a math course, examples include *hypotenuse*, *circumference*, and *denominator*.

Understanding the definitions of academic and domain-specific words and using them frequently will help you to complete assignments correctly and express your ideas clearly.

## Examples

In many of your courses, you are asked to complete tasks based on specific academic words and phrases. And, on many tests, you are asked to write essays that fulfill directions containing academic words and phrases. Here are examples:

*Support your opinion* with. . .          *Explain the relationship* between . . .

*Paraphrase* the theme of . . .          *Analyze* the causes and effects of . . .

*Create a graph to represent* . . .          *Discuss the relevance* of . . .

In a literature and writing course, you use many **domain-specific words and phrases.** Here are examples:

| | | | |
|---|---|---|---|
| oxymoron | mood | analogy | flashback |
| resolution | rhythm | character | genre |

Name _____ Date _____ Assignment _____

# Apply the Standard

**A.** Match each domain-specific word or phrase with its definition. Write the letter of the definition on the line provided.

........................................ **1.** onomatopoeia     **a.** a brief story about an interesting or amusing event

........................................ **2.** epiphany     **b.** the use of words that imitate sounds

........................................ **3.** irony     **c.** a character's sudden flash of insight into a conflict or situation

........................................ **4.** anecdote     **d.** a character or force in conflict with the main character

........................................ **5.** antagonist     **e.** a technique portraying differences between expectations and actual results

**B.** These sentences include academic words and phrases. Circle the letter of the phrase that will correctly complete each sentence.

**1.** *Bias* is a point of view that ........................................ .

    **a.** is often revealed in the third person     **c.** a person has before the facts are known

    **b.** reveals the theme of the story     **d.** is in direct contrast to that of the antagonist

**2.** A *discourse* is ........................................ .

    **a.** part of the exposition     **c.** a conflict between two or more characters

    **b.** a persuasive technique     **d.** an ongoing communication of ideas

**3.** *Subjective* statements are based on or influenced by ........................................ .

    **a.** oral traditions     **c.** popular culture

    **b.** a person's feelings or point of view     **d.** figurative language, particularly metaphors

**4.** To *discern* means to ........................................ .

    **a.** paraphrase a main idea     **c.** analyze the parts of an argument

    **b.** use facts to defend an opinion     **d.** understand the differences between things

**5.** To *evolve* is to ........................................ .

    **a.** develop through gradual changes     **c.** go back in time to establish a story's background

    **b.** anticipate or predict future events     **d.** arrive at the point of highest tension

# Performance Tasks

Name _____ Date _____ Assignment _____

# Performance Task 1A

> **Literature 1  Cite strong and thorough textual evidence to support analysis of what the text says explicitly as well as inferences drawn from the text.***

## Task: Support Analysis of a Text

Write a response to literature in which you use paraphrasing or direct quotations to support your analysis of a literary text.  As part of your response, explain what the text says explicitly, as well as any inferences or conclusions you have drawn.

### Tips for Success

Write a response to a literary selection you have read. In your response, include these elements:

✓ a thesis statement that succinctly sums up your response to the literary work

✓ an analysis of the work's content

✓ strong and thorough evidence from the text that explicitly supports your analysis

✓ inferences from the text that support your analysis

✓ language that is formal, precise, and follows the rules of standard English

### Rubric for Self-Assessment

| Criteria for Success | not very          very |
|---|---|
| How clear and succinct is your thesis statement? | 1    2    3    4    5    6 |
| How thoroughly have you analyzed the text? | 1    2    3    4    5    6 |
| How successful are you at including at least three or more quotes, paraphrases, or facts from the text to support your analysis? | 1    2    3    4    5    6 |
| How successfully have you supported your ideas with inferences from your reading? | 1    2    3    4    5    6 |
| How successful is your use of standard English? | 1    2    3    4    5    6 |
| How successfully have you used a formal style and created an appropriate tone for your audience? | 1    2    3    4    5    6 |

* Other standards covered include: Writing 9a, Writing 10, Speaking 6, Language 6.

For use with Literature 1

Name _____ Date _____ Assignment _____

# Performance Task 1B

> **Speaking and Listening 1** Initiate and participate effectively in a range of collaborative discussions (one-on-one, in groups, and teacher-led) with diverse partners on grades 9–10 topics, texts, and issues, building on others' ideas and expressing your own clearly and persuasively.

## Task: Discuss the Responses to a Text

Work one-on-one with a partner to clearly and persuasively present your responses to a literary text. Respond thoughtfully to each other's point of view and build upon each other's comments.

### Tips for Success

Participate in a one-on-one discussion about a response to a literary text. Follow these tips for success:

- ✓ prepare by reading the literary text and taking notes
- ✓ work with a partner to formulate discussion guidelines for equal and full participation
- ✓ develop questions that will evoke further discussion from your partner and propel the discussion forward in order to fully explore the work
- ✓ present your inferences from the text that support your viewpoint
- ✓ summarize your responses and those of your partner

### Rubric for Self-Assessment

| Criteria for Discussion | not very | | | | | very |
|---|---|---|---|---|---|---|
| How clearly and persuasively did you present your ideas about the text? | 1 | 2 | 3 | 4 | 5 | 6 |
| How successful were you in establishing guidelines for the discussion? | 1 | 2 | 3 | 4 | 5 | 6 |
| How well did the discussion guidelines ensure that both participants participated fully and equally? | 1 | 2 | 3 | 4 | 5 | 6 |
| How effectively did your questions help to explore the points of view presented? | 1 | 2 | 3 | 4 | 5 | 6 |
| How successfully did you build upon the comments of your partner? | 1 | 2 | 3 | 4 | 5 | 6 |
| How well did the discussion summarize the main perspectives of you and your partner? | 1 | 2 | 3 | 4 | 5 | 6 |

For use with Speaking and Listening 1

Name _____ Date _____ Assignment _____

# Performance Task 2A

> **Literature 2   Determine a theme or central idea of a text and analyze in detail its development over the course of the text, including how it emerges and is shaped and refined by specific details; provide an objective summary of the text.\***

## Task: Identify Theme

Write an essay in which you discuss the theme of a literary text. Include in your essay an objective summary of the work. Also include a thesis statement about the theme and how it develops through events and details in the text. Provide evidence from the text to support your thesis.

### Tips for Success

Write an essay about theme that includes both a summary and an argument in which you present your ideas about the work's theme. As you draft your essay, include the following:

- ✓ details about important events in the work and characters' responses to the events

- ✓ an objective summary of what happens in the work, not your opinions or judgments

- ✓ a clear, succinct statement of the work's theme

- ✓ key details from the text that show how the theme is developed

- ✓ language that is formal, precise, and follows the rules of standard English

### Rubric for Self-Assessment

| Criteria for Success | not very | | | | | very |
|---|---|---|---|---|---|---|
| How objective and concise is your summary of the work? | 1 | 2 | 3 | 4 | 5 | 6 |
| How clear is your statement of the work's theme? | 1 | 2 | 3 | 4 | 5 | 6 |
| How successfully do you identify key details from the text that show development of the theme? | 1 | 2 | 3 | 4 | 5 | 6 |
| How effectively do you use those details to support your analysis of the theme? | 1 | 2 | 3 | 4 | 5 | 6 |
| How successful is your use of standard English? | 1 | 2 | 3 | 4 | 5 | 6 |
| How successfully have you used a formal style and created an appropriate tone for your audience? | 1 | 2 | 3 | 4 | 5 | 6 |

\* Other standards covered include: Writing 2a, Writing 2b, Writing 2d, Writing 3e, Writing 4, Speaking 6, Language 3.

**For use with Literature 2**

Name _____ Date _____ Assignment _____

# Performance Task 2B

> **Speaking and Listening 4** Present information, findings, and supporting evidence clearly, concisely, and logically such that listeners can follow the line of reasoning, and the organization, development, substance, and style are appropriate to purpose, audience, and task.

## Task: Make a Presentation to a Small Group

Adapt a written analysis of a literary text and present it to a small group of classmates. Organize your analysis logically and create a style of presentation that suits your purpose and audience. Listen thoughtfully and respectfully as other members of the group present their analyses.

### Tips for Success

Present a literary analysis to a small group and listen as others present their analyses. Follow these tips for success:

✓ adapt an existing literary analysis to suit an audience of peers

✓ with group members, develop guidelines for presentations

✓ create a presentation format that is logical and easy for listeners to comprehend

✓ allow time for feedback from the audience in the form of questions or comments

✓ pay close attention as other group members make their presentations

### Rubric for Self-Assessment

| Criteria for Discussion | not very | | | | | very |
|---|---|---|---|---|---|---|
| How logical and clear was your presentation? | 1 | 2 | 3 | 4 | 5 | 6 |
| To what extent did your presentation suit your purpose and audience? | 1 | 2 | 3 | 4 | 5 | 6 |
| Based on feedback from group members, how well did you present your information? | 1 | 2 | 3 | 4 | 5 | 6 |
| How fully were you able to answer questions asked by other group members? | 1 | 2 | 3 | 4 | 5 | 6 |
| How successful were the guidelines agreed upon by the group? | 1 | 2 | 3 | 4 | 5 | 6 |
| How well were you able to follow and respond to the presentations of other group members? | 1 | 2 | 3 | 4 | 5 | 6 |

For use with Speaking and Listening 4

Name _____ Date _____ Assignment _____

# Performance Task 3A

> **Literature 3** Analyze how complex characters (e.g., those with multiple or conflicting motivations) develop over the course of a text, interact with other characters, and advance the plot or develop the theme.*

## Task: Analyze Character

Write an analysis of a complex character from one of the literary selections you have read. Use evidence from the text to support your conclusions.

### Tips for Success

Write a character analysis based on a literary selection you have read. In your analysis, include these elements:

✓ a clear thesis statement that sums up your analysis of the character

✓ a description of both direct and indirect characterization in the literary selection

✓ a discussion of the character's motivations

✓ analysis of how the nature of the character shapes the theme of the work

✓ evidence from the text that explicitly supports the analysis you present

✓ inferences from the text that support your analysis

✓ language that is formal, precise, and follows the rules of standard English

### Rubric for Self-Assessment

| Criteria for Success | not very | | | | | very |
|---|---|---|---|---|---|---|
| How clear is your thesis statement? | 1 | 2 | 3 | 4 | 5 | 6 |
| How clear a picture of the character have you drawn based on direct and indirect characterization? | 1 | 2 | 3 | 4 | 5 | 6 |
| How complete is your analysis of the character's motivation? | 1 | 2 | 3 | 4 | 5 | 6 |
| How fully have you described the character's influence on theme? | 1 | 2 | 3 | 4 | 5 | 6 |
| How well have you supported your analysis with explicit evidence from the text? | 1 | 2 | 3 | 4 | 5 | 6 |
| How thoroughly have you supported inferences you made? | 1 | 2 | 3 | 4 | 5 | 6 |
| How successful is your use of standard English? | 1 | 2 | 3 | 4 | 5 | 6 |
| How successfully have you used a formal style and created an appropriate tone for your audience? | 1 | 2 | 3 | 4 | 5 | 6 |

* Other standards covered include Writing 2, Writing 9, Writing 10, Speaking 6, Language 1, Language 6

For use with Literature 3

Name _____ Date _____ Assignment _____

# Performance Task 3B

> **Speaking and Listening 1** Initiate and participate effectively in a range of collaborative discussions (one-on-one, in groups, and teacher-led) with diverse partners on grades 9–10 topics, texts, and issues, building on others' ideas and expressing your own clearly and persuasively.

## Task: Discuss the Character Analyses

Participate in a group discussion in which you analyze a character from a literary work and respond thoughtfully to others' viewpoints.

### Tips for Success

Participate in a discussion about a character from a literary work. Follow these tips for success:

- ✓ read or re-read the literary text and take notes on your analysis of the character
- ✓ with group members, develop guidelines for equal and full participation
- ✓ prepare discussion questions that will evoke further comment from participants and propel the discussion forward
- ✓ build on the ideas of others in the group
- ✓ summarize the different character analyses presented by the group

### Rubric for Self-Assessment

| Criteria for Discussion | not very | | | | | very |
|---|---|---|---|---|---|---|
| How thoroughly did each participant analyze the literary work? | 1 | 2 | 3 | 4 | 5 | 6 |
| How clearly and effectively did you present your analysis of character? | 1 | 2 | 3 | 4 | 5 | 6 |
| How well did the discussion guidelines ensure that everyone participated fully and equally? | 1 | 2 | 3 | 4 | 5 | 6 |
| To what extent did participants build on the ideas of others? | 1 | 2 | 3 | 4 | 5 | 6 |
| How effectively did participants offer different perspectives on the characters? | 1 | 2 | 3 | 4 | 5 | 6 |
| How well did the discussion summarize the main perspectives of participants? | 1 | 2 | 3 | 4 | 5 | 6 |

Name _____ Date _____ Assignment _____

# Performance Task 4A

> **Literature 4** Determine the meaning of words and phrases as they are used in the text, including figurative and connotative meanings; analyze the cumulative impact of specific word choices on meaning and tone (e.g., how the language evokes a sense of time and place; how it sets a formal or informal tone).*

## Task: Interpret Figurative Language

Write an essay in response to a literary selection in which you analyze the author's use of figurative language, such as simile, metaphor, and personification, and explain how those language choices help evoke the time and place in which the work is set.

### Tips for Success

Develop a response to a literary selection you have read. In your response, include these elements:

- ✓ a clear thesis statement in which you set forth your main conclusion about the work

- ✓ an analysis of how the author uses figures of speech, including simile, metaphor, and personification

- ✓ an explanation of how the figurative language used in the selection helps to evoke a sense of time and place

- ✓ specific examples of figurative language from the selection that support your thesis

- ✓ language that is formal, precise, and follows the rules of standard English

### Rubric for Self-Assessment

| Criteria for Success | not very | | | | | very |
|---|---|---|---|---|---|---|
| How clear is your thesis statement? | 1 | 2 | 3 | 4 | 5 | 6 |
| How effectively have you identified and analyzed the figurative language used in the selection? | 1 | 2 | 3 | 4 | 5 | 6 |
| How successfully have you explained how the figurative language evokes the time and place of the selection? | 1 | 2 | 3 | 4 | 5 | 6 |
| How well have you used specific examples of figurative language to illustrate and support your thesis? | 1 | 2 | 3 | 4 | 5 | 6 |
| How successful is your use of standard English? | 1 | 2 | 3 | 4 | 5 | 6 |
| How successfully have you used a formal style and created an appropriate tone for your audience? | 1 | 2 | 3 | 4 | 5 | 6 |

\* Other standards covered include: Writing 3, Writing 10, Speaking 6, Language 5, Language 5a, Language 5b

For use with Literature 4

Name _____ Date _____ Assignment _____

# Performance Task 4B

> **Speaking and Listening 6** Adapt speech to a variety of contexts and tasks, demonstrating command of formal English when indicated or appropriate.

## Task: Use Figurative Language

Participate in a group activity in which you describe a person, place, or event using figurative language. Then, ask other group members to "translate" your description into formal, expository English. Afterwards, listen to and translate the descriptions presented by others.

### Tips for Success

Participate in a group activity in which you use figurative language. Follow these tips for success:

- ✓ review how authors use figures of speech, analogies, and other figurative language to create imagery in their work

- ✓ with group members, create discussion guidelines for equal and full participation

- ✓ allow time for other group members to discuss and "translate" your description

- ✓ give attention to other members of the group as they present, noting how their translations altered the impact of the description

### Rubric for Self-Assessment

| Criteria for Discussion | not very | | | | | very |
|---|---|---|---|---|---|---|
| How vivid and effective was your description? | 1 | 2 | 3 | 4 | 5 | 6 |
| How vivid and effective were the descriptions presented by the group? | 1 | 2 | 3 | 4 | 5 | 6 |
| How well did the guidelines ensure that everyone participated fully and equally? | 1 | 2 | 3 | 4 | 5 | 6 |
| How successful were participants in translating the figurative language into expository English? | 1 | 2 | 3 | 4 | 5 | 6 |
| How successful were you in noting the way the change in language altered the nature of the descriptions? | 1 | 2 | 3 | 4 | 5 | 6 |

Name _____ Date _____ Assignment _____

# Performance Task 5A

Literature 5   Analyze how an author's choices concerning how to structure a text, order events within it (e.g., parallel plots), and manipulate time (e.g., pacing, flashbacks) create such effects as mystery, tension, or surprise.*

## Task: Analyze Text Structure

Write an essay about a literary selection that uses a plot device, such as flashback, foreshadowing, or parallel plots, and explain how the author uses the device to create mystery, tension, or surprise.

### Tips for Success

Write an essay about the use of plot devices in a literary selection you have read. In your essay, include these elements:

   ✓ a clear thesis statement that sums up your analysis of the author's use of plot devices

   ✓ a brief, objective summary of the events in the story

   ✓ a discussion of how the plot's resolution is affected by the use of plot devices

   ✓ evidence from the text that explicitly supports your thesis

   ✓ inferences from the text that support your thesis

   ✓ language that is formal, precise, and follows the rules of standard English

### Rubric for Self-Assessment

| Criteria for Success | not very            very | | | | | |
|---|---|---|---|---|---|---|
| How clear is your thesis statement? | 1 | 2 | 3 | 4 | 5 | 6 |
| How objective and concise is your summary of the text? | 1 | 2 | 3 | 4 | 5 | 6 |
| How well have you analyzed the effect of stylistic devices on the resolution of the plot? | 1 | 2 | 3 | 4 | 5 | 6 |
| How well have you supported your thesis with evidence from the text? | 1 | 2 | 3 | 4 | 5 | 6 |
| How well have you supported your thesis with inferences you made during reading? | 1 | 2 | 3 | 4 | 5 | 6 |
| How successful is your use of standard English? | 1 | 2 | 3 | 4 | 5 | 6 |
| How successfully have you used a formal style and created an appropriate tone for your audience? | 1 | 2 | 3 | 4 | 5 | 6 |

* Other standards covered include: Writing 1a, Writing 1e, Writing 6, Writing 10, Speaking 5, Language 3

For use with Literature 5

Name _____ Date _____ Assignment _____

# Performance Task 5B

Speaking and Listening 5  Make strategic use of digital media (e.g., textual, graphical, audio, visual, and interactive elements) in presentations to enhance understanding of findings, reasoning, and evidence and to add interest.

## Task: Adapt a Literary Selection

Participate in a group activity in which you work with others to adapt a literary selection into another medium, such as a comic book, a short animated or live-action film, or a radio-style drama.

### Tips for Success

Participate in a group activity to adapt a literary work. Follow these tips for success:

✓ with group members, identify the literary selection and medium into which it will be adapted

✓ develop guidelines with the group for equal and full participation in the activity, including assignment of tasks and responsibilities

✓ read or re-read the literary text and take notes on key elements

✓ practice and master the technology required for the adaptation

### Rubric for Self-Assessment

| Criteria for Discussion | not very | | | | | very |
|---|---|---|---|---|---|---|
| How well did the guidelines ensure that everyone participated fully and equally? | 1 | 2 | 3 | 4 | 5 | 6 |
| How well had the participants prepared for the activity by reading and taking notes on the selected work? | 1 | 2 | 3 | 4 | 5 | 6 |
| How appropriate was the selected medium for presenting an adaptation of the literary work? | 1 | 2 | 3 | 4 | 5 | 6 |
| How well did the selected medium utilize the skills and talents of the group members? | 1 | 2 | 3 | 4 | 5 | 6 |
| How well did the adaptation present the key elements of the original literary work? | 1 | 2 | 3 | 4 | 5 | 6 |
| How effective was the group's use of technology in adding interest to the presentation? | 1 | 2 | 3 | 4 | 5 | 6 |

Name _____ Date _____ Assignment _____

# Performance Task 6A

Literature 6 **Analyze a particular point of view or cultural experience reflected in a work of literature from outside the United States, drawing on a wide reading of world literature.**

## Task: Write an Essay About Theme

Write an essay about a literary selection that was written outside of the United States. Using information from both the textbook and from outside resources, explain how the work's cultural and historical context help to shape the theme of the selection.

### Tips for Success

Write an essay about a literary selection you have read. In your essay, include these elements:

✓ a clear thesis statement that sums up your analysis of the work

✓ references from three or more carefully chosen and evaluated resources other than the textbook

✓ specific examples from the text that support your analysis

✓ inferences from the text that support your analysis

✓ language that is formal, precise, and follows the rules of standard English

### Rubric for Self-Assessment

| Criteria for Success | not very | | | | | very |
|---|---|---|---|---|---|---|
| How well does your thesis statement explain your analysis of the work? | 1 | 2 | 3 | 4 | 5 | 6 |
| How well have you used at least three or more resources other than the textbook to support your analysis? | 1 | 2 | 3 | 4 | 5 | 6 |
| How well have you supported your analysis with explicit evidence from the text? | 1 | 2 | 3 | 4 | 5 | 6 |
| How successfully have you included inferences you made during reading to support your analysis? | 1 | 2 | 3 | 4 | 5 | 6 |
| How successfully have you used formal and precise English? | 1 | 2 | 3 | 4 | 5 | 6 |

\* Other standards covered include: Reading 2, Writing 7, Writing 8, Writing 9a, Language 3, Speaking and Listening 1, Speaking and Listening 3

For use with Literature 6

Name _____ Date _____ Assignment _____

# Performance Task 6B

> **Speaking and Listening 3** Evaluate a speaker's point of view, reasoning, and use of evidence and rhetoric, identifying any fallacious reasoning or exaggerated or distorted evidence.

## Task: Evaluate a Speech

Review and critique a persuasive speech. Locate a speech online and watch it, taking notes as you watch. Then write a critique in which you evaluate the speaker's point of view and use of evidence and rhetoric. Point out any instances of faulty reasoning or weak and distorted evidence.

### Tips for Success

As you prepare your critique of a persuasive speech, follow these tips for success:

✓ take notes about effective and ineffective aspects of the speech; use the pause and rewind features to allow yourself time to take notes and to review segments of the speech

✓ note ways in which the speaker uses vocal techniques and body language to emphasize key points

✓ prepare a written evaluation of the speech, and organize your main points logically

✓ provide specific details from the speech to support your evaluation

✓ use language that is formal, precise, and follows the rules of standard English

### Rubric for Self-Assessment

| Criteria for Success | not very        very |
|---|---|
| How detailed were the notes you took while watching the speech? | 1  2  3  4  5  6 |
| How clearly did you note the speaker's use of verbal and nonverbal techniques? | 1  2  3  4  5  6 |
| How successful was your analysis of the overall effectiveness of the speech? | 1  2  3  4  5  6 |
| How logically did you present and support your main points? | 1  2  3  4  5  6 |
| How successful were you in using standard English, a formal style, and an appropriate tone? | 1  2  3  4  5  6 |

Name _____ Date _____ Assignment _____

# Performance Task 7A

> **Literature 7** Analyze the representation of a subject or a key scene in two different artistic mediums, including what is emphasized or absent in each treatment (e.g., Auden's "Musée des Beaux Arts" and Breughel's *Landscape with the Fall of Icarus*).\*

## Task: Compare a Scene or Event in Two Artistic Mediums

Write an essay about a literary work and a piece of visual art that present the same subject. In your response, compare how the author creates mood, tells a story, or establishes setting using words with the way the artist creates mood, tells a story, or establishes setting using images and colors.

### Tips for Success

Write an essay about a scene or event that is presented in more than one medium. In your response, include these elements:

- ✓ a description of the scene or event being explored
- ✓ an analysis of the possibilities and limitations of the two artistic mediums
- ✓ specific details that describe the different treatments of the event or scene
- ✓ a clear thesis statement that sums up the conclusions you have drawn
- ✓ specific evidence from both texts to support your thesis
- ✓ language that is formal, precise, and follows the rules of standard English

### Rubric for Self-Assessment

| Criteria for Success | not very       very |
|---|---|
| How well have you analyzed the scene or event presented in the two mediums? | 1  2  3  4  5  6 |
| How successfully have you created one clear statement of the conclusions you have drawn? | 1  2  3  4  5  6 |
| How well have you explained the general possibilities and limitations of the two mediums you analyzed? | 1  2  3  4  5  6 |
| How well have you explained the specific differences in the way each medium represented the subject? | 1  2  3  4  5  6 |
| How well have you supported your conclusion with explicit evidence from both mediums? | 1  2  3  4  5  6 |
| How successfully have you used a formal style and created an appropriate tone for your audience? | 1  2  3  4  5  6 |

\* Other standards covered include: Writing 2a, Writing 2b, Writing 9a, Writing 10, Language 1b, Speaking and Listening 1b, Speaking and Listening 4, Speaking and Listening 5

For use with Literature 7

349

Name _____ Date _____ Assignment _____

# Performance Task 7B

> **Speaking and Listening 4** Present information, findings, and supporting
> evidence clearly, concisely, and logically such that listeners can follow the
> line of reasoning, and the organization, development, substance, and style are
> appropriate to purpose, audience, and task.

## Task: Participate in a Small Group Presentation

Participate in a group activity in which you select a subject that is represented in more than one medium (for example, a short story and a sculpture; a painting and a poem) and create a presentation in which you compare and contrast the two representations.

### Tips for Success

Participate in a group presentation in which two artistic mediums are compared. Follow these tips for success:

- ✓ review both representations thoroughly and take detailed notes
- ✓ develop guidelines with group members for equal and full participation for each person
- ✓ create a thesis statement that all members of the team agree on
- ✓ cite evidence from the works that supports the team's thesis
- ✓ develop presentation materials that help the audience to fully understand the subject presented
- ✓ create a tone that suits the presentation's material and your audience

### Rubric for Self-Assessment

| Criteria for Discussion | not very | | | | | very |
|---|---|---|---|---|---|---|
| How well had the participants thought through their responses to the works before the discussion started? | 1 | 2 | 3 | 4 | 5 | 6 |
| How successful was the team in developing a clear thesis statement? | 1 | 2 | 3 | 4 | 5 | 6 |
| How successful was the team in using evidence from both works to support the thesis statement? | 1 | 2 | 3 | 4 | 5 | 6 |
| How successful was the team in producing materials that enhanced the presentation? | 1 | 2 | 3 | 4 | 5 | 6 |
| How successful was the team in using formal language and an appropriate tone? | 1 | 2 | 3 | 4 | 5 | 6 |

For use with Speaking and Listening 4

Name _____ Date _____ Assignment _____

# Performance Task 8A

> **Literature 9** Analyze how an author draws on and transforms source material in a specific work (e.g., how Shakespeare treats a theme or topic from Ovid or the Bible or how a later author draws on a play by Shakespeare).*

## Task: Write an Essay That Explores Source Material

Write an essay about a literary selection that draws on or transforms source material from another literary work. Analyze the changes that the author made to the characters, plot, or tone of the source material and the effect of that change.

## Tips for Success

Write about a literary work that draws on another literary work and transforms it. In your essay, include these elements:

✓ a clear thesis statement that sums up your analysis

✓ a discussion of the characters, plot, or tone of the source material and how they have been adapted

✓ evidence from the text that explicitly supports your analysis

✓ inferences from the text that support your analysis

✓ an evaluation of the effectiveness of the author's choices and the overall success of the adaptation

✓ language that is formal, precise, and follows the rules of standard English

## Rubric for Self-Assessment

| Criteria for Success | not very | | | | | very |
|---|---|---|---|---|---|---|
| How successfully have you created one clear thesis statement? | 1 | 2 | 3 | 4 | 5 | 6 |
| How deeply have you discussed the characters, plot, or tone of the source material? | 1 | 2 | 3 | 4 | 5 | 6 |
| How well does your analysis address the transformation of the source material into the newer work? | 1 | 2 | 3 | 4 | 5 | 6 |
| How effectively have you used quotes, facts, or ideas from the texts to support your analysis? | 1 | 2 | 3 | 4 | 5 | 6 |
| How well have you supported your thesis with explicit evidence from the text? | 1 | 2 | 3 | 4 | 5 | 6 |
| How successfully have you used standard English, a formal style, and an appropriate tone for your audience? | 1 | 2 | 3 | 4 | 5 | 6 |

* Other standards covered include: Writing 9a, Writing 10, Speaking 6, Language 6.

For use with Literature 9

Name _____ Date _____ Assignment _____

# Performance Task 8B

> **Speaking and Listening 1** Initiate and participate effectively in a range of collaborative discussions (one-on-one, in groups, and teacher-led) with diverse partners on grades 9–10 topics, texts, and issues, building on others' ideas and expressing your own clearly and persuasively.

## Task: Discuss the Essays

Participate in a group discussion in which group members share their essays about a literary text and the source material from which the author drew inspiration. Respond thoughtfully to the ideas of others and build upon their ideas in your discussion.

### Tips for Success

Participate in a discussion about an essay on a literary text. Follow these tips for success:

✓ review the essay you wrote about a literary text and the ways in which the author adapted source material in its retelling

✓ with the group, develop discussion guidelines for equal and full participation for each person

✓ present your ideas clearly and simply when it is your turn to speak

✓ prepare questions that will evoke further discussion from participants and propel the discussion forward

✓ identify text passages that support the different points of view presented in the essays

✓ summarize the group's different responses to the text

### Rubric for Self-Assessment

| Criteria for Discussion | not very | | | | | very |
|---|---|---|---|---|---|---|
| How well had the participants prepared for the discussion? | 1 | 2 | 3 | 4 | 5 | 6 |
| How successful was the group in establishing guidelines for equal participation in the discussion? | 1 | 2 | 3 | 4 | 5 | 6 |
| How clearly did you express your ideas about the literary work and its source material? | 1 | 2 | 3 | 4 | 5 | 6 |
| How successful were participants in asking thoughtful questions that helped explore different points of view? | 1 | 2 | 3 | 4 | 5 | 6 |
| How well did participants offer different perspectives on the work? | 1 | 2 | 3 | 4 | 5 | 6 |
| How well did the discussion summarize the main perspectives of participants? | 1 | 2 | 3 | 4 | 5 | 6 |

**For use with Speaking and Listening 1**

Name _____ Date _____ Assignment _____

# Performance Task 9A

---

**Literature 10 By the end of grade 9, read and comprehend literature, including stories, dramas, and poems, in the grades 9–10 text complexity band proficiently, with scaffolding as needed at the high end of the range.**

---

## Task: Respond to an Independent Reading

After reading a text independently, write an analysis of the text. Use textual evidence and inferences you have drawn during reading to support your analysis of it.

### Tips for Success

Present a response to independent reading you have read outside of class. In your response, include these elements:

- ✓ a short, objective summary of the text
- ✓ an analysis of the text's content
- ✓ a thesis statement that clearly sums up your response to the text
- ✓ evidence from the text that explicitly supports the opinions you present
- ✓ inferences from the text that support your response
- ✓ language that is formal, precise, and follows the rules of standard English

### Rubric for Self-Assessment

| Criteria for Discussion | not very | | | | | very |
|---|---|---|---|---|---|---|
| How clear and objective is your summary of the text? | 1 | 2 | 3 | 4 | 5 | 6 |
| How thoroughly have you analyzed the text's content? | 1 | 2 | 3 | 4 | 5 | 6 |
| How successfully have you created a clear thesis statement? | 1 | 2 | 3 | 4 | 5 | 6 |
| How well does your thesis explain your response to the work? | 1 | 2 | 3 | 4 | 5 | 6 |
| How well have you supported the thesis with explicit evidence from the text? | 1 | 2 | 3 | 4 | 5 | 6 |
| How successfully have you included inferences you made during reading to support your response? | 1 | 2 | 3 | 4 | 5 | 6 |
| How successfully have you used standard English, a formal style, and an appropriate tone for your audience? | 1 | 2 | 3 | 4 | 5 | 6 |

\* Other standards covered include: Reading 1, Writing 6, Writing 9a, Writing 10, Speaking 5, Speaking 6, Language 6.

**For use with Literature 10**

Name _____ Date _____ Assignment _____

# Performance Task 9B

> **Speaking and Listening 5** Make strategic use of digital media (e.g., textual, graphical, audio, visual, and interactive elements) in presentations to enhance understanding of findings, reasoning, and evidence and to add interest.

## Task: Make a Presentation to the Class

Create a presentation about a book you read independently by adapting an essay you wrote about it. Make use of digital media to illustrate your findings and reasoning and to add interest. Make your presentation to a group of your classmates. Listen thoughtfully as other members of the group make their presentations.

### Tips for Success

As your prepare for your presentation, follow these tips for success:

✓ carefully review your essay and adapt it from written to spoken language

✓ create presentation materials that are clear and engaging for your audience

✓ allow time for feedback from the audience in the form of questions or comments

✓ with group members, develop guidelines for presentations and discussions

✓ take notes as group members make their presentations, and respond thoughtfully

### Rubric for Self-Assessment

| Criteria for Discussion | not very | | | | | very |
|---|---|---|---|---|---|---|
| How well did you adapt your written work into a spoken presentation? | 1 | 2 | 3 | 4 | 5 | 6 |
| How well did you use digital media to create presentation materials? | 1 | 2 | 3 | 4 | 5 | 6 |
| How clear and engaging were your presentation materials? | 1 | 2 | 3 | 4 | 5 | 6 |
| Based on feedback from your classmates, how well did you present your information? | 1 | 2 | 3 | 4 | 5 | 6 |
| How well were you able to answer questions asked by classmates? | 1 | 2 | 3 | 4 | 5 | 6 |
| How successful were the guidelines in ensuring that each presenter participated equally and fully? | 1 | 2 | 3 | 4 | 5 | 6 |

For use with Speaking and Listening 5

Name _____ Date _____ Assignment _____

# Performance Task 10A

> **Informational Text 1** Cite strong and thorough textual evidence to support analysis of what the text says explicitly as well as inferences drawn from the text.*

## Task: Analyze a Text

Write an essay about an informational text you have read. In your essay, identify the central idea of the text, state whether the central idea is expressed explicitly or implicitly, and evaluate whether or not the author used sufficient details to support that idea.

### Tips for Success

Present a response to an informational text you have read. In your response, include these elements:

✓ a clear, objective summary of the text

✓ a thesis statement that sums up your response to the text

✓ evidence from the text that explicitly supports your thesis

✓ inferences from the text that support your analysis

✓ language that is formal, precise, and follows the rules of standard English

### Rubric for Self-Assessment

| Criteria for Success | not very | | | | | very |
|---|---|---|---|---|---|---|
| How clearly and objectively have you summarized the text? | 1 | 2 | 3 | 4 | 5 | 6 |
| How well have you analyzed the author's central idea and supporting details? | 1 | 2 | 3 | 4 | 5 | 6 |
| How successfuliy have you created one clear thesis statement? | 1 | 2 | 3 | 4 | 5 | 6 |
| How well have you used quotes, paraphrases, or facts from the text to support your analysis? | 1 | 2 | 3 | 4 | 5 | 6 |
| How successfully have you included inferences or conclusions you had drawn during reading? | 1 | 2 | 3 | 4 | 5 | 6 |
| How successfully have you used a formal style and an appropriate tone for your audience? | 1 | 2 | 3 | 4 | 5 | 6 |

* Other standards covered include: Writing 2, Writing 9b, Writing 10, Language 6, Speaking 1, Speaking 6

**For use with Informational Text 1**

Name _____ Date _____ Assignment _____

# Performance Task 10B

Speaking and Listening 1  Initiate and participate effectively in a range of
   collaborative discussions (one-on-one, in groups, and teacher-led) with diverse
   partners on grades 9–10 topics, texts, and issues, building on others' ideas and
   expressing your own clearly and persuasively.

## Task: Discuss the Responses to an Informational Text

Participate in a group discussion in which you present your evaluation of an informational text.
Offer thoughtful feedback on others' evaluations of informational texts, and build on the comments
of other group members to further the discussion.

### Tips for Success

Participate in a group discussion about a response to an informational text. Follow these tips for
success:

- ✓ read or re-read the informational text and take notes on your response to it
- ✓ with your group, develop discussion guidelines for equal and full
     participation
- ✓ pose questions that will evoke further discussion from group members
- ✓ build on the comments of group members to deepen the discussion
- ✓ find text passages that support the point of view presented by others
- ✓ summarize each group member's response to the text

### Rubric for Self-Assessment

| Criteria for Discussion | not very | | | | | very |
|---|---|---|---|---|---|---|
| How well had the members of the group prepared for the discussion? | 1 | 2 | 3 | 4 | 5 | 6 |
| How well did the guidelines ensure that all participants participated fully and equally? | 1 | 2 | 3 | 4 | 5 | 6 |
| How well did the group raise thoughtful questions that helped explore the points of view presented? | 1 | 2 | 3 | 4 | 5 | 6 |
| How well did the group offer different perspectives on the work? | 1 | 2 | 3 | 4 | 5 | 6 |
| How well did the group summarize the evaluations given by each member? | 1 | 2 | 3 | 4 | 5 | 6 |

For use with Speaking and Listening 1

Name _____ Date _____ Assignment _____

# Performance Task 11A

> **Informational Text 2** Determine a central idea of a text and analyze its development over the course of the text, including how it emerges and is shaped and refined by specific details; provide an objective summary of the text.*

## Task: Summarize an Informational Text

Write a response to an informational text you have read. Identify the text's central idea, or thesis, and the key supporting details the author uses to support the thesis. As part of your response, write an objective summary of the text.

### Tips for Success

Write a response to an informational text you have read. In your response, include these elements:

- ✓ a clear statement of the text's thesis

- ✓ a summary of how the text develops the thesis, focusing on the details the author uses

- ✓ paraphrase of the author's words when appropriate

- ✓ direct quotations from the text when appropriate

- ✓ language that is formal, precise, and follows the rules of standard English

### Rubric for Self-Assessment

| Criteria for Success | not very | | | | | very |
|---|---|---|---|---|---|---|
| How well do you identify and express the thesis, or central idea of the text? | 1 | 2 | 3 | 4 | 5 | 6 |
| How successfully have you identified the supporting details that shape the central idea? | 1 | 2 | 3 | 4 | 5 | 6 |
| How objective is your summary? | 1 | 2 | 3 | 4 | 5 | 6 |
| How well do you paraphrase the text in your own words? | 1 | 2 | 3 | 4 | 5 | 6 |
| How successfully have you used key quotations from the text as part of your summary? | 1 | 2 | 3 | 4 | 5 | 6 |
| How successfully have you used standard English? | 1 | 2 | 3 | 4 | 5 | 6 |
| How successfully have you used a formal style, created an appropriate tone for your audience, and used standard English? | 1 | 2 | 3 | 4 | 5 | 6 |

*Other standards covered include: Writing 2b, Writing 2e, Writing 10, Language 6, Speaking 4

**For use with Informational Text 2**

Name _____ Date _____ Assignment _____

# Performance Task 11B

**Speaking and Listening 6** Adapt speech to a variety of contexts and tasks, demonstrating command of formal English when indicated or appropriate.

## Task: Present Your Summary

Present your response to a small group of your classmates and listen as they present their responses. Give feedback on your classmates' responses and welcome their feedback on yours.

### Tips for Success

Present your response to an informational text. As a part of your presentation, include these elements:

✓ preparation by having thought about how to adapt your written response into a spoken presentation to a group

✓ visual aids that will help your audience follow your presentation

✓ time allowed for feedback from the audience in the form of questions or comments

✓ guidelines agreed upon by other members in the group for presentations

✓ attention to other members of the group as they make their presentations

### Rubric for Self-Assessment

| Criteria for Discussion | not very | | | | | very |
|---|---|---|---|---|---|---|
| How prepared were you to make your presentation? | 1 | 2 | 3 | 4 | 5 | 6 |
| How clear and helpful were your visual aids? | 1 | 2 | 3 | 4 | 5 | 6 |
| Based on feedback from other members of the group, how well did you present your information? | 1 | 2 | 3 | 4 | 5 | 6 |
| How well were you able to answer questions asked by other group members? | 1 | 2 | 3 | 4 | 5 | 6 |
| How good was your feedback on the presentations given by your classmates? | 1 | 2 | 3 | 4 | 5 | 6 |
| How successful were the guidelines in ensuring that each presenter was treated respectfully? | 1 | 2 | 3 | 4 | 5 | 6 |

For use with Speaking and Listening 6

Name _____ Date _____ Assignment _____

# Performance Task 12A

---
**Informational Text 3** Analyze how the author unfolds an analysis or series of ideas or events, including the order in which the points are made, how they are introduced and developed, and the connections that are drawn between them.*
---

## Task: Analyze an Informational Text

Write a short essay comparing and contrasting two informational texts you have read. Identify the main ideas of both texts and explain the differences and similarities in the ways the authors present the details that support their main points.

### Tips for Success

Write a short essay comparing and contrasting two informational texts you have read. In your essay, include these elements:

✓ an identification of both texts' main ideas and organizational methods used by the authors

✓ a thesis statement that succinctly sums up your observations on the differences and similarities between the texts

✓ an analysis of the content and organizational methods used in both texts

✓ explicit evidence from both texts to support your thesis

✓ language that is formal, precise, and follows the rules of standard English

### Rubric for Self-Assessment

| Criteria for Success | not very | | | | very | |
|---|---|---|---|---|---|---|
| How well do you explain both texts' main points and supporting ideas? | 1 | 2 | 3 | 4 | 5 | 6 |
| How well do you analyze the organizational techniques that the authors use to present their supporting details? | 1 | 2 | 3 | 4 | 5 | 6 |
| How successfully have you created one clear statement that sums up your observations of your comparison of the texts? | 1 | 2 | 3 | 4 | 5 | 6 |
| How well does your thesis explain your analysis of the texts? | 1 | 2 | 3 | 4 | 5 | 6 |
| How well do you support your thesis with explicit evidence from the texts? | 1 | 2 | 3 | 4 | 5 | 6 |
| How successfully have you used a formal style, created an appropriate tone for your audience, and used standard English? | 1 | 2 | 3 | 4 | 5 | 6 |

*Other standards covered include: Writing 9b, Writing 10, Language 6, Speaking 6

For use with Informational Text 3

Name _____ Date _____ Assignment _____

# Performance Task 12B

> **Speaking and Listening 4** Present information, findings, and supporting evidence clearly, concisely, and logically such that listeners can follow the line of reasoning and the organization, development, substance, and style are appropriate to purpose, audience, and task.

## Task: Create an Informational Presentation

Participate in a group informational presentation about a subject of your choice. In your presentation, use one or more of the following organizational styles to present the supporting details: cause and effect, chronological order, comparison and contrast, list, order of importance, or spatial order.

### Tips for Success

Work as a team to create an informational oral presentation. As a part of the presentation, include these elements:

- ✓ agreement among all members of the group about the topic and organizational style of the presentation
- ✓ guidelines agreed upon by the group for equal and full participation in the activity, including assignment of tasks and responsibilities
- ✓ a main idea and a clear, strong plan for presenting supporting details
- ✓ well-chosen visual aids or handouts that help your audience follow your presentation
- ✓ a tone and level of formality appropriate for your subject and your audience

### Rubric for Self-Assessment

| Criteria for Discussion | not very | | | | | very |
|---|---|---|---|---|---|---|
| How successful was the group in establishing guidelines for the presentation? | 1 | 2 | 3 | 4 | 5 | 6 |
| How well did the guidelines ensure that everyone participated fully and equally? | 1 | 2 | 3 | 4 | 5 | 6 |
| How successful was the group in coming up with a main idea and strong organizational plan for the presentation? | 1 | 2 | 3 | 4 | 5 | 6 |
| How successful was the group in creating solid reasoning in support of the main idea? | 1 | 2 | 3 | 4 | 5 | 6 |
| How successful was the group in choosing a tone and level of formality appropriate for the audience and subject matter? | 1 | 2 | 3 | 4 | 5 | 6 |

For use with Speaking and Listening 4

Name _____  Date _____  Assignment _____

# Performance Task 13A

> **Informational Text 4** Determine the meaning of words and phrases as they are used in a text, including figurative, connotative, and technical meanings; analyze the cumulative impact of specific word choices on meaning and tone (e.g., how the language of a court opinion differs from that of a newspaper).*

## Task: Analyze Tone and Language

Write a response to an informational text in which you identify the tone and describe how the author's diction and syntax help to shape that tone.

### Tips for Success

Write a response to an informational text you have read. In your response, include these elements:

- ✓ a clear thesis statement that sums up your analysis of the tone
- ✓ an analysis of the author's diction and syntax and how they shape the tone of the text
- ✓ evidence from the text that explicitly supports the analysis you present
- ✓ inferences from the text that support your analysis
- ✓ language that is formal, precise, and follows the rules of standard English

### Rubric for Self-Assessment

| Criteria for Success | not very | | | | | very |
|---|---|---|---|---|---|---|
| How well do you describe the tone of the text? | 1 | 2 | 3 | 4 | 5 | 6 |
| How well do you analyze the syntax of the text? | 1 | 2 | 3 | 4 | 5 | 6 |
| How successfully have you created one clear statement that sums up your analysis of the text? | 1 | 2 | 3 | 4 | 5 | 6 |
| How successfully have you explained how the author's use of language helps to create a tone for the text? | 1 | 2 | 3 | 4 | 5 | 6 |
| How well do you include at least three or more examples of the author's diction to support your analysis? | 1 | 2 | 3 | 4 | 5 | 6 |
| How successfully have you used a formal style, created an appropriate tone for your audience, and used standard English? | 1 | 2 | 3 | 4 | 5 | 6 |

*Other standards covered include: Writing 9b, Writing 10, Language 5a, Language 5b, Language 6, Speaking 6

For use with Informational Text 4

Name _____ Date _____ Assignment _____

# Performance Task 13B

> **Speaking and Listening 1** Initiate and participate effectively in a range of collaborative discussions (one-on-one, in groups, and teacher-led) with diverse partners on *grades 9–10 topics, texts, and issues*, building on others' ideas and expressing their own clearly and persuasively.

## Task: Discuss the Responses to a Text

Participate in a group discussion in which you explain your response to the tone and word choice of an informational text and respond thoughtfully to the points of view of others. Create a diction and tone chart that summarizes the responses of each member of the group.

### Tips for Success

Participate in a discussion about a response to an informational text. As a part of your participation in the discussion, include these elements:

✓ preparation by having read the informational text and thought through your analysis of its tone and use of language

✓ guidelines agreed upon by other members in the discussion for equal and full participation

✓ questions that will evoke further discussion and propel the discussion forward

✓ inferences from the text that support the different points of view

✓ chart reflecting the diction and tone of responses of the participants

### Rubric for Self-Assessment

| Criteria for Discussion | not very | | | | very | |
|---|---|---|---|---|---|---|
| How thoroughly did each participant seem to know the informational text and have prepared for the discussion? | 1 | 2 | 3 | 4 | 5 | 6 |
| How well had the participants thought through their analyses of the text's tone and language before the discussion started? | 1 | 2 | 3 | 4 | 5 | 6 |
| How successful was the group in establishing guidelines for the discussion that everyone participates fully and equally? | 1 | 2 | 3 | 4 | 5 | 6 |
| How well did participants offer different perspectives on the work? | 1 | 2 | 3 | 4 | 5 | 6 |
| How well did the diction and tone chart reflect the responses of each member of the group? | 1 | 2 | 3 | 4 | 5 | 6 |
| How polite and respectful of other points of view were the participants? | 1 | 2 | 3 | 4 | 5 | 6 |

For use with Speaking and Listening 1

Name _____ Date _____ Assignment _____

# Performance Task 14A

---

**Informational Text 5** Analyze in detail how an author's ideas or claims are developed and refined by particular sentences, paragraphs, or larger portions of a text (e.g., a section or chapter).*

---

## Task: Respond to an Informational Text

Present a response to an informational text you have read and found persuasive. Identify the part of the text that you feel is the most persuasive and explain why it was effective. Note where and how the author uses rhetorical devices, such as repetition, parallelism, and rhetorical questions.

### Tips for Success

Present a response to an informational text you have read. In your response, include these elements:

✓ an analysis of the text's content, including the rhetorical devices used in it

✓ a clear statement of what you feel is the most persuasive element of the text

✓ evidence from the text that explicitly illustrates your thesis

✓ inferences from the text that support the opinions presented in your response

✓ language that is formal, precise, and follows the rules of standard English

### Rubric for Self-Assessment

| Criteria for Success | not very | | | | very | |
|---|---|---|---|---|---|---|
| How well do you explain what the text is about? | 1 | 2 | 3 | 4 | 5 | 6 |
| How well do you analyze rhetorical devices the author uses? | 1 | 2 | 3 | 4 | 5 | 6 |
| How successfully have you created one clear statement of what you feel makes the text persuasive? | 1 | 2 | 3 | 4 | 5 | 6 |
| How well does your response explain your personal reaction to the text? | 1 | 2 | 3 | 4 | 5 | 6 |
| How well do you include at least three or more quotes, facts, or ideas from the text to support your analysis? | 1 | 2 | 3 | 4 | 5 | 6 |
| How successfully have you included inferences you made during reading to support your response? | 1 | 2 | 3 | 4 | 5 | 6 |
| How successfully have you used a formal style, created an appropriate tone for your audience, and used standard English? | 1 | 2 | 3 | 4 | 5 | 6 |

*Other standards covered include: Writing 2b, Writing 9b, Writing 10, Language 6, Speaking 6

For use with Informational Text 5

Name _____ Date _____ Assignment _____

# Performance Task 14B

> **Speaking and Listening 1** Initiate and participate effectively in a range of collaborative discussions (one-on-one, in groups, and teacher-led) with diverse partners on *grades 9–10 topics, texts, and issues,* building on others' ideas and expressing their own clearly and persuasively.

## Task: Discuss the Responses to a Text

Participate in a group discussion in which you explain your response to an informational text, focusing on the element of the text that you felt made it persuasive, and respond thoughtfully and respectfully to the points of view of others.

### Tips for Success

Participate in a discussion about a response to an informational text. As a part of your participation in the discussion, include these elements:

- ✓ preparation by having thought through your personal response to the informational text and your reasons for finding it persuasive
- ✓ guidelines agreed upon by all members of the discussion for equal and full participation
- ✓ questions that will evoke further discussion from participants and propel the discussion forward in order to fully explore the text
- ✓ inferences from the text that support the different points of view presented in the responses
- ✓ summaries of different responses to the text

### Rubric for Self-Assessment

| Criteria for Discussion | not very                very |
|---|---|
| How thoroughly did each participant seem to know the informational text? | 1  2  3  4  5  6 |
| How well had the participants thought through their responses to the text before the discussion started? | 1  2  3  4  5  6 |
| How successful was the group in establishing guidelines for the discussion? | 1  2  3  4  5  6 |
| How well did the guidelines ensure that everyone participated fully and equally? | 1  2  3  4  5  6 |
| How thoughtful were participants in asking probing questions that helped explore the different points of view? | 1  2  3  4  5  6 |
| How well did participants offer different perspectives on the text and the elements that they found persuasive? | 1  2  3  4  5  6 |
| How well did the discussion summarize the main perspectives of participants? | 1  2  3  4  5  6 |
| How polite and respectful of other points of view were the participants? | 1  2  3  4  5  6 |

Name _____ Date _____ Assignment _____

# Performance Task 15A

> **Informational Text 6** Determine an author's point of view or purpose in a text and analyze how an author uses rhetoric to advance that point of view or purpose.*

## Task: Respond to an Informational Text

Present a response to an informational text you have read and and analyze how the author has used rhetoric to advance point of view or purpose. Note where and how the author uses rhetorical devices, such as repetition, parallelism, and rhetorical questions.

### Tips for Success

Present a response to an informational text you have read. In your response, include these elements:

✓ an analysis of the content of the text, including the rhetorical devices used in it

✓ a clear statement of how the author uses the rhetorical device to advance the point of view or purpose

✓ evidence from the text that explicitly illustrates your thesis

✓ inferences from the text that support the opinions presented in your response

✓ language that is formal, precise, and follows the rules of standard English

### Rubric for Self-Assessment

| Criteria for Success | not very | | | | | very |
|---|---|---|---|---|---|---|
| How well do you explain what the work is about? | 1 | 2 | 3 | 4 | 5 | 6 |
| How well do you analyze rhetorical devices the author uses? | 1 | 2 | 3 | 4 | 5 | 6 |
| How successfully have you created one clear statement of what you feel makes the text persuasive? | 1 | 2 | 3 | 4 | 5 | 6 |
| How well do you support the thesis with explicit evidence from the text? | 1 | 2 | 3 | 4 | 5 | 6 |
| How successfully have you included inferences you made during reading to support your response? | 1 | 2 | 3 | 4 | 5 | 6 |
| How successfully have you used standard English? | 1 | 2 | 3 | 4 | 5 | 6 |
| How successfully have you used a formal style and created an appropriate tone for your audience? | 1 | 2 | 3 | 4 | 5 | 6 |

*Other standards covered include: Writing 2b, Writing 9b, Writing 10, Language 6, Speaking 6

For use with Informational Text 6

Name _____ Date _____ Assignment _____

# Performance Task 15B

> **Speaking and Listening 1** Initiate and participate effectively in a range of collaborative discussions (one-on-one, in groups, and teacher-led) with diverse partners on *grades 9–10 topics, texts, and issues,* building on others' ideas and expressing their own clearly and persuasively.

## Task: Discuss the Responses to a Text

Participate in a group discussion in which you explain your response to an informational text. Focus especially on the element of the text that you felt made it persuasive, and respond thoughtfully to the points of view of others.

## Tips for Success

Participate in a discussion about a response to an informational text. As a part of your participation in the discussion, include these elements:

✓ preparation by having thought through your personal response to the informational text and your reasons for finding it persuasive

✓ guidelines agreed upon by members of the discussion for equal and full participation

✓ questions that will evoke further discussion from participants

✓ inferences from the text that support the different points of view presented in the responses

✓ summaries of different responses to the text

## Rubric for Self-Assessment

| Criteria for Discussion | not very | | | | | very |
|---|---|---|---|---|---|---|
| How thoroughly did each participant seem to prepare and have thought through a response to the informational text? | 1 | 2 | 3 | 4 | 5 | 6 |
| How successful was the group in establishing guidelines for full and equal participation in the discussion? | 1 | 2 | 3 | 4 | 5 | 6 |
| How successful were participants in asking thoughtful questions that helped explore the points of view? | 1 | 2 | 3 | 4 | 5 | 6 |
| How well did the discussion summarize the main perspectives of participants? | 1 | 2 | 3 | 4 | 5 | 6 |
| How polite and respectful of other points of view were the participants? | 1 | 2 | 3 | 4 | 5 | 6 |

Name _____ Date _____ Assignment _____

# Performance Task 16A

> **Informational Text 7** Analyze various accounts of a subject told in different mediums (e.g., a person's life story in both print and multimedia), determining which details are emphasized in each account.*

## Task: Compare and Contrast

Write a short essay comparing and contrasting two different accounts of the same subject presented in different mediums. As part of your essay, identify which details are emphasized in each account and explain why different media might emphasize different elements of a subject.

### Tips for Success

Write a short essay comparing two informational texts on the same subject. In your essay, include these elements:

- ✓ an analysis of the general similarities and differences between the two mediums, including the strengths and weaknesses of both in presenting certain types of information
- ✓ an analysis of the specific similarities and differences in the way the subject is presented in the two works
- ✓ a clear thesis statement that sums up the conclusions you have drawn
- ✓ specific evidence from both texts to support your thesis
- ✓ language that is formal, precise, and follows the rules of standard English.

### Rubric for Self-Assessment

| Criteria for Success | not very | | | | | very |
|---|---|---|---|---|---|---|
| How well do you analyze the subject shown in the two accounts? | 1 | 2 | 3 | 4 | 5 | 6 |
| How successfully have you created one clear statement of the conclusions you have drawn? | 1 | 2 | 3 | 4 | 5 | 6 |
| How well do you explain the general possibilities and limitations of the two mediums you analyzed? | 1 | 2 | 3 | 4 | 5 | 6 |
| How well do you explain which specific details were emphasized in the two different works? | 1 | 2 | 3 | 4 | 5 | 6 |
| How well do you support your conclusion with explicit evidence from both works? | 1 | 2 | 3 | 4 | 5 | 6 |
| How successfully have you used a formal style, created an appropriate tone for your audience, and used standard English? | 1 | 2 | 3 | 4 | 5 | 6 |

* Other standards covered include: Writing 9b, Writing 10, Language 6, Speaking 6

For use with Informational Text 7

Name _____ Date _____ Assignment _____

# Performance Task 16B

> **Speaking and Listening 2** Integrate multiple sources of information presented in diverse media or formats (e.g., visually, quantitatively, orally) evaluating the credibility and accuracy of each source.

## Task: Create a Comparison Chart

Participate in a group activity in which you create a chart or presentation that graphically represents the differences between two works in different media but about the same subject. As you create the chart, try to think about the difference the medium makes when presenting information.

### Tips for Success

Discuss the multiple sources of information and participate in a group activity to create a chart or presentation. As a part of your participation in the activity, include these elements:

- ✓ preparation by having read both works and thought through the similarities and differences between them

- ✓ preparation by having thought about why different details are emphasized in different media

- ✓ guidelines agreed upon by the group for equal and full participation of each person

- ✓ careful thought and group discussion about what type of chart or presentation the team will need to represent the differences between the works

- ✓ a clear, easy-to-read chart or presentation as a final product

### Rubric for Self-Assessment

| Criteria for Discussion | not very | | | | | very |
|---|---|---|---|---|---|---|
| How thoroughly did each participant seem to know both works and have thought through the two mediums before the discussion started? | 1 | 2 | 3 | 4 | 5 | 6 |
| How successful was the group in establishing guidelines for equal participation in creating the chart or presentation? | 1 | 2 | 3 | 4 | 5 | 6 |
| How successful was the team in developing a chart or presentation that represented the differences and similarities between the two works? | 1 | 2 | 3 | 4 | 5 | 6 |
| How clear and understandable was the final product? | 1 | 2 | 3 | 4 | 5 | 6 |

For use with Speaking and Listening 2

Name _____ Date _____ Assignment _____

# Performance Task 17A

Informational Text 8  Delineate and evaluate the argument and specific claims in a text, assessing whether the reasoning is valid and the evidence is relevant and sufficient; identify false statements and fallacious reasoning.*

## Task: Evaluate an Argument

Write a short essay about an informational text you have read that presents an argument. As part of your response, analyze the author's argument and evaluate its credibility.

### Tips for Success

Write a short essay about an informational text you have read. In your essay, include these elements:

- ✓ a clear thesis statement in which you sum up your analysis of the author's argument and credibility

- ✓ a discussion of whether the argument was clear, logical, and well-reasoned

- ✓ an explanation of whether or not the evidence presented was credible and comprehensive

- ✓ evidence from the text that supports and illustrates your analysis

- ✓ language that is formal, precise, and follows the rules of standard English

### Rubric for Self-Assessment

| Criteria for Success | not very | | | | | very |
|---|---|---|---|---|---|---|
| How well do you analyze the text and evaluate the argument in it? | 1 | 2 | 3 | 4 | 5 | 6 |
| How well does your thesis explain your analysis of the author's argument? | 1 | 2 | 3 | 4 | 5 | 6 |
| To what extent have you determined if the argument was logical and well-reasoned? | 1 | 2 | 3 | 4 | 5 | 6 |
| How well are you able to identify and evaluate the evidence and reasoning the author uses to support the argument? | 1 | 2 | 3 | 4 | 5 | 6 |
| How well do you use quotes, fact, or ideas from the text to support and illustrate your thesis? | 1 | 2 | 3 | 4 | 5 | 6 |
| How successfully have you used standard English? | 1 | 2 | 3 | 4 | 5 | 6 |
| How successfully have you used a formal style and created an appropriate tone for your audience? | 1 | 2 | 3 | 4 | 5 | 6 |

*Other standards covered include: Writing 9b, Writing 10, Language 6, Speaking 2, Speaking 3, Speaking 6

For use with Informational Text 8

Name _____  Date _____  Assignment _____

# Performance Task 17B

**Speaking and Listening 3**  Evaluate a speaker's point of view, reasoning, and use of evidence and rhetoric, identifying any fallacious reasoning or exaggerated or distorted evidence.

## Task: Evaluate Essays

Work with a partner to review and critique a short essay about the argument in an informational text. Read your essay aloud to your partner and evaluate both how well he or she analyzed the author's reasoning and the credibility of the argument.

### Tips for Success

Discuss with a partner an essay about an informational text. As a part of your participation in the discussion, include these elements:

- ✓ preparation by having read the informational text and thought through your own analysis of it
- ✓ thoughtful attention to your partner's reading of his or her essay
- ✓ guidelines agreed upon by you and your partner for critiques
- ✓ questions that will evoke further discussion from your partner to explore the work fully
- ✓ a written outline of your evaluation of your partner's essay to supplement your verbal critique

### Rubric for Self-Assessment

| Criteria for Discussion | not very | | | | | very |
|---|---|---|---|---|---|---|
| How successful was your partner in creating one clear statement of his or her analysis of the text? | 1 | 2 | 3 | 4 | 5 | 6 |
| How well does your partner's thesis explain his or her evaluation of the author's credibility? | 1 | 2 | 3 | 4 | 5 | 6 |
| How successful was your partner in determining if the argument was logical and well-reasoned? | 1 | 2 | 3 | 4 | 5 | 6 |
| How well was your partner able to identify and evaluate the evidence the author uses to support the argument? | 1 | 2 | 3 | 4 | 5 | 6 |
| How well did your partner use at least three quotes, facts, or ideas from the text to support and illustrate his or her thesis? | 1 | 2 | 3 | 4 | 5 | 6 |
| How successful was your partner in using a formal style, creating an appropriate tone, and using standard English? | 1 | 2 | 3 | 4 | 5 | 6 |

Name _____  Date _____  Assignment _____

# Performance Task 18A

> **Informational Text 9** Analyze seminal U.S. documents of historical and literary significance (e.g., Washington's Farewell Address, the Gettysburg Address, Roosevelt's Four Freedoms speech, King's "Letter from Birmingham Jail"), including how they address related themes and concepts.*

## Task: Analyze a Speech

Write a response to a document that is significant in U.S. history. For your response, analyze the main theme or significance of the text and explain what images and details the author uses to convey that theme.

### Tips for Success

Write a response to a significant historical document you have read and include these elements:

✓ an analysis of the document's main idea and the significance of the document

✓ an explanation of the rhetoric, figurative language, and expository techniques used to present the supporting details of the document

✓ a thesis statement that succinctly sums up your analysis

✓ explicit evidence from the text to support your thesis

✓ language that is formal, precise, and follows the rules of standard English

### Rubric for Self-Assessment

| Criteria for Success | not very | | | | | very |
|---|---|---|---|---|---|---|
| How well do you explain the text's main point and significance? | 1 | 2 | 3 | 4 | 5 | 6 |
| How well do you analyze the technique or techniques the author uses to present the supporting details? | 1 | 2 | 3 | 4 | 5 | 6 |
| How successfully have you created one clear statement of your analysis of the work? | 1 | 2 | 3 | 4 | 5 | 6 |
| How well does your thesis sum up your analysis of the work? | 1 | 2 | 3 | 4 | 5 | 6 |
| How well do you support the thesis with explicit evidence from the text? | 1 | 2 | 3 | 4 | 5 | 6 |
| How successfully have you used standard English? | 1 | 2 | 3 | 4 | 5 | 6 |
| How successfully have you used a formal style and created an appropriate tone for your audience? | 1 | 2 | 3 | 4 | 5 | 6 |

*Other standards covered include: Writing 7, Writing 9b, Writing 10, Speaking 6, Language 6

For use with Informational Text 9

Name _____ Date _____ Assignment _____

# Performance Task 18B

---

**Speaking and Listening 4** Present information, findings, and supporting evidence clearly, concisely, and logically such that listeners can follow the line of reasoning and the organization, development, substance, and style are appropriate to purpose, audience, and task.

---

## Task: Give a Group Presentation

Participate in a group activity in which you do further research on the context and significance of a historical document and give a group presentation about it to the class.

### Tips for Success

Participate in a group activity to create a presentation. As a part of your participation in the activity, include these elements:

✓ research into the historical document, using credible, well-chosen sources

✓ guidelines agreed upon by all members of the presentation team for equal and full participation of each person

✓ clear point of view, organization, and line of reasoning for the presentation that have been agreed to by all members of the presentation team

✓ materials that support the presentation's point of view and help the audience to fully understand the subject presented

✓ tone that is appropriate for the presentation's subject and for your audience

### Rubric for Self-Assessment

| Criteria for Discussion | not very | | | | | very |
|---|---|---|---|---|---|---|
| How successful was the team in finding information about the history, context, and significance of the document? | 1 | 2 | 3 | 4 | 5 | 6 |
| How successful was the group in creating guidelines that enabled full participation by all of the group members? | 1 | 2 | 3 | 4 | 5 | 6 |
| How successful was the presentation team in developing a clear point of view, organization, and line of reasoning for the presentation? | 1 | 2 | 3 | 4 | 5 | 6 |
| How successful was the team in using formal language, an appropriate tone, and standard English? | 1 | 2 | 3 | 4 | 5 | 6 |

Name _____ Date _____ Assignment _____

# Performance Task 19A

---

Informational Text 10   By the end of grade 10, read and comprehend literary nonfiction, in the grades 9–10 text complexity band proficiently, with scaffolding as needed at the high end of the range.

---

## Task: Respond to an Independent Reading

Read a book of literary nonfiction listed for your class as independent reading. Then write a response to the book using textual evidence and inferences you have drawn from the text to support your analysis of it.

### Tips for Success

Present a response to a work of literary nonfiction you have read outside of class. In your response, include these elements:

✓ a short summary of the work and an analysis of the work's contents

✓ a thesis statement that succinctly sums up your personal response to the work

✓ evidence from the text that explicitly supports the opinions you present

✓ inferences from the text that support the opinions presented in your response

✓ language that is formal, precise, and follows the rules of standard English

### Rubric for Self-Assessment

| Criteria for Success | not very           very |
|---|---|
| How well do you summarize the book and analyze its content? | 1  2  3  4  5  6 |
| How successfully have you created one clear thesis statement of your response to the work? | 1  2  3  4  5  6 |
| How well does your thesis explain your feelings about the work? | 1  2  3  4  5  6 |
| How well do you include at least three or more quotes, facts, or ideas from the text to support your analysis? | 1  2  3  4  5  6 |
| How well do you support the thesis with explicit evidence from the text? | 1  2  3  4  5  6 |
| How successfully have you included inferences you made during reading to support your response? | 1  2  3  4  5  6 |
| How successfully have you used a formal style, created an appropriate tone for your audience, and used standard English? | 1  2  3  4  5  6 |

*Other standards covered include: Reading 1, Writing 9a, Writing 10, Speaking 5, Speaking 6, Language 6.

For use with Informational Text 10

Name _____ Date _____ Assignment _____

# Performance Task 19B

> **Speaking and Listening 5** Make strategic use of digital media (e.g., textual, graphical, audio, visual, and interactive elements) in presentations to enhance understanding of findings, reasoning, and evidence and to add interest.

## Task: Make a Presentation to a Small Group

Create a short presentation about the book you read, making use of digital media to illustrate your points. Make your presentation to a small group of your classmates. Listen thoughtfully as other members of the group make their presentations.

### Tips for Success

Make a presentation to a small group about a book you have read and listen as others make their presentations. As a part of your participation, include these elements:

✓ preparation by having carefully reviewed your book and thought about ways to present it

✓ guidelines agreed upon by other members in the group for presentations

✓ multimedia presentation materials that are clear and engaging for your audience

✓ time allowed for feedback from the audience in the form of questions or comments

✓ attention to other members of the group as they make their presentations

### Rubric for Self-Assessment

| Criteria for Discussion | not very | | | | | very |
|---|---|---|---|---|---|---|
| How carefully had you reviewed your book and thought about ways to present it? | 1 | 2 | 3 | 4 | 5 | 6 |
| How successful were the group guidelines for full and equal participation? | 1 | 2 | 3 | 4 | 5 | 6 |
| How effectively did you use digital media to create presentation materials? | 1 | 2 | 3 | 4 | 5 | 6 |
| How clear and engaging were your presentation materials? | 1 | 2 | 3 | 4 | 5 | 6 |
| Based on feedback from your classmates, how well did you present your information? | 1 | 2 | 3 | 4 | 5 | 6 |
| How well were you able to answer questions asked by classmates? | 1 | 2 | 3 | 4 | 5 | 6 |
| How well did you listen to presentations by other groups? | 1 | 2 | 3 | 4 | 5 | 6 |